THEOLOGY IN HYMNS?

THEOLOGY IN HYMNS?

A Study of the Relationship of
Doxology and Theology
According to
*A Collection of Hymns for the
Use of
the People Called Methodists* (1780)

Teresa Berger

Translated by
Timothy E. Kimbrough

KINGSWOOD BOOKS

An Imprint of Abingdon Press
Nashville, Tennessee

THEOLOGY IN HYMNS?
A STUDY OF THE RELATIONSHIP OF DOXOLOGY AND THEOLOGY ACCORDING
TO *A COLLECTION OF HYMNS FOR THE USE OF THE PEOPLE CALLED METHODISTS*
(1780)

Alle Rechte vorbehalten: Oros Verlag, Altenberge 1989
© Oros Verlag, Altenberge/Germany 1989

English translation Copyright © 1995 by Abingdon Press

95 96 97 98 99 00 01 02 03 04 — 10 9 8 7 6 5 4 3 2 1

Library of Congress Cataloging-in-Publication Data

Berger, Teresa.
   [Theologie in Hymnen? English]
   Theology in hymns? : a study of the relationship of doxology and theology according to A collection of hymns for the use of the people called Methodists (1780) / Teresa Berger : translated by Timothy Edward Kimbrough.
     p.   cm.
   Includes bibliographical references.
   ISBN 0-687-00281-8
   1. Wesley, John, 1703-1791. Collection of hymns for the use of the people called Methodists. 2. Wesley, Charles, 1707-1788. 3. Methodist Church—Hymns—History and criticism. 4. Theology. 5. Doxology. I. Title.
BV415.A1B4713 1995   95-9648
264'.0702—dc20   CIP

Scripture quotations, unless otherwise noted, are from the New Revised Standard Version Bible, Copyright © 1989 by the Division of Christian Education of the National Council of the Churches of Christ in the USA. Used by permission.

Those noted KJV are from the King James Version of the Bible.

Printed in the United States of America on recycled, acid-free paper.

Contents

PART II

Translator's Note

This book is a translation of *Theologie in Hymnen? Zum Verhältnis von Theologie und Doxologie am Beispiel der "Collection of Hymns for the Use of the People called Methodists" (1780)*, published in a single volume by Telos Verlag, Altenberge. The volume was first published in 1989, sixth in the series *Münsteraner Theologische Abhandlungen (MThA)*. The translation has been made from the German original, but it incorporates several additions and corrections that Dr. Berger wished to have inserted in the text. The bibliography has also been brought up-to-date through the Fall of 1994.

I wish to express my indebtedness for the help provided me in various ways to the Rev. Dr. S T Kimbrough, Jr. and Rex Matthews; to the vestry and people of the Church of the Holy Family, Chapel Hill, North Carolina for their continual kindness and forbearance; to the University of the South, School of Theology, Sewanee, Tennessee, especially to Dr. Samuel R. Williamson, Vice-Chancellor and President, and the Rev. Robert S. Creamer, Jr., Executive Director of Church Relations, for the invaluable resources of their library and campus made available to me during my work on this translation; to my wife, Darlene, for her patience; and not the least to Dr. Teresa Berger for her several suggestions and the privilege of working with this text.

Timothy E. Kimbrough
Chapel Hill, North Carolina
Advent, 1994

Foreword
(To the English Edition)

The present book is a thoroughly revised and updated version of my book *Theologie in Hymnen?* (1989), which itself was based on my 1989 dissertation for the Catholic Faculty of the University of Münster, Germany.

I thank the translator, the Rev. Timothy E. Kimbrough, who brought to the task of translating not only his knowledge of German but also his familiarity with the Wesley hymns. I thank the Center for Studies in the Wesleyan Tradition of Duke University Divinity School and its director, Dean Dennis Campbell, for funding the translation of the book. I thank the editorial board of Kingswood Books for accepting the manuscript in their series.

The original German version of this book was dedicated to the faculty of the Divinity School of Duke University, where over the last ten years I have found a home for my research and my teaching. There is no reason whatsoever for this dedication to change. If I should single out a particular group of people at the Divinity School who have supported me in a special way, it would be the women faculty and administrators. To them, and to all others who have supported me through the long process of research, translation, and new publication of this book, I am deeply grateful.

Teresa Berger

PART I

CHAPTER 1

Definition of the Theme

A. Purpose, Range, and Parameters of This Study

This work is prompted by two different, yet related, concerns. First, it is rooted within the newly awakened interest in the doxological traditions of the churches that has grown increasingly in recent years. I am committed to this newly awakened theological interest in doxological traditions and the accompanying scholarly discussion. The second characteristic perspective of this work is closely tied to a peculiarity of this new theological discussion: generally this discussion is not conducted on the basis of doxological material itself but rather remains on a theoretical level. This bypassing of specific doxological material itself produces certain consequences that are often not foreseen. What is said theologically about doxology and its relationship to theological reflection often seems to lie beyond doxological speech and is not easily verified in the doxological material itself.

For this reason the following considerations on the relationship of doxology to theology are consciously placed within the context of a study of specific doxological material. The relevant literature supports this methodology by insisting that the "special nature" and the peculiar character of doxological speech has not yet been adequately researched. For example, shortly after the Second Vatican Council, the German theologian, Alois Stenzel, when referring to liturgical language wrote in the Roman Catholic standard reference work *Mysterium Salutis*, "Research into liturgical language has the wonderful and tiresome prerogative of being 'ground-breaking' in every sense of the word—everywhere you turn there is unexplored territory."[1] What is said here in reference to liturgical language may also be said of doxological language in the broader sense. It remains, for the most part, a stepchild of theological inquiry.

With this initial outline as to the reason for this study the following becomes clear: my purpose is twofold—although each aspect will serve the other. (1) At its heart, this study will pursue a detailed exploration of a specific doxological tradition, namely that of Wesleyan hymnody as reflected in the 1780 *A Collection of Hymns for the Use of the People Called Methodists*. On a very basic level, specific doxological texts will be understood and examined carefully as the object and theme of theological inquiry. (2) In dealing with *A Collection of Hymns for the Use of the People Called Methodists,* however, a broader context will be kept in mind, one which, in the final analysis, is motivated by a question that extends well beyond the study of Wesleyan hymnody: What is the essence of doxological speech and the relationship of doxology to theology? In effect, what is the relationship of the language of prayer and praise directed to God to that of scholarly reflection on the history of God's relationship with humankind, and the cosmos?

It goes without saying that answers to such basic questions cannot be found by way of Wesleyan hymnody alone. Thus, this study will not, nor can it, be about the task of attempting to resolve the question of how doxology relates to theology. Rather, this study will present a theological reading of specific doxological texts, which hopefully will produce some preliminary findings and criteria for relating doxological speech to theological reflection. I note, however, that the relationship between doxology and theology will not be construed, in what follows, in terms of a simplistic "usefulness" of doxology for theology. After all, more is involved here than simply illustrating every theological idea with a doxological quotation. Such a simplistic way of construing the relationship between doxology and theology, as will be shown, is untenable. This study will therefore consider the relationship of doxology to theology deliberately within the context of the theological reading of doxological material itself, without the theological reading of this particular material being understood as the final word on the relationship of doxology to theology. This would be a crude overestimation of and place excessive demands on the chosen doxological material. The connection between the theological study of doxological texts and reflection on the relationship of doxology to theology will have to be established more cautiously than a simplistic "use" of doxology for theology would permit.

Before returning to this tension between the theological study of doxological texts, on the one hand, and the reflection on doxology and theology, on the other, which provides the structure for this study, a few key concepts must be defined. Four such concepts and themes will be considered as follows: the concept of doxology (as understood by this study), the question as to whether there is a

"Theology in Hymns," the liturgical and ecumenical potential of this study, and the concept of the constitutive multilingual nature of faith. We begin with a few considerations on the concept of doxology.

1. The Concept of "Doxology"

This study will use the term *doxology* in a broader sense than is generally customary in liturgiology, where doxology is defined as "an expression of praise directed toward the Triune God . . . , which completes liturgical prayer, both by intensifying and directing it toward its goal."[2] The concept of "doxology" as a *terminus technicus* for such a narrowly defined liturgical unit is the product of recent liturgiological research.[3] It prescribes a very narrow usage for the term. The basic concept of "doxology," determinative for this study, issues from a much broader understanding. It also, however, transcends an aliturgical, *formgeschichtliche* definition, which sees the basic form of doxology as having the following elements: the naming of the recipient of praise, a doxological predicate, and a concluding ascription of praise.[4] Yet my definition of "doxology" is not so broadly drawn as it sometimes is in systematic theology, where it may include all prayer, whether lamentation, petition, thanksgiving, or praise.

For the purposes of this study, it is between these narrow and broad definitions that the concept "doxology," i.e., doxological speech, is found. Doxology is here understood as the explicit and implicit speech[5] of praise, confession of faith, prayer, and thanksgiving, as directed to God for God's glorification. Such doxological speech is found most often in prayers, hymnic confessions, and songs. For the purpose of the present study, the doxological character and intention of any given statement provide the determining criteria for designating a statement as doxological speech. In order to prevent any misunderstanding, note that the preceding description of the term *doxology* does not and does not intend to constitute a (new) definition, but rather provides a working hypothesis that helps delineate the field of exploration. So as not to restrict too sharply the field of exploration, the description of the term *doxology* has been kept intentionally rather broad. One thing should be clear from this description of the term: whether or not a statement takes the classic form of a (liturgical) doxology is secondary. In this way,

17

the narrow liturgiological definition of doxology is indeed broadened, but in such a way that the essence of doxology, as the language of praise to God, remains intact without becoming synonymous with the term *prayer*.

With such a description of the term *doxology*, this study commits itself to a moderate, and it is hoped, consensus-building, position within the scholarly discussion on the relationship of doxological speech to theological reflection. There are a few involved in the scholarly discussion who appropriate an even broader concept of doxology. For example, the theologian Dietrich Ritschl writes:

> By "doxological language" we mean the whole complex of utterances (in the Bible and later church tradition) which are *directly* prayer, i.e., petitions, thanksgiving, praises, etc., or *indirectly* related to prayer, such as liturgies, including narrative parts, and names, titles, ascriptions, designations, attributes and even "definitions" used with regard to Yahweh or Jesus, but not necessarily addressed to God.[6]

Without question such a definition can be meaningful. It describes the fundamental doxological orientation of all prayers and liturgies. The special concerns of this study, however, warrant a more narrow definition lest the area of exploration be without boundaries.

There are also some involved in the scholarly discussion who operate with an extremely narrow concept of doxology. Their view takes a specialized form of prayer, namely adoration, and elevates it over all other forms of praise and thanksgiving. In my opinion, this does not adequately take into account the doxological character and intention, for example, of thanksgiving or of hymnic confessions. The description of doxology embraced by this study provides the inclusion of these forms of doxological speech. In principle, this description of doxology takes a middle position between extremely narrow (liturgiological) and extremely broad (often those of systematic theology) definitions.

As the fundamental question on the relationship of doxology to theology is reviewed, the distinction between "cultic speech," that is, the language of the liturgy, and "the language of (private) devotion,"[7] often inadequately addressed by scholarly discussion, becomes important. The lack of appreciation for this distinction is especially true within Protestant theology and is attributable to obvious theological prejudgments. To differentiate between the language of the liturgy and the language of devotion, however, appears to be important for the following reason: while the speech of individual doxological devotion is difficult to grasp and analyze, the language of the liturgy has long been easily accessible and (since it is theologically more explicit and responsive) more readily subject to theological analysis. Even if the essential features of both forms of doxological speech seem identical, important differences are detected when reviewed in light of their relationship to theological reflection, especially when considering the question of doxology as a *locus theologicus.*

These differences are not limited to speech form alone (the language of the liturgy is often stylized, standardized, and ritualized,[8] while the language of devotion is formed by the speech of the individual at prayer). Neither are the differences solely attributable to limited accessibility for scholarly reflection. Rather, in the case of individual devotional language, the differences are to be found in the "bearers" of the language of the liturgy and the language of devotion. The language of the liturgy is not the private expression of the faith of an individual believer but rather the expression of faith of the (assembled) People of God standing in a long tradition of shared, public, and communal doxological speech. It is obvious that the language of the liturgy, as such, is (and must be) theologically more accessible and accountable than the language of private devotion.

These differences will play an important role in establishing the relationship of doxological speech to theological reflection. Naturally, it will not be as easy to identify the differences between the language of devotion and liturgical language in the hymns of Christian worship as the linguistic distinction made here might suggest. The hymns of Charles Wesley provide an excellent example of how devotional texts, when once a part of liturgical language, may again be integrated into the language of devotion. The transitions between both forms of religious speech are fluid and often exist solely, as mentioned above, in the different "bearers" of this speech in a given period of time.

2. "Theology in Hymns?"

Enough, for the moment, on doxology and its meaning for the present study. We turn now to the question of how doxological speech, as presently defined, relates to the doxological text material that will serve as the object of this study: Wesleyan hymnody. This question is best answered by addressing the justification for having chosen hymn texts in the first place as an example of doxological material.

It must be emphasized that not all hymns qua hymnic material are to be understood as doxology—even though hymn singing itself might suggest this. There are also many forms of confession of faith served by hymnic expression that are not explicitly doxological; for example, the so-called songs of "lamentation" in the Hebrew Bible. It must be added, however, that when it comes to Wesleyan hymnody, particularly as represented in *A Collection of Hymns for the Use of the People Called Methodists*, we are dealing almost exclusively with doxological hymn texts. This is a result, on the one hand, of the particular experience of faith at the heart of this collection and, on the other hand, of the selection process used for this hymnbook. Thus, Wesleyan hymnody offers a fine example of "doxology in hymns," the study of which will have something to say about "theology in hymns," which in turn will make a contribution to the fundamental question of the relationship of doxological speech to theological reflection.

But why even attempt to address this fundamental question with hymn texts—instead of another more obvious genre of doxological speech (for example, that of the Eucharistic prayer)? A variety of reasons speak for the decision to choose hymn texts. First, the category "hymnody" is a genre of doxological speech that would be held in common by practically all Christian traditions, whatever the form (this is important for the liturgical and ecumenical implications of this study). The same could not be said, for example, of the genre of many other fixed liturgical formularies, and certainly not of Eucharistic prayers (however regrettable this may be). From the liturgical and ecumenical perspective of this study it is particularly important to note that living, vital hymnody is not only the property of "liturgical" communities. On the contrary, so-called "nonliturgical" communities often cultivate especially vigorous hymn singing at worship. Hymns are then a genre of "doxological speech" that is held in common by the so-called liturgical and nonliturgical traditions alike. In spite of the importance of hymn traditions for the life of practically all Christian communities, theological reflection on hymns remains a stepchild of scholarly inquiry. Several important prerequisites, however, are missing before one can think of supplementing a doctrinal theology with a "theology in hymns."[9] The choice of *hymn* texts for this study therefore provides a good opportunity to press forward into an area as yet relatively unexplored theologically.

Finally, the choice of hymn texts for the study of the essential characteristics of doxological speech and its relationship to theological reflection is especially appropriate because hymnic texts comprise the bulk of doxological material in general.[10] After all, the most measured and effective exercise of doxology seems to rest not in the spoken but in the sung word. In the present study, this characteristic of doxology is taken into account by way of the texts chosen for examination.

It should also be noted that hymnody is one of the variable elements in worship and thus constitutes liturgical language or "cultic speech" with connections to the "language of devotion," which are often still quite recognizable. Not infrequently, texts originally devotional and private in character are found in the context of liturgical language. If the essential elements of both types of doxological speech are identical, it would seem important to choose texts for study that can belong to both types, liturgical language and the language of private devotion. Hymnody used in worship fits this description. Moreover, it is nowhere nearly as static in most traditions as, for example, the Eucharistic prayer. Thus, it demonstrates more clearly the imprint and interaction of a particular period and its theology. This, too, is important for the present study.

After this brief justification of the choice of hymn texts for the present study, there is yet another word to say about the title of this inquiry: "Theology in Hymns." The title is not new.[11] In 1737, Johann Jacob Gottschaldt (1688–1759) published a hymnbook with the title *Theologia in Hymnis*. Today, the term "theology in hymns" is often used as a short form for attempting theological interpretation of doxological material. Without a doubt this is an important and rewarding task for theological inquiry, even biblical inquiry, as well as that of church history, the history of dogma, liturgiology, theology (in the narrow sense of the word), and other disciplines, for example, pastoral theology. At the same time, however, the term "theology in hymns" prompts fundamental questions and problems that are

21

often not asked by studies with this leitmotif and thus remain unanswered. The following problem is implied in the term "theology in hymns": assuming that a *theological* study of doxological material is both suitable and appropriate, this fact would not change the way in which the study was done (theological) nor would it change the type of material studied (doxological). The question then must be asked: In what sense can one speak of a "theology in hymns," without missing the essential characteristics and intention of doxological-hymnic expression? It would appear as if the phrase "theology in hymns," suggests that the manner in which a text is to be studied forces the text to change its character in order to be consistent with the method of study. But is it possible for a scholarly, theological analysis of doxological-hymnic expression to take place under such mechanisms without it becoming inadequate? This question, prompted by the term "theology in hymns," is the one that motivates the present study. Thus, the term "theology in hymns," and the questions relevant to the relationship between theology and hymns point to the fundamental problem of the title of the study.

It remains a key phrase for this study and its title, one that until now has eluded more precise definition. It is a question of the term *theology* or, as the case may be, theological reflection. This is not the place to review all the many faceted efforts at understanding and defining this term. That would be of secondary importance for the present study, which is primarily concerned with the particular form of doxology. But since the particular form of doxology is to be explored by way of its relationship to theological reflection, it seems worthwhile, at this point, to mark the difference between these two forms of faith expression, however briefly. (This study presupposes, of course, that these two forms of faith expression cannot be separated from each other, but are instead closely related.) This characterization will help clarify the manner in which the term *theology* or, as the case may be, theological reflection, is used by this study.

I will limit myself to but a few remarks here. The real exploration of this theme can only take place in the last part of this study. Briefly, the intrinsic and manifest differences between "doxological speech" and "theological reflection" for which a consensus can be found even in widely differing definitions of the nature of theology are as follows: Theological reflection employs, principally, the scholarly language of theological discipline and addresses, primarily, the church (and the academic community). Doxology uses as its medium, in most cases, the *genus poeticum*, and addresses itself, primarily, to God. Theological reflection is argumentative and descriptive (of and about God's history with humankind and the cosmos). Doxology is ascriptive (to God). Theology strives for coherence and lucidity while doxology strives for transparency. Theological reflection intends theological clarity and abstraction. Doxology intends *orthodoxa* as the proper praise of God and is, finally, without agenda. Doxological speech is also often shared by more communities than theological reflection: when theological differences exist people are often still able to sing and pray together. Further differences between doxology and theology are easily identified. The last part of this study will return to these differences.

These brief observations on the relationship of doxology to theology make clear that the present study is working with a fairly narrow definition of theology. Even those who work with a broader definition would not contest the fundamental characteristics of doxological speech and theological reflection, described by this study, though they may stress different definitions for the two forms of speech. Clearly, this short description has not said everything that needs to be said about this study's understanding of theology[12] (and its relationship to doxology). But with this study's theme defined and terms initially clarified, the following remarks are reserved for two of its fundamental aspects, which will motivate and accompany it throughout. They have to do with the liturgical and ecumenical dimensions of doxological material and with the concept of the "constitutive multilingual nature" of the faith. First, a few remarks on the liturgical and ecumenical dimensions of this study.

3. Liturgical and Ecumenical Perspectives

The liturgical and ecumenical dimensions of the present study will be determined, first of all, by the choice of doxological texts that will serve as its foundation; namely, a selection of hymns from early Methodism by Charles Wesley, the cofounder of the largest newly formed church besides Pentecostalism of the modern era. Why this doxological material? The choice of Wesleyan hymnody as an example of hymnic-doxological speech was prompted, in part, by the bilateral dialogue between the Roman Catholic Church and the World Methodist Council, which has produced five joint reports since its beginning shortly after the Second Vatican Council. In these reports, Methodists have continually pointed to the hymns of Charles Wesley as pivotal to their community's expression of faith.[13] An ideal of Methodist theological reflection, clearly informed by this positioning of Wesley's hymns, finds expression in the formulation, "a theology that can be sung(!)."[14] The Roman Catholic members of the joint commission also acknowledged, "that the hymns of Charles Wesley, a rich source of Methodist spirituality, find echoes and recognition in the Catholic soul."[15] At the same time, all members emphasized the need to promote a common use of hymns in worship.[16] In any case, Wesleyan hymnody has clearly demonstrated its relevance to ecumenical relations and dialogue. It is a fundamental expression of Methodism's faith, both in its historical development and present reality.

But the liturgical-ecumenical dimension of the present study extends beyond the consideration given ecumenical dialogues (even if these are important for theological study and teaching). What is true for Methodism, in some similar measure, may be true for all churches and ecclesial communities. In Methodism, a community that has no normative dogmatic theology of its own except by way of the sermons and exegetical notes of John Wesley, Wesleyan hymnody provides one such hidden norm. In many ways one could say that it is these hymns that shape the actual identity of Methodism.

What is manifest for Methodism may also hold for other churches and ecclesial communities. The heart and soul of these communities may be found not in normative dogmatic statements, but rather in doxological traditions and their practice. No simple priority for doxology over theology should be postulated from this. Only note that liturgy, the doxological practice *par excellence*, "is the summit toward which the activity of the church is directed; it is also the fount from which all her power flows," as formulated by the Constitution on the Sacred Liturgy of the Second Vatican Council (SC 10). Doxological practice is named here as the essence of the *communio sanctorum* and the self-realization of the church. In light of this interpretation, the doxological and liturgical traditions of the church need to be given more careful consideration in systematic, ecumenical, and confessional theologies than has been the case until now. Specifically, this would mean that every systematic, ecumenical, and confessional theology would need to take up the doxological traditions of the churches (the prayers, hymns, and liturgies) not simply their dogmatic statements. Only once this is guaranteed can one be certain that dogmatic theology will not be isolated from the life of prayer that has formed the church.

A further observation must be added to this emphasis on the importance of doxological traditions within the life of the churches: "that members of divided churches find it much easier to pray and witness together than to formulate common dogmatic statements. In other words, the members of one church have little difficulty in appropriating for themselves the prayers and preaching of another church."[17] This squares with the notion that while churches of diverse confessions have waged the grimmest of battles with one another, the hymns of the churches have always transcended confessional lines and thus accomplished a "concealed ecumenism"[18] long before ecumenism became officially fashionable. The ecumenical potential of common doxological language and the central positioning of doxological traditions in the lives of the churches make doxological material an important field for ecumenical study.

It is apparent that the liturgical-ecumenical dimensions of this study are multilayered and are as related to the choice of material to be studied as they are to the broader context in which this study is pursued. Finally, proceeding in this fashion makes a case for the serious study of the ecumenical dimension in all theological research, particularly in connection with confessional themes. In this day and age, one should no longer formulate theology independent of "the separated brothers and sisters."

4. The Constitutive Multilingual Nature of Faith

The constitutive multilingual nature of faith (Richard Schaeffler) has, in no small way, given rise to the multiplicity of church traditions and ecclesial communities. This constitutive multilingual nature of faith provides one of the starting points for the present study. Even though the present study will work primarily with two forms of this multilingual faith, that of doxological speech and theological reflection, this should not hide the fact that the response of faith to the call of God is always multifaceted and that this multifacetedness is intrinsic for faith.[19] Three important and fundamental expressions of this multifaceted language of faith may be characterized by the threefold formula, *leiturgia-martyria-diakonia,* often used in recent

25

Roman Catholic discussions.[20] For the present study, it is important to allow for the legitimate, peculiar characteristics of these three fundamental faith expressions, and the tension between them, so that any tendency to dissolve one of them into another might be resisted.

At the same time it must be emphasized that the peculiar characteristics of these faith expressions cannot be understood independently from one another, never mind conceiving of a conflict between them. That all share a comprehensive framework, namely the response of faith to the saving grace of God, is undeniable. Thus, a fundamental partnership within the constitutive multilingual nature of faith has to be noted here. The entire faith response of humankind is complete only when *all* forms are taken together. The intrinsic multifaceted language of faith is insisted upon here specifically in order to avoid the impression that the present study might assume a duality of forms in the expression of faith (doxology and theology), thus resulting in a gross oversimplification of the issue.

The above notwithstanding, in theological discussion the tension between differing expressions of faith is often understood by the coupling of terms: faith and works, liturgy and life, *lex orandi* and *lex credendi*. The question must be asked: Do such couplings of terms do justice to the characteristics of each faith expression and to the multifaceted nature of the language of faith? Or do they lead inevitably to a regrettable one-sidedness? Is it not only in the light of the partnership between all faith expressions that each is adequately grasped?

With the aid of these questions it becomes clear, at least for the present study, that an inquiry into the relationship between doxological speech and theological reflection does not want to suggest a fundamental duality in the forms of faith expression, which could be analyzed and perhaps even synthesized. Rather, the present study will consider one specific connection within the multifaceted language of faith, which needs clarification. It is not implausible that light may be cast through such a study on other connections and their partnership within the multilingual nature of faith.

B. The Development and Goal of the Study

Having stated the proposed definition of this study's theme in the introduction above, the study will develop as follows: the presentation of the contemporary discussion on the relationship of doxology and theology and its context occupies chapter 2. This presentation is divided into several fields of theological inquiry: the Roman Catholic study of liturgy (A); Protestant systematic theology (B); Orthodox theology (C); and ecumenical discussions (D). In spite of specific questions and perspectives raised within these various fields of theological inquiry, it is clear that they share a common interest as far as the present study is concerned: the relationship of doxological speech to theological reflection, in its broadest sense.

Following the presentation of the contemporary discussion on the relationship of doxology and theology, the second part of this book will turn to the study of a particular doxological tradition, that of *A Collection of Hymns for the Use of the People Called Methodists* (chapter 3). An introductory section describes the historical, theological, and spiritual context of this Methodist hymnbook (A). An excursus then sheds some light on the contemporary research into Wesleyan hymnody within which this study takes place. The second section will describe the specific characteristics of Wesleyan hymnody (B), in order to secure a starting point for the individual interpretations of theological themes and hymns that will follow. The last part of the chapter (C) is the heart of this part of the study. It is dedicated to a detailed theological interpretation of the central themes of *A Collection of Hymns for the Use of the People Called Methodists*.

Following the analysis of the scholarly discussion on the relationship of doxology and theology in part 1 (chapters 1 and 2) and the exploration of specific doxological texts in part 2 (chapter 3), part 3 attempts to describe the essential characteristics of doxological speech in its relationship to theological reflection (chapter 4). A more careful analysis of the peculiar characteristics of doxology must first be secured. This chapter approaches this task by way of three guiding questions, which will, at the same time, delineate three sections of this chapter. What are the characteristics of doxological speech (A)? What criteria are required for an acknowledgement of its legitimacy (B)? How will they be tested (C)?

The fourth and last section (D) attempts to present for discussion this study's characterization of the relationship of doxological speech to theological reflection. As has already been emphasized, nothing more than a preliminary finding should be expected from this section. This preliminary finding will, obviously, need to be tested by further studies of other doxological traditions and modified accordingly. In this way, this third section should not be taken as the last word on this theme but rather as a *prolegomenon* to further considerations given to the relationship between doxology and theology.

A further word must be added here in regard to the three parts of this study, or as the case may be, the specific role of the second part, which deals with Wesleyan hymnody. It may appear that the analysis of *A Collection of Hymns for the Use of the People Called Methodists* of 1780 forms an erratic block of material within the fundamental consideration of the relationship of doxological speech to theological reflection. This impression is not far from the truth. On the one hand, parts 1 and 3 could be understood as the ongoing development of a particular line of reasoning, which even (and especially?) without part 2 would yield a coherent analysis. On the other hand, part 2, the actual study of Wesleyan hymnody, could stand on its own as contributing to the field of Charles Wesley research, without the framing discussions of parts 1 and 3.

Why then, connect these three parts into a single study? First, these two themes (parts 1 and 3, on the one hand, and part 2, on the other) evolved simultaneously. In some sense, their division is artificial and secondary (even if the finished study creates the opposite impression). As these themes were developed they formed and productively influenced one another. This is not, however, to be understood simplistically in the sense of doxological texts being immediately applicable in theological reflection, as emphasized at the beginning of this study. The tension-filled relationship between doxological speech and theological reflection prohibits, in my opinion, such a direct conclusion. The connection between the two themes of this study is perhaps better described by the "contextualization" of deliberations on the relationship of doxology and theology by way of a study of concrete doxological material: these deliberations will be developed within the study of specific doxological texts so that this context will help determine and form the discussion.

This study, then, cannot be about providing a quotation from Wesleyan hymnody for every theological conclusion presented. To begin and proceed in such a fashion would not be helpful in determining the complex relationship between doxology and theology.

The connection between the two themes of this study is more indirect, circumspect, and guarded. Perhaps a Pauline image would be helpful here in interpreting the connection between this study's three parts. The second part, the concrete study of a specific doxological tradition, might be characterized as "the thorn in the flesh" of the discussion on the relationship of doxology and theology—"to keep [them] from being too elated" (2 Cor. 12:7). In other words, this second part is not undertaken in order to produce immediate illustrations for the execution of the third part, but rather, stated cautiously, in order to provide a context for reflection that would ensure that the conclusions are not established in a doxological vacuum. I would suggest that this is the glue that holds the three parts of this study together and justifies their collection into a single study.

CHAPTER 2

Doxology and Theology:
The Recent Discussion

In this first phase of the present study the context for inquiry into the relationship between doxology and theology will be established. It will become clear that this inquiry does not exist in a vacuum, but rather is surrounded by the multifaceted pursuit of related questions.

Even though consideration of the relationship between theology and doxology (as an explicit problem) has long stood in the shadow of other theological challenges, several points of departure for the consideration of this question have emerged in the twentieth century. They can be traced to a variety of factors found, most notably, in four fields of theological inquiry. Each individual field of inquiry has, for the most part, had little influence on the others—a fact that is losing its import now with the growing importance of ecumenical inquiry into the relationship between doxology and theology. The hope remains that an effective exchange of information may yet emerge between the various fields of theological inquiry dealing with the relationship between theology and doxology, even if the reasons, goals, and means of their study remain dissimilar. The fields of inquiry to be addressed include: Roman Catholic liturgiology, Protestant systematics, the Orthodox tradition, and ecumenical dialogue.

What follows will present briefly the historical points of departure and differing modes of inquiry as well as the development and treatment of the theme within the four identified fields of inquiry. In spite of differences in terminology and varying theological emphases, I hope to show that these fields of theological study are fundamentally concerned with the same theme and that the connection between these different discourses is significant.

A. *Roman Catholic Liturgiology:* ut legem credendi lex statuat supplicandi

Until recently, when Roman Catholic theology was challenged by the question of the relationship between theology and doxology, one could find very little material on the subject. This did not mean, however, that the topic did not receive any attention within Roman Catholic circles. Rather, the forum in which the discussion of this topic took place was not necessarily identified as (dogmatic) theology. Second, the discussion that took place was not conducted, in terms of the language used in the present study, on the relationship of "theology" and "doxology." "Doxology" within the Roman Catholic tradition can only be understood by way of a strong connection to the liturgical tradition of the church. Accordingly, the main point of interest in this topic was centered on the language of the liturgy (not the language of individual devotion) and its relationship to dogma and theology.

Taking these two factors into account, a continuous and important discussion is to be found within Roman Catholicism, at least in the twentieth century,[1] on the relationship of theology and doxology, more specifically on the relationship of dogma, dogmatics, and liturgy. This discussion is largely found within the field of liturgiology and is guided by the following Patristic axiom: *ut legem credendi lex statuat supplicandi*[2]—even though it cannot be overlooked that the discussion often ignored the very limited original meaning of the phrase. It is no accident that this axiom is often reduced to the oscillating phrase *lex orandi—lex credendi*, which, when taken out of context, can be drawn into a variety of constructs rarely having anything in common with the phrase's origin.

The interest of Roman Catholic liturgiology in the axiom just quoted, which is attributed to Tiro Prosper of Aquitaine (ca. A.D. 390–455), a disciple of Augustine,[3] cannot be explained by the quickly increasing importance of the liturgical movement in the first half of this century alone, even though, without a doubt, this was the most influential factor. Rather, two other factors must be taken into account even though, in the end, they prove antagonistic to one another. The first has to do with the interest that this early church axiom (born of the struggle with semi-Pelagianism) generated during the Modernist Controversy. Two influential books by the English Modernist George Tyrrell (1861–1909) took their titles from the substance of Prosper's axiom.[4] This starting point was also adopted, most notably, by Tyrrell's article entitled "The Relation of Theology to Devotion."[5] The author argued for the historical and dogmatic priority of the *lex orandi* as opposed to the *lex credendi*, a position met with great mistrust by the Roman Catholic magisterium of his day.

That Prosper's axiom, in spite of Tyrrell's interest, avoided the suspicion of heresy and was able to rise to such prominence in the twentieth century, is likely attributable to the second factor from which interest in the axiom was generated. In seeking to substantiate Marian dogma, the church's magisterium seized on Prosper's axiom: In order to demonstrate the lengthy tradition of the announced dogma, Pope Pius IX explicitly referred to the liturgy when the immaculate conception of Mary was pronounced dogma in 1854. The reference to the liturgy, however, was not an isolated reference within this context of dogmatic justification. The liturgical tradition as such was not important, but rather the fact that it (according to Pius IX) faithfully mirrored the convictions of the magisterium: the church's teaching office had introduced and furthered, throughout the history of the church, an emphasis on Mary's *immaculata conceptio* in various liturgical texts and rites.

Similar reasoning can also be found in other papal proclamations on the liturgy.[6] The importance of the *lex orandi* is guaranteed by its subordination to the church's magisterium. This kind of "liturgical proof-texting" can even lead to a papal reversal of the early church axiom, as found in the 1947 encyclical of Pius XII, *Mediator Dei*. The Pope claims boldly, *"lex credendi legem statuat supplicandi."*[7] It is noteworthy that this interpretation, that is, this reversal, of Prosper's axiom was taken up again recently. The Roman Catholic liturgiologist, Walter Dürig, under the influence of *Mediator Dei* maintained that the liturgy could never generate dogma, rather it must always follow and be subordinate to dogma as taught by the magisterium.[8]

The Modernist Controversy and papal proclamations were not, however, the central areas in which Roman Catholic theology dealt with the question on the relationship of dogma, dogmatics, and liturgy. Instead, this question surfaced particularly in liturgiology, which in this century has been revolutionized by the Liturgical Movement. The question that first faced Roman Catholic theologians at the beginning of the Liturgical Movement centered on the utilization of the liturgy as a didactic medium and a source for theological reflection. This was an attempt to "theologically revalue" the liturgy, which (understood as a part of the church's tradition) was to take its place next to, and subordinate to, dogma and the magisterium—not above them as the Modernists had envisioned it. Such a "theological revaluation" of the liturgy must be seen against the background of a liturgy that had for centuries already ceased to influence and form (Western) theology in any significant way—one has only to note the matter of course taken in outlining sacramental theology quite independently of liturgical rites and texts. In this sense, the attempt to "revalue" the liturgy theologically was long overdue, even if the manner in which it was presented at the beginning of the twentieth century would not necessarily persist. At the same time, it must not be forgotten that this "theological revaluation" of the liturgy was part of a comprehensive paradigm shift in the understanding of liturgy and thus in the self-apprehension of liturgiology. This paradigm shift made critical contributions to the theological interpretation of liturgical rites and texts.

In his article, "Die Liturgie als dogmatische Erkenntnisquelle," the Paderborn professor of dogmatics, Johannes Brinktrine (1889–1965) provides a good example of the attempt to establish a relationship between liturgy and dogmatics from the theological perspective of his day. The article, written in 1929, is dedicated to a description of criteria for the *certain* proof of doctrine by way of the liturgy.[9] The author refers first to the Eucharistic canon, the reliability of which, as a source of dogmatic knowledge, is secured because the Council of Trent declared it *ab omne errorum purum.* Brinktrine also made a case for the theologically normative validity of rubrics and symbols since these were established by the church and the church could not err in matters pertaining to sacramental validity, especially in the Eucharist. During this time similar tendencies to use the liturgy for proof-texting doctrinal teaching were not unusual, in later years especially with reference to the encyclical *Mediator Dei.*[10] The well-loved catchphrase, *Liturgie als gebetetes Dogma* (the liturgy as prayed dogma), appears to have its origin within this context.[11] It echoes the assertion of Pope Pius XI that the liturgy signifies the most important tool of the church's teaching office.[12] It must not be forgotten, however, that this assertion continued to assume a relatively narrow understanding of the nature of the liturgy which, strictly speaking, did not do justice to the essence of the liturgical event. Within this narrow understanding of the liturgy, the dogmatic status of a conglomeration of texts, ceremonies, and rites authorized by the church was being reflected upon, not the substance of the dialogue between God and humankind in the liturgical celebration of the church and its relationship to the confession of faith.

Of course, it was clear from the beginning that this dogmatic "utilitarianism" would not do justice to the actual essence of the liturgy. The Jesuit theologian, Johann Baptist Umberg (born in 1875), already inadvertently pointed this out in his article on liturgical style and dogmatics published in 1926.[13] The author, who at the same time was involved in the nascent controversy over the *Mysterientheologie* of Odo Casel, emphasized the peculiar character of liturgical speech and action and warned against its direct employment in dogmatic theology. Umberg's emphasis was not only appropriate in view of the attempts at a (in the last analysis utilitarian) dogmatic revaluation of the liturgy but also in light of papal use of the liturgy for proclamations from the magisterium. The liturgiologist Joseph Pascher repeated and refined Umberg's warning at the beginning of the 1960s in a far more exacting fashion, when the liturgical witness was being considered as one of the markers for the doctrine of Mary as *mediatrix omnium gratiarum.* In his article "Theologische Erkenntnis aus der Liturgie," Pascher stressed that even if liturgical rites and texts implied notions of Mary as a mediator of grace, this should not, under any circumstances, be understood as a theological-dogmatic assertion. Liturgical language must be recognized and respected as a "special type" of language.[14] Pascher's article signaled the beginning of an important reversal. The pursuit of the relationship between dogma, dogmatic theology, and liturgy, that is, between theological and liturgical language, has been approached in recent decades with far more caution than at the turn of this century. Increasingly, notions that maintain direct and immediate connections between liturgy and theology, erasing the peculiar nature of liturgical language while unilaterally making use of and subordinating liturgy to theology, are losing credibility.[15]

Viewed from yet another perspective, the whole equation and interchangeability of *lex orandi . . . lex credendi* had become suspect. Historical studies on Prosper of Aquitaine's writings produced a far more narrow (and thus more concrete) definition of the early church axiom than had been previously recognized.[16] Above all, it became clear that Prosper's method did not necessarily (as had been assumed) represent a theological argument based on tradition but rather on Holy Scripture. As a student of Augustine, Prosper, in conflict with semi-Pelagianism, referred to the Holy Scriptures as that with which the liturgy of the church must be consistent. The

Pauline command to pray for all humankind, rightly obeyed in the intercessions of the church, demonstrates the necessity of an all-saving grace. Thus, according to Prosper, it holds true: *ut legem credendi lex statuat supplicandi.*

Within the Liturgical Movement itself, which is largely responsible for the renewed central positioning of the liturgy in the life of the twentieth-century church, yet another aspect of the relationship of theology and liturgy has been given considerable attention. Theologians such as the Benedictine Odo Casel (1886–1948) had set aside neoscholastic theology. Theology was now grounded in and interpreted by the liturgical mystery. It was to be understood, primarily, as sacramental theology.[17]

The whole framework for the question of the relationship between liturgy and theology was changed again with and after the Second Vatican Council, particularly in connection with its call for liturgical renewal and reform. The following three things should be noted: (1) The autocracy of the Roman canon, held as "inerrant" since the Council of Trent, was broken, while many of the ceremonies and rubrics that still maintained dogmatic importance at the turn of the century disappeared. (2) At the same time, the renewal of the liturgy was, in the end, an act of the church's teaching office (unless, of course, one argues that the liturgy had so recaptured its primitive power in the liturgical renewal that the magisterium had no choice but to recognize it officially). But, on the whole, the relationship between the liturgy and the teaching office of the church, despite all the changes in liturgical life, was never truly affected. (3) With the translation of liturgical texts into native languages a new interest in the peculiarity of liturgical language emerged that began to clarify the poetic and ritual character of liturgical language.

The consequences of conciliar and postconciliar liturgical renewal for the discussion on the relationship of the *lex orandi* to the *lex credendi* were manifested, above all, in a considerable broadening of horizons. It was no longer a question of how liturgical texts, ceremonies, and rubrics related to dogmatic proclamations. The focus shifted to questions about the nature of the liturgy itself. For the first time its peculiar character was taken seriously. The essence of the liturgy, indeed, the essence of liturgical action was no longer characterized by its close ties to dogma and the magisterium. Rather, attention turned to the poetic and doxological peculiarities of the *lex orandi.* Interest in a direct and functional utilization of the liturgy as a *locus theologicus* waned.

At the same time, an increasing interest in liturgical questions slowly emerged among dogmatic theologians. Notable are the contributions of Edward Schillebeeckx[18] and Karl Lehmann[19] as well as the theological considerations of Walter Kasper[20] and Frans Jozef van Beecks. But, on the whole, it must be said, that Roman Catholic dogmatic theology has remained curiously untouched by the liturgiological discussion on the relationship of theology to liturgy. This was recently apparent in the *Festschrift* in honor of the German liturgiologist, Emil Joseph Lengeling, which appeared under the title *Liturgie—ein vergessenes Thema der Theologie?*[21] Even though the term *theology* here does not strictly refer to dogmatic theology, but rather to all theological disciplines, still the contribution of the dogmatic theologian to this *Festschrift* is telling. The Münster dogmatic theologian and student of Karl Rahner, Herbert Vorgrimler, reviewed "Liturgie als Thema der Dogmatik." Prompted by the conclusions of the Second Vatican Council, he began by recognizing the liturgy as a core theme of all theology. Indeed, liturgical theology has advanced to become a field of its own among the theological disciplines and should be of greater concern to those who work in dogmatic theology. According to Vorgrimler, after Holy Scripture, which serves as the primary source of faith, the liturgy is the most important witness of faith the tradition offers and the most important tool of the church's magisterium. Thus, he writes, "If the liturgy is not simply a witness of the faith of the people of God (and that, at best, by way of acclamation), but rather an expression of the church's teaching office, then dogmatic theology has the right to ask the fundamental question, how and when does the liturgy, as an expression of the church's teaching office, function with binding force."[22]

Though the question posed by Vorgrimler is not answered, it does paint an interesting picture of the fundamental understanding of liturgy. The liturgy is defined as "an instrument of the ordinary (and extra-ordinary) teaching office of the church," by which is implied that the church's hierarchy should also serve as the actual bearer and subject of the liturgy.[23] The question remains as to whether dogmatic theology, in this case, does not introduce problems into the study of liturgy that in their essence are incompatible with, or at least of secondary importance to, the dialogue between liturgiology and dogmatic theology. This recalls an earlier dogmatic theology that embraced a utilitarian view of the liturgy—a view that is not conducive to making liturgy "the central theme of theology" as the introduction to the *Festschrift* demanded.[24] Here one glimpses a reason for the conspicuous apathy of dogmatic theology in the relationship of theology and liturgy/doxology: until recently, dogmatic theology has not fully appreciated or engaged the power of the paradigm shift in liturgical understanding in the twentieth century.

An article by Maria-Judith Krahe (a Benedictine influenced by Odo Casel) points the discussion on this matter in a new direction. In her often overlooked article, "Psalmen, Hymnen und Lieder, wie der Geist sie eingibt," she attempts to understand theology on four different levels, as the programmatic subtitle indicates: "Doxologie als Ursprung und Ziel aller Theologie." The term *theology* is used in the broadest sense of the word, including theology as the speech *of* God, *from* God, *about* God, and *to* God. According to Krahe, theology exists only where these different levels of understanding are integrated. As an outstanding example of such an integrated "primitive" theology, she cites the hymn in the Letter to the Ephesians (Eph. 1:3-14), and writes:

> The content of such a "primitive" theology—the mystery of God's will to save—determines its speech, its *Sitz im Leben* in the community, and its task. It also, however, names the prerequisites for those who would work with this theology: faith, hearing, being filled with the Holy Spirit upon the forgiveness of sins, the life in Christ. These are the fundamentals on which all theologies must be founded, even if theological differentiation and scholarly development take them beyond the Letter to the Ephesians. The development could not and cannot stand still in this "primitive" form. The paradigm by which all theologians and theologies are measured, however, remains constant.[25]

The liturgiologist Aidan Kavanagh, OSB, takes a similar tack in his book, *On Liturgical Theology*, published in 1985. Kavanagh's thoughts are reported here in somewhat greater detail for he wishes to redirect previous notions of the liturgy as subjugated to the teaching office and dogma into a recognition of the liturgy's intrinsic value vis-à-vis dogmatics. Specifically, he accords the liturgy a place prior to theology. From the beginning, Kavanagh is clear about what interests him and what does not: "liturgical theology" is not meant to suggest a dogmatic tract on the liturgy, or a systematic theology built on liturgical material. Rather, according to Kavanagh, the adjective *liturgical* indicates that theology is to be formulated from the liturgical action that makes possible, determines, and forms it. In principle, the entire book turns on this assertion. Kavanagh begins with the customary distinction between *theologia prima* and *theologia secunda*, thus naming the liturgy as *theologia prima* in much the same way as the Orthodox theologian Alexander Schmemann (to whom the book is dedicated): "the liturgy . . . 'is not an *authority* or a *locus theologicus*; it is the ontological condition of theology.'" [26] Since, for Kavanagh, theology in its broadest sense represents a reflection on the communion between God and humankind, it is clear that the community at prayer before God must be the starting point and center of all theology. A key term used by the author in this connection is *orthodoxia*, referring to the authentic worship of God. Kavanagh sees its relationship to the *theologia secunda* as consistent with Prosper's axiom *ut legem credendi lex statuat supplicandi*, according particular importance to the verb: liturgy constitutes and forms theology. He distances himself from Geoffrey Wainwright's assertion that theology does serve a certain function vis-à-vis the liturgy, on the one hand, while, on the other, providing for the systematic study of the liturgy: "The liturgy is neither structured nor does it operate in such a way as to provide doctrinal conclusions."[27] Nevertheless, the liturgy is not given over to haphazard development and growth. According to Kavanagh four "canonical" regulations order it: the canon of Holy Scripture, the canon of the baptismal confession of faith, the Eucharistic canon, and canon law. Based on this assertion, Kavanagh returns to his starting point and develops it as follows:

> I have insisted so far upon the liturgical act as the primary theological act in a church's life because it is the first act of critical reflection triggered by faith-encounters with the presence of the living God in the midst of those who assemble precisely for this end. As such, the liturgical dialectic of encounter, change, and adjustment to change amounts to a reflective and lived theology which is native to all the members of the faithful assembly.[28]

So much for Kavanagh's original contributions. The author obviously attempts in *On Liturgical Theology* to draw conclusions for theological reflection and dogmatic work from an interpretation of the liturgy—one that views the liturgy as crucial and fundamental to Christian life and thought.

It is clear that liturgiological claims with regard to the meaning of the liturgy in the life of the church are rarely taken seriously by dogmatic theology. However, several important new attempts to build bridges between these two fields must be noted. The Jesuit Lothar Lies, in his article entitled "Theologie als eulogisches Handeln,"[29] attempts to demonstrate how the essence of theology has a Eucharistic structure. His starting point is as simple as it is obvious. Since the Eucharist functions as the source and high point of the church's life, theology, as reflection on faith, must also be a reflection in and of this source. Lies points to four elements present in the Eucharist that determine the meaning of the Eucharist: *anamnesis, epiclesis*, real presence, and sacrifice.

The Jesuit Edward J. Kilmartin embraces a similar perspective in a short chapter ("Theology as Theology of the Liturgy") of his book *Christian Liturgy*, published in 1988. Assuming the central place of the liturgy in the life of the church, the author demands that every theology must accept as its task reflection on the theology of liturgy. (The axiom *lex orandi—lex credendi*, never quoted in *Christian Liturgy* in its original form, is interpreted by Kilmartin as follows: "the law of prayer is the law of belief, and vice versa.")[30]

The dogmatic theologian Catherine Mowry LaCugna, chooses a similar premise to that of Kilmartin in her article "Can Liturgy ever again be a Source for Theology?" when determining the relationship between liturgy and theology based on the individual "doxological moments" of each: "liturgy and theology are *intrinsically* related to each other because the 'inner moment' of both is doxology."[31] LaCugna uses the doxological alignment of theology and liturgy to outline a relationship that emphasizes their interdependency on each other.

How is the preceding review of discussion within Roman Catholic liturgiology useful and what interest does it hold for the present study? Above all, it appears that the significance of the liturgy and its understanding (and thus the essence of the doxological traditions of the church) has been recognized and significantly furthered. The "value" of the liturgy will no longer be sought for the purpose of determining its use for dogma, theology, and the teaching office of the church. But rather its peculiar nature will be respected as having its own contribution to make as a specific form of faith expression.[32] This study is to be understood as a part of this attempt to discern the particular contribution of doxological traditions to the overall expression of faith of the people of God.

B. Protestant Systematic Theology: The Linguistic Differences Between Dogmatics and the Language of Faith

Protestant theology, in comparison to Roman Catholic theology, relies on a different methodology when addressing the relationship between theology and doxology. For Protestant theology, the nature of the relationship between theology and doxology is not primarily a liturgical concern, but rather a theological one. Thus, it should come as no surprise that, until recently, the discussion in this field has not centered exclusively on the relationship between theology and doxology, but rather on the broader question of linguistic differences between dogmatic speech and the language of faith. This represents an important shift in emphasis when compared to the discussion within Roman Catholic liturgical theology. If Roman Catholic liturgiology has been chiefly concerned with "cultic speech," that is, the language of the liturgy, then Protestant theology has engaged the language of devotion more intensively. Of course, the entire framework for addressing this question must be seen within the broader context of "a turning to linguistics"[33] (*linguistische Wende*) by theologians of the last several decades.

Interest in the linguistic differences between dogmatic speech and the language of faith was initially awakened by way of a Christological debate, where it soon found a controversial formulation. Note the distinction drawn between theological and poetical/doxological/liturgical speech by several authors in John Hick's book, *The Myth of God Incarnate*, published in 1977. This distinction suggests an affirmation of the classical language of the incarnation in doxological terms while at the same time rejecting this language in the dogmatic sphere. Other more tentative studies in this area have exercised greater influence and contributed to an increasing interest in the question of the relationship between theology and doxology. The most important examples of these studies are noted below since they will hopefully have a lasting impact on the scholarly debate.

Gerhard Ebeling considers the relationship between dogmatic speech and the language of faith in his *Dogmatik des christlichen Glaubens*. While he identifies similarities (particularly in distinguishing both from the language of science) and differences,[34] Ebeling insists that the development of more precise categories for theological and doxological linguistic theory is required before a detailed discussion can continue. Ebeling's interest in doxological speech, in the broadest sense of the word (he writes specifically of "prayer"), is particularly clear in his book, *Dogmatik des christlichen Glaubens*, where he refers to "prayer as the key to the doctrine of God."[35]

Of course, Ebeling is not the first Protestant systematic theologian to take up the theme of prayer and worship in his work. Others who deserve mention here include: Karl Barth, Peter Brunner, Regin Prenter, Edmund Schlink, and Vilmos Vajta.[36] It was, however, not until the British Methodist, Geoffrey Wainwright, published his book *Doxology* (1980) that a Protestant systematic theology had taken worship as its fundamental point of reference.[37] Wainwright places the early church phrase *lex orandi—lex credendi* at the heart of his systematic theology. This orientation alone (up until this time Prosper's axiom had played virtually no role whatsoever in Protestant systematic theology) was enough to keep the author of *Doxology* from working in isolation from Roman Catholic liturgiology. As might be assumed by the use of the Patristic leitmotiv, Wainwright concentrates exclusively on the liturgical traditions of the church, specifically on liturgical language, rather than "prayer" or the language of an individual's devotional life. More than once, Wainwright reminds the reader that his work represents a systematic theology first, and second—indirectly, as it were—a theology of liturgy. The author is, after all, a professor of systematic theology. Accordingly, he designates his task and goal with the subtitle of *Doxology*, "A *systematic* theology." It is also not difficult to spot the priorities of systematic theology in the overall structure of the book (the chapter titles are reminiscent of the classical themes of [Protestant] dogmatic theology). *Doxology* is distinguished from other attempts at Protestant systematic theology by the perspective from which the theology is pursued. Wainwright is the first among (Protestant) systematic theologians to take seriously the liturgy as a *locus theologicus,* that is, as the primary context for the exercise and expression of faith and reflection upon it. In the words of the title of an article by Wainwright that would appear later: "the worship of God is both a source and a theme of theology."[38]

What is the nature of the relationship between liturgy and theology for which *Doxology* makes its case? In one sense, the entire book is devoted to answering this question, but particularly the two central chapters entitled "Lex Orandi" and "Lex Credendi" take up this task. The early church axiom, to which these chapters are dedicated, is the foundation of Wainwright's work. Wainwright, by way of this starting point, postulates a deep interdependence between liturgy and theology. The book cannot escape, however, the centuries-old separation of theology and liturgy and thus never addresses—as a problem—their interdependence methodologically. For Wainwright, the great benefit liturgical traditions have for theology becomes apparent when the exercise of worship and the liturgical expression of faith are embraced as sources for theological reflection (given Wainwright's premise, one critic's question, suggesting that, for example, Basil's Eucharistic anaphora might have provided a more fitting way for structuring this systematic theology, cannot be dismissed). In articles to follow, Wainwright gives greater emphasis to the interdependence of the *theologia prima* (doxology/liturgy) and the *theologia secunda* (dogma/theology), for example, when he defends himself against "liturgical fundamentalism."[39] Already in *Doxology* he attempts to establish criteria that will allow the liturgy to function as *locus theologicus*.[40] However, the fundamental interdependence between theology and liturgy that allows for the interpretation of liturgical traditions as theological reflection is never called into question. When it comes to this issue, Wainwright seems more at home in the Roman Catholic liturgiological debate than in that of Protestant systematic theology. Even his focus on liturgical tradition and the language of the liturgy (as opposed to more general reflections on the "language of prayer," which usually has meant on the "language of devotion") is unusual within the context of a Protestant systematic theology.

One year after the appearance of *Doxology,* the German Lutheran theologian Gerhard Sauter published his article, "Reden von Gott im Gebet." The author emphasized the need to view theology not only as speech about God but also as speech directed to God. More than

43

this, he suggests that in theology, speech directed to God should be given priority over speech about God. Sauter's clear association of doxology to the liturgy is noteworthy (one wonders, immediately, whether *Doxology* had already begun to bear fruit): "the authentic place of doxology is in the liturgical worship of God."[41]

This unequivocal linking of doxology and liturgy, as mentioned above, is not always recognizable in Protestant systematic theology. The following two examples will help support this point. Wolfhart Pannenberg takes up the question of analogical and doxological speech with his article, "Analogy and Doxology,"[42] first published in 1963 as part of a *Festschrift* for Edmund Schlink (Pannenberg employs the ideas of Edmund Schlink, whose position I will reference later). The author notes that doxology makes use of analogy but never intends analogy as such. In the act of prayer analogy is transcended. The person praising God offers her "I" and thus also the conceptual clarity of her speech. As a matter of formality one notes that Pannenberg's essay is devoid of any quotations from doxological material (not to mention references to liturgical rites and texts).

With their book *Jubilate* (1984) Daniel W. Hardy and David F. Ford serve as another example of the interest of Protestant systematic theology in doxological speech, but, like Pannenberg, they neglect the liturgy in their study. The authors concentrate on the concept of "praise" as the fundamental and central category of relationship to God and thus understand it as the fundamental and central reason for Christian being. They postulate a close connection between praise and the knowledge of God:

> The interplay of knowing and praising God is the theme of this book. Their inseparability is simply stated: knowing this God is to know a glory and love that evokes all our astonishment, thanks and praise, praising this God is a matter of affirming truth as well as expressing adoration and love. [43]

Jubilate's theme is an important one. The fundamental doxological orientation of Christian existence has been neglected by theologians for much too long (particularly in the theological traditions of the West). The book attempts to expose and fill this void. The subtitle of the British edition, *Theology in Praise*, indicates that the authors were not interested in forming a new exotic theology but rather sought to have doxology, as the beginning point for Christian living and Christian knowledge, seen as formative in the theological enterprise. As important and interesting as this essay is, it is all the more astounding that the authors turned a blind eye to the liturgy! It is hard to believe that two hundred pages of a "doxological theology" would not contain a single serious reference to the liturgical traditions of the church,[44] to say nothing of but one concrete example of a liturgical text. One must ask how the authors succeeded in shutting the liturgy so completely out of their considerations, especially when one reads in the appendix, "It is, of course, true that praise appears, perhaps most specifically, in worship."[45] Instinctively, one wishes that the authors had taken the title of their own book more seriously: the Latin *Jubilate* is plural. So much for contributions on the theme of "doxology" from within Protestantism that are clearly formulated without reference to the worship of the church.

At this point, the position of Dietrich Ritschl in his book *The Logic of Theology* (1984) must be noted as an important new contribution to the discussion surrounding the linguistic differences between dogmatic speech and the language of faith within Protestant systematic theology. The author, a Swiss Reformed theologian, sees the beginning of theological reflection in prayer itself. In his opinion, however, the extent to which doxology takes priority over theology must still be determined. On the other hand, Ritschl in no way obliges doxology strictly to the liturgical worship of God—it is not clear whether he is speaking of liturgical language, the language of devotion, or both, or whether he simply counts such distinctions as irrelevant for his methodology from the very beginning. The following thesis is, however, of crucial importance to Ritschl: Doxological speech, as transfigured speech, must never become the premise for argumentative and descriptive lines of theological reasoning. Ritschl had already written earlier along the same lines: "Doxological speech must not be made the *beginning* of theological analyses; . . . Prayers must not be analyzed; they must be prayed."[46] Here the linguistic differences between theological and doxological speech are taken seriously. The question remains, however: How can doxological traditions (particularly the doxological language of the liturgy, which often carries theological weight) be made to nourish and inform theological reflection?

This short review of the discussion within Protestant systematic theology demonstrates the growing interest in the relationship between the language of faith and dogmatic speech. It is easy to see how, as a consequence of this discussion, the term *doxology* will no longer be counted as foreign to systematic theology. Similarly, themes like those of "prayer" and "worship" are afforded more space than was the case a few years ago[47]—even though the doctrine of prayer has been recently characterized as "a neglected theme of Protestant theology."[48]

The results of this newly awakened interest in the doxological traditions of the church remain inconclusive. In the meantime, however, two distinct emphases have emerged. While they are not necessarily contradictory, they do represent two specific models for interpretation that maintain slightly different foci. The first calls attention to the *differences* between theological and doxological speech while the second emphasizes the *continuity* between them both, understanding doxology as the source and goal of all theology. Those who represent the first perspective often work with a narrow definition of theology (e.g., theology is understood as "meta-language" to use one of the catchwords) and often limit their understanding of doxology to devotional speech. Thus, doxology appears subject to other laws of being and function than those of theological reflection. The supporters of this position mark the discontinuity between doxological and theological speech with varying intensity. The various positions run the gamut from suggesting there is hardly any connection between the two to the assertion that the two are so connected as to suggest a continuum. In each case, however, all agree there are differences.

Representatives of the second position concentrate their energies on the close connection between the two expressions of faith and often interpret doxology within a liturgical context. Even when the particularities of the two languages of faith are not denied, there is little interest in and emphasis placed on these particularities. It is, rather, the interdependence of theology and doxology, or respectively, the priority of doxology over theology that attracts the attention of these theologians. Representatives of this position often tend to a less clear-cut definition of "theology." One favorite model for analysis assumes a continuum between doxology as *theologia prima* and theology as *theologia secunda*. Unfortunately, there is a buildup

46

of assertions about the priority of doxology over theology among these theologians, which usually cannot be substantiated, but which is nevertheless claimed as self-evident: "Dogmatic theology has its origin in the worship of God; similarly, the creeds in hymnody, and the catechism in the liturgy."[49] "The doctrine of God is not doxology per se, but it must lead one into and serve doxology."[50] "[T]heology has its origin in worship."[51] "Theology begins and ends in prayer . . . . The church prayed before it undertook the formulation of theology."[52] "Worship . . . is the point of departure for theological reflection."[53] "[T]he liturgy . . . is the tap root of all of our theology."[54] The list of quotations could continue endlessly. The findings read much like foregone conclusions. Substantiation is rarely provided and the consequences of these positions (particularly for the theological enterprise) seem uncertain. This much, however, is clear: Doxology and liturgical worship have begun to emerge as an area of interest within Protestant systematic theology. Behind the varying positions described above lie common questions: What is the relationship of doxology to theology? And what weight do doxological traditions carry for and within the theological enterprise?

C. The Orthodox Tradition: Liturgy as Theology and Theology as Doxology

When the Orthodox tradition is considered, it becomes particularly clear just how dependent the discussion on the relationship of theology and doxology is on the definition of these basic theological terms. A quick glance at this tradition is, thus, important for the present study. This is not the only reason, however, for including a brief review of the Orthodox position here. The Orthodox tradition has become an important dialogue partner for Western theology in this century, in part due to several Orthodox theologians in Europe and North America, who have been and are competent interpreters of their tradition. Furthermore, the influence of Orthodox theology in the ecumenical movement has grown steadily, resulting in its more intensive pursuit by Western theology. As far as the specific theme of this study is concerned, note particularly the intensity with which Orthodox theologians have engaged the discussion on the relationship of theology and doxology.[55] The uneasiness in Western theology over the estrangement of academic theology from spiritual and liturgical life provided a welcome opportunity for Orthodox theologians to point to the Eastern tradition, which, in their opinion, was not, and in principle, could never be subject to such an estrangement. The Orthodox theologian, Anastasios Kallis, who teaches in Germany, argues that this is attributable to the specific understanding of theology in the Orthodox tradition (as it has received it faithfully from the Patristic era). According to Kallis, Eastern theology is not characterized primarily by an orientation toward theoretical theological knowledge of but rather by the search for communion with God, or, in other words, a share in the life of the Triune God:

> In its purest form it [theology] is not rational but spiritual, and it finds expression not in the logical but the doxo-logical. In its highest form of expression it makes use of the "language" of liturgical life and thus finds itself anchored in the prayers of the church, the beginning and end of all theological study.[56]

It is easy to see how, in light of these and similar assertions, the Western tradition in describing the Eastern tradition increasingly adopts a position that moves the liturgy to center stage.[57] The Orthodox liturgy is portrayed as the concentrated self-realization of the Orthodox church. On the other hand, some interpretations of Eastern liturgies continually speak of its theological character or of its theological function. This is particularly noticeable, in light of the Eastern liturgical texts themselves, which are generally characterized by a poetical and hymnic style more intensive than that of their Western partners. It was not without good reason that the catchphrase "theology in hymns" was born in this context.[58] The close connection between liturgy and theology in the Orthodox tradition results in an emphasis on the theological dimension of the liturgy, on the one hand, while, on the other, allowing for a fundamental doxological orientation of all theological understanding—both positions claim to be rooted in the Patristic tradition as embraced by Orthodox theologians. It appears that the Orthodox understanding of God (which, in principle, comes the closest to an apophatic theology) and the understanding of dogma (which is closely connected with the liturgy and which provides the groundwork for all theology) play important roles in this interdependence between liturgy and theology.

It must not, however, be forgotten that Orthodox theologians have repeatedly warned against simply interpreting the liturgy as a *locus theologicus* among others. The Orthodox tradition, as Alexander Schmemann writes, points to a relationship between liturgy and theology that is far more radical: "Liturgical tradition is not an 'authority' or a *locus theologicus*; it is the ontological condition of theology." [59] The concept of "liturgical theology" [60] finds its validity here, of course with a far more basic meaning than customarily afforded by the Western tradition. This is especially evident when one considers the so-called "Eucharistic ecclesiology," as developed at the turn of the century from Patristic principles by exiled Russian theologians and embraced with great interest in the West. Eucharistic ecclesiology was not simply about securing a place for the Eucharist within the doctrine of the church. Rather, ecclesiology was to be shaped and interpreted by the Eucharistic celebration. These and similar presuppositions are characteristic of the Orthodox tradition. Everything that theology is, and can be, is determined and formed by the liturgy.

After the description of the discussion on the relationship between theology and doxology within Roman Catholic liturgiology and Protestant systematic theology, it is easy to see the influence of the Orthodox tradition on some of the representatives of both these disciplines. The following section will demonstrate the influence of the Orthodox tradition on ecumenical discussion. A closing observation by Anastasios Kallis indicates that Orthodox theologians are prepared to recognize and use the ecumenical potential of their position:

> The multiplicity of liturgical traditions in the East and West, more apparent in centuries past, points inevitably to the ecumenical dimension of liturgical theology, which, in turn, highlights the diversity of faith expressions (not as a pointer to division but to catholicity). . . . The newly won appreciation for the churches of God throughout the world and their complementary diversity is best introduced by the liturgies which variously express and accent the common and authentic faith. [61]

D. The Ecumenical Discussion: Communion in Doxology as the Source and High Point of Church Unity

In recent years, the question surrounding the relationship between theology and doxology has become more urgent for ecumenical discussion. As was the case for the fields of study discussed above, this question is addressed in the ecumenical movement from a particular point of view. Broadly speaking, the ecumenical discussion is about defining a relationship between the spiritual and theological traditions of the churches (or as in recent years, between the traditions of the churches and other religious traditions)[62] that could provide a basis for consensus and communion. The question of a communion in doxology that recognizes the liturgy as the source and high point of the church's unity has emerged as a specific challenge for the ecumenical movement.

A variety of factors have contributed to the growing interest in the doxological-liturgical traditions of the churches. Certainly, the influence of the liturgical movement, which quickly crossed the boundaries of the Roman Catholic Church to include practically all churches, played an important role. Even so-called nonliturgical communities were suddenly finding the center of their church life in the liturgical worship of God. A further consequence of the liturgical movement, namely the thorough liturgical reforms in almost every denomination, helped bring churches separated because of differences in their worship closer to one another. These reforms were often based on the recognition of primitive sources, that is, on the recognition of the churches' common traditions, and led to an important convergence of new liturgical rites and texts.

This newly awakened interest among the separated churches in their liturgical worship of God was not lost on the World Council of Churches.[63] In 1937, meeting in Edinburgh, the Second World Conference on Faith and Order proposed, in its report, a study of various worship structures and forms as characteristic for the various churches and ecclesial communities. A "Theological Commission on Worship" was formed, which published its report entitled *Ways of Worship* in 1951. The report was largely descriptive. The account given of various worship traditions among the separated churches led to the assessment of worship as *the* benchmark for the existing divisions: "In worship we meet the problem, nay rather the sin of the disunion of the church in its sharpest form."[64] At the same time the report notes the growing importance of worship as a theological theme for the ecumenical movement. It states that "ways of worship are never built up in a theoretical way by drawing liturgical consequences from dogmatic tenets. Rather the creed is born of worship . . . worship is the living form of faith."[65]

These rudiments of reassessing the importance of worship for ecumenical discussions were taken up and furthered by the Fourth World Conference on Faith and Order (Montreal, 1963) in its report entitled "Worship and the Oneness of Christ's Church." This report names worship as "the central and determinative act of the church's life"[66] for the first time in ecumenical dialogue. Rightly so, addressing liturgical questions was seen as one of the main tasks of ecumenical dialogue. A rather lengthy but relevant citation bears quoting:

> The study of worship has often been regarded as one of the "compartments" of ecumenical conversation. It has often been controlled by theological assumptions not directly related to the actual worshipping life of the church. But if theology is to reflect the whole faith of the church, and if (as we believe) it is in *leitourgia* that the church is to find the fulfillment of its life, then it is essential that we let that *leitourgia* speak for itself. It is of crucial importance that we should investigate its forms and structures, its language and spirit, in the expectation that this process may throw new light upon various theological positions and affirmations, perhaps even lend new meaning to them, and thus open new possibilities in ecumenical dialogue. Clearly this is one of the main tasks facing the churches in the coming decades.[67]

Agreeing with this premise the mandate of the conference charged that "a fresh approach be made to the relationship between theology and worship, so that . . . as a definitive step beyond current practice, our entire theological work may be informed by a fresh sensitivity to the demands and problems of Christian worship."[68]

It soon became apparent, however, that the interest and urgency manifested in this report would not be sustained in the ecumenical movement. Fifteen years would pass before a working paper of a subcommittee within the World Council of Churches would reference the need for a liturgical expression of the increasing theological-dogmatic consensus between the churches.[69] Even the so-called Lima Liturgy, seen by many as the liturgical parallel to the Faith and Order text *Baptism, Eucharist, Ministry* was not conceived as such. It is an incidental liturgy written by the theologian (at first Reformed, then Roman Catholic) and Taizé monk Max Thurian, as a Eucharistic liturgy for the 1982 Lima meeting of the Commission on Faith and Order. Its positive reception worldwide in conjunction with the document *Baptism, Eucharist, Ministry* came as a complete surprise.

In the meantime, however, important considerations arose regarding the emphasis on "Eucharistic vision" as introduced by the World Council of Churches' Sixth General Assembly in Vancouver (1983). The following question became urgent: Should not a solution for the ecumenical problem of Eucharistic sharing be sought and found, strictly speaking, by way of the liturgy? It seemed problematic, for example, to recognize the Lima Liturgy as a liturgy that contained all the constitutive elements of a valid Eucharist only then to retreat from its common celebration.[70]

Of course, ecumenical consideration given to the liturgy as the source and high point of the churches' unity cannot be limited to official documents of the World Council of Churches. Individual theologians have continually returned to this theme and produced important contributions for ecumenical discussion. So far as the significance of a communion in doxology for the unity of the church is concerned, Edmund Schlink (+1984), the German Lutheran theologian, clearly deserves to be mentioned first. I refer, at some length, to Schlink's position first developed four decades ago, since its relevance for the present has not diminished and is still a task of the ecumenical movement. Cited repeatedly in ecumenical discussions, Schlink proceeded from the following position: "that members of divided churches find it much easier to pray and witness together than to formulate common dogmatic statements."[71] Schlink assumed this position as the starting point for his reflection on the structure of dogmatic statements amid the essential forms of religious speech (his use of the phrase "theological statement"[72] is misleading, in my opinion). When viewed in the light of a doxological language community, dogmatic speech seems to be *the* obstacle to unity. The question followed, how could this obstacle be removed without forsaking or simply ignoring dogmatic statements? Schlink's last book *Ökumenische Dogmatik* (1983) attempted to address this question. The author claims to develop the whole of his dogmatic theology by paying close attention to the structure of dogmatic statements. Here he writes similarly to his first observations on this theme:

> As I began this task, one observation, which I had made before and which was consistently corroborated in ecumenical conversation with Orthodox churches, in my participation in the Second Vatican Council and in meetings with many other churches, remained important to

me. It is often possible to achieve a common statement based on the structure of prayer or on a proclamation about the same theme, otherwise impossible from the vantage of dogmatic teaching.[73]

What is at issue for Schlink in these observations? He begins with various fundamental forms of religious speech (prayer, doxology, witness, teaching, and confession of faith) and notes that each exhibits a different structure and that each represents a different category of speech to and of God. How do the differences in structure affect the speech content? Schlink assumes that there are elementary forms for the expression of faith (for Schlink, the recognition of Christ as Lord and Savior is the first and fundamental act of faith expression). The elementary forms for the expression of faith have not been maintained in the theological and dogmatic development of the church, according to Schlink. He accords the Orthodox churches alone a certain elementary doxological structure in dogma,[74] even though they too have experienced shifts in structure. For Schlink, however, any connection between worship and dogmatic statements has been lost for the most part within the theological and dogmatic development in the West. Individual structural elements of the single expression of the faith developed into manifold different dogmatic statements. Thus, for example, doxological references to God turned into metaphysical doctrinal statements about God.

Another example for the (theologically controversial) structural differences in dogmatic speech can be found, according to Schlink, in the difference between Protestant and Tridentine statements on justification.[75] The language of Luther's teaching is closest in structure to that of proclamation, while the Tridentine decree on justification uses the language of dogmatic description. The differing structures of these two statements lead to opposing perspectives on the subject of justification, which would not appear so pronounced had the specific categories of speech about the subject been given more attention. (Schlink, by the way, cites the teaching on predestination as the most radical example of a shift in language structure: "Instead of a thankful recognition of the abundance of God's grace [which alone can save], and instead of God's eternal loving decree, we are confronted with the problem of determinism, in the face of whose awful logic, the voice of doxology is silenced. This is what happens when expressions of doxology are isolated and incorporated into the structure of theoretical instruction.")[76]

In his *Ökumenische Dogmatik* Schlink draws the following conclusion from the recognition of shifts in the use of language: "I considered the many structures of statements of faith . . . and observed that the content of faith could not be expressed equally in all. Rather, in most cases, the translation of a statement of faith from one structure into another seems necessary in order to identify the actual differences in statements subject to debate."[77] In effect, Schlink called for a new methodology for the interpretation of theologically normative statements in an ecumenical context. He has in mind here, above all, doctrinal language whose content belongs to the language of prayer or proclamation but has been transposed into dogmatic language. A "retranslation of dogmatic language from secondary structures to those primary"[78] is needed in order to make possible an ecumenical consensus or even some basic understanding between the churches. The call for a retranslation of dogmatic language into the basic structures does not represent an escape into a doxological language community that ignores dogmatic speech. Schlink repeatedly made this clear: "In no sense may one avoid the task of working for a dogmatic consensus."[79] Rather, the realization is taken seriously here that for a genuine understanding of theological-dogmatic statements the structure of normative maxims (the primary as well as the secondary structure) would need to be considered. The various statements of the divided churches cannot be compared on the basis of their content alone. They must be retranslated into the fundamental structures of Christian faith statements in order for their true meaning to be recognized. Schlink hoped that such a retranslation would make it easier for the divided churches to discern the legitimate and meaningful language of the common Christian faith in the normative statements of other churches.

Of course, Schlink was not the first to establish the ecumenical potential of communion in doxology. It had long been present and effective in the hymnic traditions of the churches.[80] But Schlink was nevertheless one of the first theologians who did formulate theological-ecumenical conclusions from this observation.

The importance of the doxological, liturgical, and hymnic traditions of the churches for ecumenical dialogue is readily apparent. Other ecumenically engaged theologians have followed Schlink in his appraisal of doxological traditions and their importance in the search for church unity. Geoffrey Wainwright, for example, writes of the liturgy as the primary medium of any ecumenical consensus, which also implies its use as the possible focus of dogmatic unity between the churches.[81] In his book *Ökumenische Glaubenseinheit aus eucharistischer Überlieferung* (1976) written in the context of ecumenical dialogue between the Roman Catholic and Orthodox churches, Hans-Joachim Schulz, a Roman Catholic specialist on Eastern churches, dared a similar approach. The author, who refers to Edmund Schlink[82] among others, calls for a reconsideration of the Patristic deposit of faith and its eucharistically, doxologically determined structure as the basis for contemporary dogmatic consensus between the churches. According to Schulz, the celebration of the Eucharist is *the* place where the church finds a representative articulation of the faith. Thus, it is also the central place of ecumenical unity in faith.

This review of the ecumenical discussion makes clear that the doxological traditions of the churches have gained increasing importance in the search for church unity,[83] even if there is not yet an ecumenical consensus concerning the relationship between the theological and doxological traditions among the churches. An important contribution might be made with the development of shared doxological traditions.

E. Summary

What conclusions can be drawn from this presentation of the discussion on doxology and theology within Roman Catholic liturgiology, Protestant systematics, the Orthodox tradition, and ecumenical dialogue? Without a doubt, a bewildering multiplicity of emphases is to be found. Roman Catholic liturgiology debates the relationship of the *lex orandi* to the *lex credendi* while Protestant systematic theology takes as its theme the question of linguistic differences between doxological and theological speech. On the other hand, the Orthodox tradition accepts as a foregone conclusion the theological character of liturgical language and the doxological roots and orientation of theology. And those in ecumenical dialogue seek the meaning of communion in doxology for church unity.

In spite of the bewildering multiplicity of presumptions and perspectives (which, in the final analysis, are often based on *terminological* differences) it does not seem too misguided to surmise some common interest behind the differing perspectives—broadly speaking, a newly awakened interest in the doxological-liturgical-hymnic traditions of the churches. The (re)discovery of the importance of these traditions for contemporary theology of course raises the following question: How are they to be used and interpreted? On this point, note particularly that a certain prior understanding of the nature of theology, the meaning of worship, and the vision of God and the church in a given ecclesial tradition conditions the way doxological-liturgical-hymnic materials are engaged. Conversely, all fields of study here described seem to share the notion that the peculiar nature of these materials is to be determined more and more in relationship to theological reflection. Thus, the question emerges, as a common concern: What meaning do doxological traditions have in relationship to theological reflection?

What results are to be observed in relation to this question? This question can only be answered meaningfully in the particular context provided by each individual field of theological study. Thus, the emphasis, within Roman Catholic liturgiology, on the specific nature of the liturgy, finds its meaning only against the background of a strict linking and subordination of the liturgy to the teaching office of the church for centuries. Within Protestant systematic theology the interest in doxology becomes meaningful in the light of the long period of theological lack of interest in worship. The close linking of theology and doxology in the Orthodox tradition must be seen in the context of a "primitive" (in the sense of Patristic) definition of theology. And to provide an understanding of the question within ecumenical dialogue, the experience of communion in doxology between the divided churches is of fundamental importance.

It is easy to see how the differing contexts influence each study and determine the envisioned field of possible solutions. Yet unmistakably it appears that the various discussions do have a common fundamental problem to address—in its broadest sense, the question of the nature of doxology and its relationship to theology. The following provisional results seem to hold true for all fields of study. First (and fundamentally), awareness of the importance of doxological traditions for theological reflection has been steadily increasing. At the same time, the doxological traditions have come to be respected as a topic for theological reflection (though sometimes more in theory than practice). Furthermore, the specific characteristics of these traditions are more readily accepted and respected, even though there is not always a clear consensus on their definition. Finally, all appear of one mind regarding the need to define the relationship between doxology and theology. But the manner in which this relationship is to be defined remains controversial, particularly when considering if and how doxology is to be the source, the fundamental prerequisite, or the context of theology.

Of course, these questions point to differing understandings of the essence of theology and of church worship in each of the individual fields of study as described above. Precisely for this reason, whatever agreement is found between them should not be taken lightly. After all, the deliberations of Roman Catholic liturgiology, Protestant systematic theology, and the Orthodox tradition have proceeded over long periods of time in isolation from one another. Ecumenical dialogue may provide a sign of hope, for the principal questions remain open and answers proffered by individual traditions will only gain acceptance as they become ecumenically viable.

Even with all the newly awakened interest in the doxological traditions of the churches, the question regarding the relationship of doxology and theology is rarely tied to the witness of specific doxological sources. The question (and answers to it) is often addressed on a theoretical level and not by way of specific doxological material. It is on this point that this study attempts to chart new territory by intentionally placing the debate on the relationship of doxology and theology in the context of the study of a specific doxological tradition. The following section of this work is dedicated to the study of a specific doxological tradition—namely, a portion of Charles Wesley's hymnody, "one of the classics of Christian doxology,"[84]—as one of early Methodism's expressions of faith.

PART II

CHAPTER 3

Theology in Hymns?
A Collection of Hymns for the Use of the People Called Methodists

A. Introduction

1. The Historical, Theological, and Spiritual Context of *A Collection of Hymns for the Use of the People Called Methodists*

The hymns of Charles Wesley are inseparably connected with the beginning of the Methodist renewal movement within the Anglican church in the eighteenth century. The formation of the Methodist movement (as well as that of the evangelicals who remained in the Anglican church) was not first and foremost attributable to theological differences with the mother church. On the contrary, at first, the faith and traditional teaching of the *ecclesia anglicana* provided the foundation upon which Methodism was to be built. It was largely contemporary problems facing the Church of England and spiritual reasons that gave rise to the new movement. The movement can be understood, principally, as a (Pietist) response to the rigidity of the Anglican church during the English Enlightenment and to the threat of Rationalism and Deism. The Methodist movement, like continental European Pietism, was primarily a renewal movement seeking heartfelt Christian living within an existing church community.

At the beginning John (1703–1791) and his brother, Charles (1707–1788), were marked by high church Anglican spirituality. However, nonconformist influences in the home (the paternal and maternal grandparents were Puritans of conviction) and a certain interest in Mystical Spiritualism were also present. While enrolled as students at Oxford, the brothers and some friends undertook a strict and systematic rule of piety and good works that earned them names like "Holy Club" and "Methodists." During this time John began an intensive (and unceasing) study of the Church Fathers (East and West), the writings of German and French Mystics, Jansenists, and high church Anglican authors.

The encounter with various forms of German Pietism, however, would prove crucial for the two brothers and the actual beginning of the Methodist movement. In 1735, on board ship during their trip to the North American colony of Georgia where they were to work as missionaries, John and Charles met some members of the Moravian community (Herrnhuter). The encounter with these immigrants, which would continue in the colonies with Pietists from Salzburg and Halle, introduced the brothers to a living and warm life of faith that deeply impressed them. Interestingly enough, it provided the impetus for the development of their own hymnody as an expression of Wesleyan spirituality. John was not only impressed by the regular hours of singing observed by the Moravians, he also learned German during the Atlantic crossing, apparently by way of the *Gesang-Buch der Gemeine Herrn-Huth* (1735) and the *Neues Geistreiches Gesang-Buch* (1714), which had been published by the Pietist Johann Anastasius Freylinghausen of Halle (1670–1739).

In Georgia, John Wesley translated thirty-three hymns from these Pietist hymnbooks into English,[1] which even today are still considered small masterpieces. For example, note the translation of the first stanza of the Ernst Lange (1650–1727) hymn, "O Gott, Du Tiefe sonder Grund":

> O God, thou bottomless abyss,
>   Thee to perfection who can know?
> O height immense, what words suffice
>   Thy countless attributes to show?
> Unfathomable depths thou art!
>   O plunge me in thy mercy's sea;
> Void of true wisdom is my heart,
>   With love embrace and cover me!
> While thee all-infinite I set
>   By faith before my ravished eye,
> My weakness bends beneath the weight;
>   O'erpowered I sink, I faint, I die.[2]

> O Gott du Tiefe sonder Grund!
>   Wie kann ich Dich zu Gnüge kennen?
> Du große Höh, wie soll mein Mund
>   Dich nach den Eigenschaften nennen?
> Du bist ein unbegreiflich Meer
>   ich sencke mich in Dein Erbarmen.
> Mein Herz ist rechter Weisheit leer
>   umfasse mich mit Deinen Armen.
> Ich stellte Dich zwar mir

und anderen gerne für
doch werd ich meiner Schwachheit innen.
Weil alles, was Du bist nur End und Anfang ist,
verlier ich drüber alle Sinnen.[3]

The influence of German Pietism on John Wesley was not limited to the translation of a few hymns. In 1738, when John and Charles Wesley returned to England from their unsuccessful mission in Georgia it was through the influence of Peter Böhler (1712–1775), a Moravian and friend of Nikolaus Ludwig Graf von Zinzendorf (1700–1760) that both brothers experienced "conversion."[4] On May 21 of the same year, after several days of intense internal struggle during which he had read Martin Luther's commentary on the Epistle to the Galatians, Charles wrote, "I now found myself at peace with God, and rejoiced in hope of loving Christ. I knew that by faith I stood."[5] What came to be regarded as the classic description of Methodist conversion, however, came from John who three days later in a society meeting (of evangelical Anglicans or Moravians) in London had a life-changing experience. That night those gathered heard the reading of Martin Luther's Preface to the Epistle to the Romans (one of the Lutheran texts of choice among Pietists[6]). John Wesley's well-known description of this evening is found in his diary:

In the evening I went very unwillingly to a society in Aldersgate Street, where one was reading Luther's Preface to the Epistle to the Romans. About a quarter before nine, while he was describing the change which God works in the heart through faith in Christ, I felt my heart strangely warmed. I felt I did trust in Christ, Christ alone for my salvation, and an assurance was given me that he had taken away my sins, even mine, and saved me from the law of sin and death.[7]

It was, however, left to Charles Wesley to recount this experience poetically. There are two well-known Wesley hymns in particular that deal specifically with the experience of conversion. Below I quote from the first stanza of each hymn:

Where shall my wond'ring soul begin?
How shall I all to heaven aspire?
A slave redeemed from death and sin,
A brand plucked from eternal fire,

> How shall I equal triumphs raise,
> or sing my great Deliverer's praise?[8]

The following hymn indicates, like the hymn quoted above, a near speechless amazement at the conversion experience:

> And can it be, that I should gain
>   An interest in my Saviour's blood?
> Died he for me, who caused his pain?
>   For me? Who him to death pursued?
> Amazing love! How can it be
> That Thou, my God, shouldst die for me?[9]

Shortly after John's conversion experience, he traveled to Herrnhut and Marienborn where he believed he had found the realization of primitive Christian living.[10] In the period following his return, however, a division emerged between John and some of the followers of Zinzendorf in England, whom he accused of mystical Pietism and tendencies toward Antinomianism. In spite of this, the character of the emerging Methodist movement was significantly marked by Pietist thought and the embrace (or, as the case may be, the restructuring) within Pietism of the concerns of the Reformation. In Pietism, for example, the teaching on justification by faith alone came to be associated with an emphasis on the personal experience of salvation by new birth, while the assurance of salvation came to be connected with the struggle for moral perfection. An appreciation of the "law" or "works" within the appropriation of salvation became characteristic of Methodism in contrast to Luther. Doctrinal struggles within the Pietist movement were often fought out with other Pietists. Along with distancing themselves from Moravians for fear of their mystical Quietism, the Wesleys also disagreed strongly with the view of salvation held by followers of George Whitefield (1714–1770) who had been influenced by Calvinist thought (and a strict view of predestination).

In the years that followed 1738, the Methodist renewal movement itself began to grow, spurred on by the intense and frequent preaching of the Wesleys and their followers who, after the pulpits in Anglican churches were increasingly denied them, began to hold massive open air gatherings. The movement spread, particularly among common people who, hit hard by the early beginnings of the

Industrial Revolution, were drawn, in no small measure, by Methodism's engagement of social concerns.

Even though the Wesleys were initially anxious to strengthen the ties of their followers to the Church of England, the negative reception by the church made this increasingly difficult. In the beginning, Methodist Anglicans simply continued with their ordered worship and the celebration of the sacrament for a worship life but supplemented it with preaching missions that would include stories of personal salvation, and communal singing. Charles Wesley, responding to the need for texts to be sung, became the tireless writer of new hymns for the Methodist renewal movement. The formation and growth of the whole movement was accompanied by the ongoing publication of new hymns, most of which were written by Charles Wesley. *A Collection of Hymns for the Use of the People Called Methodists,* published in 1780, was without a doubt the most important of these hymnbooks.

In spite of the close connection with the established church, Methodist communities began to organize themselves (in the manner of many Pietists) into small groups ("societies," as they were also known by the evangelical renewal movement within the Church of England, albeit without the same level of organization) under the care of lay leaders. From 1744 on, an annual conference of "Methodist" preachers was held, which would later become the focus of oversight in the movement. The established church's repeated refusals to acknowledge the Methodist renewal movement as well as the movement's development of independent organizational structures led to the unavoidable break with the mother church, which was made official in 1795 following John Wesley's death. During his life John Wesley had held fast to the concept of "Methodist Societies within the Church of England," even though his ordinations for the North American Methodist societies were clearly beyond the boundaries of the *ecclesia anglicana.* Thus, Methodism became (not counting Pentecostalism) the largest new church of modern times instead of the Anglican renewal movement it was meant to be.

2. The Author of Methodist Hymnody: Charles Wesley

As indicated by this brief review of its formation, the Methodist movement was primarily driven by the person of John Wesley. Charles Wesley, not only in his lifetime but also in the reception and history of Methodism, has stood in the shadow of his brother. It is therefore necessary to look more carefully at Charles Wesley himself in order to focus on the author of Methodist hymnody. Even though Charles Wesley is no longer to be characterized as "the first Methodist" (Frederick Gill),[11] it was Charles who first tried to implement the communal attempt at "holy living" at Oxford in 1729 (under the advisement and then leadership of his brother). Charles, too, was the first to have a personal experience of "conversion"—John's came three days after Charles's. More than this, it would appear that the hymns of Charles Wesley have had a much greater influence on the identity and sense of community experienced by members of Methodist churches than, for example, the *Sermons on Several Occasions* by John or his *Explanatory Notes upon the New Testament*, which, together with the *Minutes* of the Conferences, comprised the official "doctrinal standards" of British Methodism. Almost every Methodist is familiar with several Wesley hymns, while few could recount the writings of John. Still, it cannot be disputed: John's energy and vision fueled the nascent movement—his life, more so than that of Charles, was synonymous with the formation of the Methodist movement.

Charles Wesley, born as the eighteenth child of the Wesley family, appears to have had an innate gift for communication by way of poetry. A solid background in the classics along with the influence of his father, Samuel Wesley, Sr., and his brother, Samuel (both of whom were hymn writers[12]), led Charles to express himself frequently in verse long before his conversion. Like the poets of the Augustan Age before him, he practiced writing the classics of Greek and Latin literature in stanza form. The widespread (pious) assumption that his conversion first freed the creative spirit within him birthing the poet, Charles Wesley, is false. It is clear, however, that with his experience of conversion, a whole new theme for his poetry appeared and with the growing Methodist renewal movement an entirely new audience began to emerge. This fact, both as cause and incentive, may account for Wesley's incredible productivity: the entire Wesley corpus is estimated at nine thousand poems and hymns.[13] If this astronomical number is divided by days over the length of fifty years, then Wesley would have had to write ten lines of poetry a day to have produced the entire poetical corpus.[14]

The poetical medium was so firmly ingrained in Charles Wesley as his mode of expression that almost everything he had to say (not just on religious matters) was expressed through poetry. No small portion of his poetry is dedicated to nonreligious themes. He wrote love poetry, commented on political issues and events of the day, from an earthquake in Lisbon to the loss of the thirteen North American colonies. It was, however, his religious hymns and poems that would have the greatest impact. Even in these, the breadth of themes is astounding. The hymns of his conversion are those best known, but it must not be overlooked that Wesley dedicated volumes of hymns to other themes as well: the Eucharist (*Hymns on the Lord's Supper*, 1745), the Trinity (*Hymns to the Trinity*, 1746), the Holy Scriptures (*Short Hymns on Select Passages of the Holy Scriptures*, 1762), Christmas (*Hymns for the Nativity of Our Lord*, 1745), Easter (*Hymns for the Lord's Resurrection*, 1746) and other occasions of the church year.

With all the attention given to the hymns of Charles Wesley as his primary and preferred medium of expression, it must not be forgotten that Wesley also experienced great success as a preacher, even though very few of his sermons remain. Only in his fragmentary journal does one get a glimpse at the frequency with which he was engaged as a preacher.[15] His activities as a preacher were intensive during the early 1740s when the Methodist movement began to form and spread through massive gatherings and preaching missions in the open air. In the 1750s Charles Wesley began to withdraw from this form of evangelism and commit his energies to the Methodist societies in Bristol and London.

Poetry remained his preferred form of expression until the end of his life. Just shortly before his death he dictated the following lines (known more likely for having been written at a time close to his death rather than for their literary quality):

> In age and feebleness extreme,
>> Who shall a helpless worm redeem?
> Jesus! my only hope Thou art,
>> Strength of my failing flesh and heart;
> Oh! could I catch one smile from Thee,
>> And drop into eternity![16]

After his death in 1788, the following notice appeared in the Minutes of the Methodist Conference:

Mr. Charles Wesley, who, after spending fourscore years with much sorrow and pain, quietly retired into Abraham's bosom. He had no disease; but after gradual decay of some months, "The weary wheels of life stood still at last." His least praise was, his talent for poetry, although Dr. [Isaac] Watts did not scruple to say that "that single poem Wrestling Jacob is worth all the stanzas which I have ever written."[17]

3. *A Collection of Hymns for the Use of the People Called Methodists:* A Hymnbook as a "Methodist Manifesto"

The hymns of Charles Wesley became well known, above all, through the many hymnbooks whose publications accompanied the birth and growth of the Methodist renewal movement. The *Collection* was not the first hymnbook published by the Wesley brothers but it is surely the most important. The edition published in 1780 was to have been the standard-bearer for use in Methodist societies: "a hymn-book as might be generally used in all our congregations," as John Wesley wrote in a foreword to the book.[18] The many different hymnbooks published by the Wesleys up until that point seemed to have introduced more confusion than enrichment among the Methodist societies and prompted the need for a harmonization of editions. A brief overview of the hymnbooks published through 1780 will demonstrate this.

It was one year prior to his conversion experience that John Wesley issued his first hymnbook while in the colony of Georgia (meetings with German Pietists and exposure to their hymnbooks and hymn-sings had influenced him considerably). It bore the title *A Collection of Psalms and Hymns*[19] and was, in many respects, a first attempt at such an endeavor: It appears that this small edition was the first hymnbook ever to be published in North America (Lewis Timothy printed it in the then Charles-Town). More than this, it was the first hymnbook designed for parish use within the Anglican Communion, which knew nothing at this time, officially, of hymn singing in the liturgy (the *Book of Common Prayer* contained only psalm paraphrases and metrical settings of liturgical texts for singing).[20] And finally, this edition stands at the beginning of a long line of hymnbooks published by the Wesley brothers for the Methodist societies.

A Collection of Psalms and Hymns contained seventy psalms and hymns, which were divided into three sections corresponding to the most important days in the liturgical week: Sunday, Wednesday and Friday, as well as Saturday. The first section, dedicated to Sunday as the first day, the beginning and high point of the week, contains psalms and hymns whose thematic content suggests the subheadings of praise and prayer. The second section is dedicated to the traditional fast days of each week and contains psalms and hymns of repentance and penance. The last section is dedicated to Saturday and follows the theme of creation. This first hymnbook, like all others that would follow it, was a collection of psalms and hymns from a variety of sources. It is interesting to note that *A Collection of Psalms and Hymns* not only begins the production of Wesley hymnbooks but also concludes it. In 1784 a hymnbook by this title was published, a full third of which was identical to the first *A Collection of Psalms and Hymns.*

John Wesley drew on the hymns of Isaac Watts, George Herbert, Thomas Ken, Samuel Wesley, Sr., Samuel Wesley, Jr. (among others), and included for the 1737 volume five of his own translations of hymns from German Pietists.[21] Not a single hymn of Charles Wesley was to be found in this collection. The same was true for *A Collection of Psalms and Hymns*, which John published in England one year later.[22] Only a few details distinguished this hymnbook from the first publication. A third hymnbook by the same title appeared in 1741 that would survive many editions. Its second edition contained several hymns of Charles Wesley and from this time on he would become the source for the hymns of the nascent Methodist movement. In 1739, 1740, and 1742 the two brothers produced the three-volume *Hymns and Sacred Poems*, which consisted almost exclusively of Wesley hymns. A portion of these was used to create the 1753 collection entitled *Hymns and Spiritual Songs, intended for the Use of Real Christians of all Denominations.*[23] Though this small book contained only forty-eight hymns, it would go through thirty editions. A few years earlier a hymnbook appeared designed for use in similar circles, though perhaps without the explicit ecumenical orientation: *Hymns for those that seek and those that have Redemption in the Blood of Jesus Christ* (1747). In 1761 John published a new standard hymnbook for the Methodist societies that included melodies: *Select Hymns with Tunes Annext; Designed chiefly for the Use of the People called Methodists.* The 133 hymns contained therein had all appeared in earlier hymnbooks of the Wesley brothers.

This brief overview shows clearly that John Wesley had already made several attempts at creating a "standard" hymnbook for Methodist societies before the creation of the *Collection*. An early draft of this 1780 hymnbook was penned in 1773, but John needed years before bringing the finished product to publication. His foreword to the hymnbook demonstrates clearly what his expectations for the book were:

> What we want is a collection neither too large, that it may be cheap and portable, nor too small, that it may contain a sufficient variety for all ordinary occasions. Such a hymn-book you have now before you. It is not so large as to be either cumbersome or expensive. And it is large enough to contain such a variety of hymns as will not soon be worn threadbare. It is large enough to contain all the important truths of our most holy religion, whether speculative or practical; yea, to illustrate them all, and to prove them both by Scripture and reason. And this is done in a regular order. The hymns are not carelessly jumbled together, but carefully ranged under proper heads, according to the experience of real Christians. So that this book is in effect a little body of experimental and practical divinity. . . . I am persuaded that no such hymn-book as this has yet been published in the English language. In what other publication of the kind have you so distinct and full an account of scriptural Christianity? Such a declaration of the heights and depths of religion, speculative and practical? So strong cautions against the most plausible errors, particularly those that are now most prevalent? And so clear directions for making our calling and election sure, for perfecting holiness in the fear of God?[24]

As its many editions and printings indicate, the hymnbook accompanied by the above foreword more than fulfilled the hopes and expectations of its editor. But even this "final" hymnbook did not represent the end of Wesley's hymnbook production. In 1785 an abridged version of the *Collection* appeared under the title *A Pocket Hymnbook, for the Use of Christians of all Denominations*—only to have a new edition of the same issued two years later under the same title. This hymnbook was the last in a long line of hymnbooks produced by the Wesleys. The 1780 *Collection*, however, was and is the premiere collection. The Congregationalist Bernard Lord Manning (1892–1941) rightly observed (with the concurrence of many) of this book:

This little book . . . ranks in Christian literature with the Psalms, the Book of Common Prayer, the Canon of the Mass. In its own way, it is perfect, unapproachable, elemental in its perfection. You cannot alter it, except to mar it; it is a work of supreme devotional art by a religious genius.[25]

Most of the 525 hymns that appear in this book come from the hand of Charles Wesley. Several are, however, written by John Wesley, several by Isaac Watts, one each by the two Samuel Wesleys, one by George Herbert, and two by the Cambridge Platonist Henry More (1614–1687). Most of the hymns were edited, in some form or another, by John Wesley. He also included nineteen of the thirty-three translated hymns from German Pietists, which he completed while in Georgia. John often used the hymns of his brother that had appeared in earlier hymnbooks, and the *Collection* represents no departure from this method: no Wesley hymn was used in this volume that had not previously been published.

Still, the simple enumeration of the different sources for this hymnbook does not reveal its distinct character. As John mentions in his foreword, the various hymns for this book were collected and ordered according to a specific principle: "the experience of real Christians."[26] This principle used in the *Collection* is, in the final analysis, that of *Pilgrim's Progress*[27]—the poetical biography of a Christian. Instead of using the church year or the fundamentals of the faith as his point of orientation, John Wesley organizes this hymnbook according to the personal experience of salvation for the "real" Christian. A brief review of the structure of the *Collection* shows how this personal experience of salvation is conceived. The first part of the hymnbook is reminiscent of an introduction. The first segment is dedicated to conversion ("Exhorting and beseeching sinners to return to God"). Segments that follow describe various themes for proclamation: "describing 1. The pleasantness of Religion; 2. The goodness of God; 3. Death; 4. Judgment; 5. Heaven; [and] 6. Hell." A third segment, which appears under the heading "Praying for a Blessing," consists expressly of prayers and petitions. The second part of the book is devoted to the tension held between the outward ("formal") and the personal ("inward") experience of religion. Both sides of this tension are addressed in separate segments. The third part of the hymnbook turns on the personal experience of salvation. The first segment speaks of "Praying for Repentance." The second is devoted to those who suffer under the burden of their sins ("For Mourners convinced of Sin"). The next segment contains hymns written "For Mourners brought to the Birth." A segment for those "Convinced of Backsliding" follows immediately thereafter. The closing segment to this part of the hymnbook is devoted to those who have experienced redemption afresh ("Recovered"). The fourth part of the book is directed to believers and their various experiences: "For Believers Rejoicing, Fighting, Praying, Watching, Working, Suffering, Groaning for full Redemption, Brought to the Birth, Saved, Interceding for the World." The last part of the book focuses on the Methodist societies. The hymns here speak to the assemblies of the renewal movement: "For the Society, Meeting, Giving Thanks, Praying, [and] Parting."

This brief review of the structure of the *Collection* demonstrates how this structure traces the path of believers from the turning from sin, to conversion, to the life of faith. Such a method for organization was unusual in Wesley's day. It neglected altogether the "objective" tools for organization like the church year or Christian doctrine. It must not be forgotten, however, that as this hymnbook was being published the Methodist movement was still a renewal movement within the Anglican church. Technically speaking, its members were devoted to the worship of the mother church and attended the meetings of the Methodist societies as a supplement to religious life in their parish. If the structure of the *Collection* were compared with other hymnbooks of the day it would fall outside the bounds of the usual and customary. Hymnbooks in the English-speaking world either followed no specific ordering principle or provided a series of unrelated headings such as "Paraphrases of Scripture" or "On the Eucharist." Only the Evangelical-Anglican *Olney Hymns* by William Cowper (1731–1800) and John Newton (1725–1807) come close, in the final section, to approximating the ordering principle used by the *Collection*. This hymnbook contains themes reminiscent of a believer's personal experience of salvation, but never with the kind of detail provided by Wesley. The title of this last section reads, "On the Progress and Changes of the Spiritual Life"[28] and is divided into the following segments: Solemn Addresses to Sinners—Seeking, Pleading, Hoping—Conflict—Comfort—Dedication and Surrender—Cautions—Praise—Short Hymns: Before Sermon, after Sermon, Gloria Patri. Though the *Olney Hymns* appeared in 1779, one year prior to the *Collection*, the organization of the *Collection* was already in place several years earlier. On the other hand, Newton was also making plans for such a hymnbook at the beginning of the 1770s. The source for the new and conspicuous ordering principle of these two hymnbooks has never been clearly identified. One thing, however, appears to be certain and too often overlooked by researchers—the structure of the *Collection* is (more) understandable when one looks beyond examples from the English-speaking world and begins to consider examples from the German Pietists, who, after all, inspired the Wesleys to work on their first hymnbook (perhaps it is no coincidence that John Wesley, in his foreword to the new hymnbook, writes of it being unique among *English-speaking* peoples).

Even if a direct connection could be made between the *Olney Hymns* and the Wesleyan *Collection* (which seems entirely possible to me—John Wesley and John Newton knew each other) this would only establish the influence of Wesley over Newton. Toward the end of the 1750s, when Wesley had taken his place as a well-known leader of the evangelical renewal movement (and had acquired considerable experience in the publication of hymnbooks), Newton sought out Wesley for his advice and counsel. Thus, it seems fruitless to dwell on attempts at establishing strict chronological priority between the *Collection* and the *Olney Hymns*.

A closer look at German Pietism may provide helpful clues to understanding the framework for organization in the *Collection*. The seventeenth- and eighteenth-century hymnbooks of German Pietism distinguish themselves by the special emphasis placed on the spiritual life of believers—though this is usually integrated into an ordering principle that is not at odds with the theological, catechetical, and liturgical emphases of earlier hymnbooks.[29] But their main concern remains clear: Johann Anastasius Freylinghausen left little for debate in formulating an ordering principle for his *Neues Geistreiches Gesang-Buch* (1714), in which everything "must be organized according to the economy and order of salvation."[30] The connections between the hymnbooks of German Pietism and the *Collection* can be observed in even greater detail, however. Wesley invariably provides the most space for hymns that were also the main interest of the German Pietists, namely hymns for the various circumstances in the spiritual lives of believers. When the hymnbooks of German

73

Pietism are compared with the 1780 *Collection*, the structure of the latter seems to expand on a premise characteristic of the former: the focus on the individual's spiritual life from the time of conversion to the incorporation into the fellowship of believers. It is obvious that an individualized *ordo salutis* lies hidden in the ordering principle used for the *Collection*. But its ordering principle is a long way away from, say, those utilized for hymnbooks edited by the adherents of Protestant Orthodoxy, who drew on the *theological and dogmatic themes* of the *ordo salutis*.[31] Wesley found the ordering principle for his hymnbook by concentrating on the *inner experience* of the individual believer.

The hymn of Charles Wesley placed by John at the beginning of the collection has an almost programmatic character for what is to follow in the remainder of the hymnbook. It functions, by way of its placement, as an introduction to and interpretation of the *Collection*.

4. A Prelude to *A Collection of Hymns for the Use of the People Called Methodists:* "O For a Thousand Tongues to Sing"

Practically every Methodist hymnbook since the *Collection* has opened with this hymn and by no coincidence. It has become the leitmotif of Methodist singing and one of the most important witnesses to Methodist spirituality—notwithstanding the fact that the hymn as published by John Wesley in *A Collection of Hymns for the Use of the People Called Methodists* does not in every way accurately reflect the one written by Charles Wesley forty years earlier. It is, however, the latter version that is necessary to the establishment of proper context and interpretation.

The original hymn carries the heading "For the Anniversary Day of One's Conversion," which provides it with a most specific *Sitz im Leben*. It is likely that Charles Wesley wrote the text as a memorial on the first anniversary of his own conversion. This is an indicator of the central (spiritual) meaning of the moment of conversion within the Methodist renewal movement. Charles Wesley may have been simply expressing gratitude for his own conversion, but, at the same time, as indicated by the title, he also provides all participants in this nascent renewal movement with a tool for the expression of their individual (and corporate) fundamental experience of conversion. Thus, the hymn's *Sitz im Leben* is found in the spiritual life of each member of the community who has experienced both conversion and the urgent need for proclamation. With this in mind it is easy to see why this hymn has introduced practically every Methodist hymnbook since the *Collection* in 1780.

I cite below the hymn in its entirety as originally written by Charles Wesley at the very beginning of the Methodist renewal movement. The famous abridged version "O for a Thousand Tongues to Sing," as published in the *Collection,* is important for historical reasons but does not demonstrate the hymn's original intention quite so clearly as the longer version. But first, the text of the hymn:

> Glory to God, and praise, and love   (1)
> > Be ever, ever given,
> By saints below, and saints above,
> > The church in earth and heaven.

> On this glad day the glorious Sun   (2)
> > Of Righteousness arose;
> On my benighted soul He shone,
> > And fill'd it with repose.

> Sudden expired the legal strife;   (3)
> > 'Twas then I ceased to grieve;
> My second, real, living life
> > I then began to live.

> Then with my *heart* I first believed,   (4)
> > Believed with faith Divine;
> Power with the Holy Ghost received
> > To call the Saviour *mine.*

> I felt my Lord's atoning blood   (5)
> > Close to *my* soul applied;
> *Me, me* He loved—the Son of God
> > For *me,* for *me* He died!

> I found, and own'd His promise true,   (6)
> > Ascertain'd of my part;
> My pardon pass'd in heaven I *knew,*
> > When written on my heart.

O for a thousand tongues to sing   (7)
    My dear Redeemer's praise!
The glories of my God and King,
    The triumphs of His grace.

My gracious Master, and my God,   (8)
    Assist me to proclaim,
To spread through all the earth abroad
    The honours of Thy name.

Jesus, the name that charms our fears,   (9)
    That bids our sorrows cease;
'Tis music in the sinner's ears,
    'Tis life, and health, and peace!

He breaks the power of cancell'd sin,   (10)
    He sets the prisoner free;
His blood can make the foulest clean,
    His blood avail'd for me.

He speaks; and, listening to His voice,   (11)
    New life the dead receive,
The mournful, broken hearts rejoice,
    The humble poor *believe.*

Hear Him, ye deaf; His praise, ye dumb,   (12)
    Your loosen'd tongues employ;
Ye blind, behold your Saviour come;
    And leap, ye lame, for joy.

Look unto Him, ye nations; own   (13)
    Your God, ye fallen race!
Look, and be saved through faith alone;
    Be justified by grace!

See all your sins on Jesus laid;   (14)
    The Lamb of God was slain,
His soul was once an offering made
    For *every soul* of man.

Harlots, and publicans, and thieves   (15)
    In holy triumph join;

Saved is the sinner that believes
    From crimes as great as mine.

Murderers, and all ye hellish crew,   (16)
    Ye sons of lust and pride,
Believe the Saviour died for you;
    For me the Saviour died.

Awake from guilty nature's sleep,   (17)
    And Christ shall give you light,
Cast all your sins into the deep,
    And wash the *Ethiop* white.

With me, your chief, you then shall *know*,   (18)
    Shall feel your sins forgiven;
Anticipate your heaven below,
    And own that love is heaven.[32]

The hymn begins with a doxological prelude—like no small number of Charles Wesley's hymns:[33] "Glory to God, and praise." The language and content of this beginning are picked up and amplified in stanza 7: "My dear Redeemer's praise! The glories of my God and King." The ecclesiological context of the doxology in the opening stanza is noteworthy, particularly in light of the description of the individual's conversion that follows. This individual experience of conversion appears to be put into context by the introductory doxology, which calls on the *ecclesia militans* and the *ecclesia triumphans* throughout the ages to praise God.

With this doxological and ecclesiological context secured at the beginning, stanzas 2 through 6 provide a description of that day on which Charles Wesley experienced his conversion, referenced in the title of the hymn (as mentioned above, for Charles this can be dated precisely: May 21, 1738). Stanza 2 uses traditional language to describe the day on which the Sun of Righteousness broke through the cover of darkness of his soul. The next stanza makes clear that the advent of the Sun of Righteousness will mean an end to "the legal strife." Stanza 13 will provide a corresponding emphasis on the *sola fide* of the Reformation (reminiscent of the important role played by Luther's commentary on the Epistle to the Galatians in Charles Wesley's conversion experience). The beginning of new life ("My second, real, living life") comes only by faith, a faith, as indicated in stanza 4, given by God and flowing from the heart. This same stanza foreshadows the theme of the following stanza, which will be explored throughout the rest of the hymn, namely the Pauline/Lutheran *pro me*. It appears throughout the hymn in many variations by way of different poetical devices (in this stanza Wesley uses a double epizeuxis, or the immediate repetition of a word or phrase): "Me, me He loved . . . For me, for me He died!" The central concept that lies behind the phrase "I felt . . . (the) blood . . . applied" (stanza 5) is closely related to that of the *pro me*, and like the *pro me* is followed throughout the hymn. This phrase is used as a code word for the application of salvation and its reception by an individual in conversion.

Stanza 7 closes the first part of the hymn as it began with a doxology and simultaneously introduces the next part of the hymn, which moves toward proclamation by recounting the personal experience of conversion.[34] This stanza of doxology picks up thematically where the opening stanza of the hymn left off, broadening its expression of praise in the witness born to personal conversion. For example, God, the one to whom the doxology is addressed, is referred to more precisely as "My dear Redeemer," and "the triumphs of His grace" are specifically named as the reason for praise. Moreover, the entire doxology presented in stanza 7 is more personal, warm, and exuberant than that of the opening stanza. The doxology of stanza 7 marks and provides the transition from the descriptive to the kerygmatic section of this hymn. The following stanza is already part of the kerygmatic section but is nevertheless distinguished as the only stanza in the entire hymn that is recognizably a prayer. This prayer forms a petition for assistance in the proclamation of the gospel. As the previous stanza closed extolling the "triumphs of His [God's] grace," the prayer in this stanza is reminiscent of the emphasis on grace, when addressing "My *gracious* Master, and my God, Assist me to proclaim." This prayer also establishes simultaneously the breadth and theme of proclamation: "To spread through all the earth abroad The honours of Thy Name."

The earth or world of which Charles Wesley writes is best summed up and personified when he refers to the "sinner" and the "prisoner." And the Good News to be proclaimed is best summed up and personified in the single word *Jesus*. Stanzas 9 through 11 provide a description of Jesus. The connection between stanza 8, which, as a prayer, asks for assistance in proclamation, and these stanzas is noteworthy. As the prayer ends with a description of the proclamation's purpose, "To spread . . . The honours of Thy name," so the following stanza begins with the single word *Jesus,* the name of God "that charms our fears" (here Charles Wesley employs the poetic device of anadiplosis). Wesley clearly associates a description of the person of Jesus with a soteriological perspective: the recognition of God comes with and is the knowledge and experience of salvation. Thus, the soteriological categories of proclamation are adapted to the experiences of those to whom the proclamation is addressed. For prisoners, Jesus becomes liberator. For the (spiritually) dead, Jesus becomes giver of life. And for the sorrowful, he becomes joy.

If stanzas 9 through 11 can be characterized as an indirect proclamation of the gospel by way of describing the person of Jesus, then the last seven stanzas of the hymn are dedicated explicitly to proclamation. Charles Wesley speaks directly to his audience and presents them with a host of challenges in the imperative mode. Fifteen such imperatives can be found in the last seven stanzas, leaving the impression of one great call to spiritual awakening.

Stanza 12 employs biblical language in calling for the deaf to hear, the blind to see, and the lame to leap. Stanza 13 broadens the circle of those to whom the hymn is addressed: "all nations, ye nations," which are described as the "fallen race," in the same way that the whole earth is described as "sinner" at the outset of the hymn. The call to conversion directed to everyone is unmistakable: "Be saved through faith alone, be justified by grace!" There is no mistaking the Methodist appropriation of the emphasis of the Reformation on justification by faith alone in this proclamation. The universal offer of salvation is emphasized once more in the following stanza: "For every soul of man." Stanzas 15 and 16 slowly move from the language of Scripture to the vocabulary of the day. Those addressed in the hymn are now referred to as "Harlots, and publicans, and thieves . . . sons of lust and pride." It is interesting to note the way in which Charles Wesley repeatedly places himself (or as the case may be, his sins) on the same level with his audience: "crimes as great as mine; the Saviour died for you; For me the Saviour died." The reference to himself as "chief among sinners" (Pauline in origin) is the most striking (and typical for Charles Wesley) example of this. The imagery of darkness preceding redemption is taken up, once again, in stanza 17, as the biblical call is issued to awake from the sleep of sin and receive the light of Christ. The stanza closes with yet another provocative biblical image.

The last stanza adopts a theme found often in the works of Charles Wesley. He envisions the moment of conversion (and thus, also, the forgiveness of sin) as an eschatological event. Heaven is found on earth in the experience of God's love. This experience is the anticipation of the coming glory: "Anticipate your heaven below." This eschatological perspective is found in many of Charles Wesley's hymns. In fact, it is so prevalent as to lead one Methodist lover of Wesley hymns to observe that Wesley had "the habit . . . of ending his hymns, whatever their burden, in the courts of heaven. Into the earthly songs of praise breaks the music of the archangels."[35]

When viewed as a whole, this hymn, from beginning to end, reflects subject material and literary devices typical for Charles Wesley and found in many of his hymns. Among these are included: the focus on soteriological categories, the central meaning of experience (i.e., the experience of conversion), and the frequent use of the term *blood* (also found in Pietism) to refer to the redemption of the cross and its appropriation by the faithful ("the blood applied"). Furthermore, an emphasis on the importance of the name of God (for Wesley, to know and recognize God's name became a synonym for reconciliation) and the use of eschatological categories to describe the new life must be included in this list. Two themes not addressed in this hymn, which were nevertheless important to Charles Wesley are: (1) the believer's participation in the divine nature; and (2) Wesley's multifaceted preoccupation with ethical components of the new life, especially as it pertained to Christian perfection, a theme frequently discussed within the Methodist renewal movement. These notwithstanding, the hymn can still be counted, for the most part, as a summary of the central ideas found in Charles Wesley's poetical works and more specifically in *A Collection of Hymns for the Use of the People Called Methodists.*

A few issues remain to be dealt with following this interpretation of the first hymn from the *Collection*. First, a more precise analysis of speaker and addressee in this hymn is important (even if the addressee is likely fictional). Like many of Charles Wesley's hymns, this one also employs a dialogical framework. The speaker is the redeemed "I" who reflects on the day of his or her conversion. Thus, the first part of the hymn is directed towards God, beginning and ending with a doxology. The prayer in stanza 8, formed on the basis of the description of the speaker's conversion, serves as further witness to this. The second part of the hymn is driven by proclamation and is directed to everyone who needs to hear the Good News. Shifting dialogue partners is a literary device often employed by Charles Wesley. Especially with the hymn heading "For the Anniversary Day of One's Conversion" the dialogical structure demonstrates that Wesleyan spirituality is not primarily concerned with the pious introspection of the converted individual but rather with proclamation.

The following is to be said about this hymn's theme and its development: as announced in the title, it addresses the experience of salvation in conversion. On the one hand, this is developed by way of a doxology that gives thanks for the events of the past, while, on the other hand, sounding the call to proclamation in the present. The event and experience of conversion are reflected in and referred to with many varying images and from constantly changing vantage points. The subjective experience shares the central focus of the hymn with the objective reason for the experience, namely the saving acts of God in the death and resurrection of Jesus Christ. Both of these aspects are tightly interwoven.

A consideration of sources used for this hymn reveals that this hymn, like many of the hymns of Charles Wesley, is formed first and foremost by its proximity to Holy Scripture. Not so much in the sense that biblical themes are assumed and reworked; Charles Wesley's "biblicism" runs much deeper. His use of language moves within the biblical world, its pictures, vocabulary, and imagery. Wesley, the poet, speaks the language of Scripture as if it were his mother tongue. In the nine stanzas of the abbreviated hymn, as it appears in the 1780 *Collection*,[36] over twenty references to Scripture, of all different kinds, can be identified. To be sure, this poetical biblicism is the most important facet to identify among the sources used by Charles Wesley. However, it points to yet another important element: the manner through which many hymns take up the Psalms. It is clear that Charles Wesley relied heavily on liturgical traditions, specifically on the Anglican *Book of Common Prayer* and its translation of the Psalms. The influence of the Anglican liturgy and its powerful language on Wesleyan poetry should not be underestimated. (The whole of early Methodism was much more involved in the liturgical life of the Anglican church than one might presume given later developments—remember particularly Charles Wesley's Eucharistic hymns in this connection.) A third important influence on the content of Wesleyan poetry is the tradition of the Reformation, which manifests itself for Wesley in the Lutheran *pro me* and *solus Christus, sola gratia, sola fide*. Wesley's conversion experience, as mentioned earlier, is closely connected with Luther's commentary on the Epistle to the Galatians. The tradition of the Reformation found here, however, is not pure but rather one received and lived by German Pietists. The hymn just described, with its emphasis on conversion, the personal experience of salvation, and the call to proclamation, stands as witness to this Pietist heritage.

So much for the traditions reflected throughout Charles Wesley's poetical work. It is easy to see how these traditions have left their mark on the language and form of this hymn. Furthermore, the hymn is also characterized by a tendency toward a certain overabundance of emotive language particularly apparent in the doxological stanza: "O for a thousand tongues to sing, My dear Redeemer's praise." The many exclamation points used by Charles Wesley in his hymns would also support this observation. The emotive quality of the language used ("dear Redeemer; glad day") is also characteristic of Wesleyan hymnody, perhaps representing, at least in part, the legacy of Pietism, a legacy that Charles's brother, John, sought to suppress at various places in the 1780 collection of hymns. This may account for the exclusion of the decidedly emotional "Jesu, Lover of My Soul"[37] from the *A Collection of Hymns for the Use of the People Called Methodists.*

The following may be said about the linguistic form of Wesley's conversion hymn: the first part provides through its doxological framing an atmosphere of explicit praise, praise for conversion which, however, by its very nature is also a profession of faith. By contrast, the second part of the hymn is entirely devoted to proclamation. Didactic elements are not to be found even though other Wesley hymns are given to catechetical emphases.

The form of speech utilized provides one of the first clues as to the identity of those for whom the hymn is written. The part devoted to proclamation states precisely that the hymn is addressed to the hearers of the Methodist message, which calls everyone to conversion. The first part of the hymn, with its doxological retrospective on conversion, provides the individual member of the Methodist renewal movement with a medium for expressing his or her own experience. However, in making the experience of conversion the common foundation, it also provides a certain identity for those who come to claim this hymn as their own.[38] Thus, this hymn takes on significance for both the individual and the community.

John Wesley chose this hymn of his brother as the first listed in the opening section of the 1780 hymnbook entitled "Exhorting and beseeching to return to God." It is worth noting that John Wesley did not include the first part of the hymn, but rather began directly with the doxological stanza 7. Thus, the retrospective description of the day of conversion, which prompts proclamation for Charles Wesley, is left out altogether. A doxological beginning, the ensuing prayer, and the stanzas that announce the call to conversion are what remain. Nevertheless this hymn, as it stands (in spite of or because of its abbreviated form) has become representative of the Methodist movement and its hymnody.

Excursus: The Current State of Research[39]

The literary overview that follows concentrates exclusively on Charles Wesley,[40] particularly his fundamental contribution to developing Methodism: Wesleyan hymnody. The study of Charles Wesley and Wesleyan hymnody has only recently received an essential tool, namely a critical edition of the *Collection* published by John Wesley in 1780. The first adequate critical edition of this hymnbook appeared in 1983 as a separate volume in a new, critical edition of *The Works of John Welsey.*[41] Until recently this was the only Charles Wesley material available in a critical edition. The new edition of the 1780 *Collection* fulfills the demands of critical scholarship quite well. Its introduction outlines the origins and sources of the *Collection*, the theological and literary characteristics of Charles Wesley's hymns, the editorial work of John Wesley, and the reception of Wesleyan hymnody within Methodism. The greatest accomplishment of this edition, however, rests in the publication of the hymnbook itself. For the first time a whole variety of helpful aids are made available with each hymn text: references to the place of first publication, the original length of each text (thereby highlighting the editorial privilege exercised by John Wesley), the variations of earlier editions, and the biblical and literary references upon which Charles Wesley drew. This thorough edition of the 1780 *Collection* provides the foundation for any scholarly review of Wesleyan hymnody, even though it includes only about five hundred of Charles Wesley's hymns (from a total output of some nine thousand hymns and poems). In the meantime, another critical edition of Wesleyan poetical work has appeared: *The Unpublished Poetry of Charles Wesley*, edited by S T Kimbrough, Jr. and Oliver A. Beckerlegge (1988 –1991). This three-volume work contains well over one thousand unpublished or partially unpublished Charles Wesley texts. This work also meets the requirements of a scholarly edition.

A further development has contributed to an essential improvement for the basis of Charles Wesley research. Over roughly the past thirty years, the English-speaking world, in the context of a general renaissance of John Wesley studies, has seen an increased number of publications that analyze the poetical works of Charles Wesley from a theological perspective. A brief overview of the previous direction of research makes clear that this development of theological inquiry represents progress, when compared with earlier primary emphases on Charles Wesley and his works.

As one might expect, from the beginning the most intensive interest in Methodism was to be found in the English-speaking world. With the expansion of Methodism to North America both England *and* the United States became the locus of interest in Methodism. During the nineteenth century, both countries produced numerous publications on the Methodist movement. These publications, of many varieties, however, often represented similar directions. For a good part they were historical biographies, frequently belonging to the genre of devotional literature written by Methodists for Methodists. An inventory of Methodist literature written between 1773 and 1869 reveals a total of 2,254 titles, 320 of which are biographies.[42] These historical and biographical emphases are also evident in the works on Charles Wesley.

The biographies that repeatedly described *The Life of the Reverend Charles Wesley, M.A.*[43] offered little variation from one another even in their tables of contents. A detailed description of the family home is followed by references to Charles Wesley's studies at Oxford, with a special emphasis on the emerging development of a strict and systematic rule of life with regard to personal piety and good works. The time spent by the two Wesley brothers in the North American colony of Georgia as Anglican clerics and missionaries is often pictured as bleak. Only the encounters with German Pietists seem to shed light on the horizon. Against the bleak background of the American colonial experience, however, the Wesley conversions after their return from Georgia appear in a bright light. The few days before and after the conversions are frequently described in great detail. Descriptions of the rapid spread of the Methodist renewal movement follow, which include the picture of its amazing success, as well as the difficulties it confronted. It is at this point in the history of Methodism that Charles, when compared to John, begins to step into the background. Thus, the biographies, from this point on, concentrate without exception on Charles's remaining contribution to the Methodist movement, namely his hymns.

Not a few of the biographies, as already mentioned, have titles that belie the categorization of devotional literature. Charles Wesley is presented as the *Poet Preacher* by Charles Adams (1859), as the *Poet of Methodism* by John Kirk (1860), and as the *Poet of the Evangelical Revival* by Frank Colquhoun. Such publications are not restricted to the nineteenth century. One still finds contributions of a similar style in the twentieth century: Charles Wesley is described as the *Evangelist and Poet* by F. Luke Wiseman (1932), as the *Singer of the Evangelical Revival* by Elmer T. Clark (1957), and—more specifically!—as the *Singer of Six Thousand Songs* by Elizabeth P. Myers (1965), and *The First Methodist* by Frederick C. Gill (1964).

Historical interest in the Wesleys was not, however, exclusively restricted to the devotional literature of the nineteenth century, but also found expression in the first complete editions of the Wesleys' works. Of those editions that dealt with Charles and his poetical work, George Osborn's *The Poetical Works of John and Charles Wesley*, published between 1868 and 1872, is of considerable importance.[44] Even if Osborn's work does not meet today's critical demands, it remained, for a long time, the only source where many Wesley texts were published and accessible. Thomas Jackson's attempt to publish Charles Wesley's *Journal* (1849)[45] and a complete biography with considerable autobiographical material (1841) suffered from less than exacting academic standards. Nevertheless, it remains a gold mine of detailed information and autobiographical material for every new biography of Charles Wesley, even though it tends toward hagiography in many places.

Until recently the only published edition of Charles Wesley's sermons was a collection published in 1816 by his wife. For the most part, however, the sermons have proved to be unauthentic. They were indeed preached by Charles but most of them originated from his brother John. A small critical edition of six heretofore unpublished Charles Wesley sermons, however, has now been made available (1987).

There is practically no new satisfactory critical publication of the historical/biographical material available on Charles Wesley, much less a theological biography as Martin Schmidt has written on John Wesley. One must continue, for the most part, to rely on the production of popular scholarship.[46] This holds true even for the 1988 biography of Charles Wesley by Arnold A. Dallimore, an author who is well known for his biography of George Whitefield. The volume, published under the title *A Heart Set Free*, is fairly balanced and Dallimore's treatment of Wesley is not uncritical. Charles is described as a poet, preacher, and proclaimer of the gospel. But even Dallimore includes generalizations such as portraying Charles Wesley as "undoubtedly the greatest of all Christian hymn composers,"[47] which simply cannot be accepted without question. Furthermore, Dallimore does not really go beyond the information already provided by Thomas Jackson in his biography of Charles Wesley 150 years earlier.

In the twentieth century, the interest in Charles Wesley, up to this time often historical and biographical, has shifted to his poetical work from various perspectives.[48] The first group of publications concentrated on the literary characteristics of the texts and the traditions that they assimilated. Henry Bett's *The Hymns of Methodism in their Literary Relations* (1913) best represents this method of inquiry. The author respects the poetical works of Charles Wesley as literature, a point of view minimized, so far, in his opinion. Bett himself claims that the hymns of Methodism constitute the finest body of devotional verse in the English language.[49] Bett's study focuses on the sources and traditions assimilated in the hymns of Charles Wesley (writings of the Church Fathers, influences of the *Book of Common Prayer*, and other literature). His catalog of criteria for distinguishing between the hymns of John and Charles remains the standard work referred to by all ensuing research attempts.[50] Though research efforts to resolve the problem of precise authorship in several individual Wesley texts continue, a satisfactory solution has yet to be found. The pioneering work of Henry Bett is, however, not to be diminished thereby. With his detailed delineation of the sources of the hymns, Bett was one of the first to analyze and present the various traditions from which Charles Wesley drew for his hymn writing.

The other principal studies of the Wesleyan poetical corpus that fall into this group of publications tend to have a more explicitly literary interest. Such volumes include Robert Newton Flew's *Hymns of Charles Wesley: A Study of Their Structure* (1953), and, notably, Frank Baker's edition of poetical texts, *Representative Verse of Charles Wesley* (1962), as well as Baker's introduction to this volume,[51] which in 1964 was published separately and specifically discusses the literary characteristics of Wesley texts. This introduction appeared in an expanded edition for the 1988 Wesley anniversary celebration. Seen strictly from the point of view of literary criticism very little attention has been devoted to the work of Charles Wesley. Donald Davie's chapter on "The Classicism of Charles Wesley" in his book *Purity of Diction in English Verse* (1953) is a notable exception. One of the questions raised by Davie's chapter, however, is subject to continuing debate among those devoted to Wesley studies. What is Charles Wesley's relationship to Romanticism? Does he serve as a forerunner of Romanticism or are his ties to the Classicism of the Augustan Age too strong to shake?[52] Whatever the outcome, the debate in and of itself seems to me to be of limited value. After all, the placement of the Wesleyan poetical corpus as such is not really in question here. Rather, the debate should focus on the placement of an entire group of poets from the period of late Classicism who began to include elements of Romanticism. Charles Wesley is but one of these poets and probably not the best example to be used in the resolution of this question as to their status between Classicism and Romanticism.

Theological interest in the poetical texts of Charles Wesley began to surface almost simultaneously with publications concerned with a more literary focus. This interest in theology leads us to the second group of twentieth-century publications on Wesley's work. The 1940s saw the publication of two works by J. Ernest Rattenbury often cited for prompting a number of subsequent theological inquiries.

The attempt at theological analysis in Rattenbury's *Evangelical Doctrines of Charles Wesley's Hymns* (1941) and *The Eucharistic Hymns of John and Charles Wesley* (1948) remain standard reference points consistently acknowledged in more recent studies along similar themes. *The Hymns of Wesley and Watts* (1942), a collection of lectures by the Congregationalist Bernard L. Manning, and the short book of George H. Findlay, *Christ's Standard Bearer* (1956), are to be noted at this point even though they straddle the fence separating literary inquiry from the theological. Findlay, in particular, after introductory pages on literary characteristics (he devotes an entire chapter to the use of the exclamation point in the hymns!) explores questions of content and themes suggested by key words within the hymns. Neither book takes as its subject the whole Wesleyan poetical corpus but rather looks specifically at the 1780 *A Collection of Hymns for the Use of the People Called Methodists.*

More detailed theological analysis of Wesley's poetical work has surfaced during the last thirty years, taking the form of dissertations from England, and in particular, the USA. It could almost be referred to as a Charles Wesley renaissance, which, however, appears to be focusing on his theological legacy rather than renewed interest in his biography. The dissertations of James Dale, *The Theological and Literary Qualities of the Poetry of Charles Welsey in Relation to the Standards of His Age* (1960), and Gilbert L. Morris, *Imagery in the Hymns of Charles Wesley* (1969), combine literary and theological inquiry. Dale's thesis attempts to establish Charles Wesley as a Classicist of the Augustan Age as opposed to a poet with early Romanticist tendencies. This work also provides important insight into the relationship between poetical form and religious witness in the Wesleyan writings.[53] Morris's dissertation explores, in detail, the colorful language of three hundred representative Charles Wesley hymns. In contrast to the above, the dissertations of Barbara Ann Welch, *Charles Wesley and the Celebrations of Evangelical Experience* (1971), James C. Ekrut, *Universal Redemption, Assurance of Salvation, and Christian Perfection in the Hymns of Charles Wesley, With Poetic Analyses and Tune Examples* (1978), James A. Townsend, *Feelings Related to Assurance in Charles Wesley's Hymns* (1979), and John R. Tyson's *Charles Wesley's Theology of the Cross: An Examination of the Theology and Method of Charles Wesley as Seen in His Doctrine of the Atonement* (1983), provide primarily theological insight.

With nearly one thousand pages, John Tyson's dissertation is the most exhaustive theological examination of Charles Wesley's hymns to date.[54] The author uses detailed word and motif studies in examining the soteriological center of Wesley's legacy. His study has led Tyson to believe that Charles Wesley is an important theologian, often underrated. Presumably, this conclusion motivated him to continue his work on Charles Wesley beyond his dissertation. In 1986, Tyson's book describing Wesley's teaching on sanctification was published and characterized, in the subtitle, as "A Biographical and Theological Study." Three years later, Tyson published a collection of selected Charles Wesley texts as an introduction to Wesley's life and work under the title *Charles Wesley: A Reader*.[55] Craig Gallaway,[56] in his 1988 dissertation, focused on an understanding of the presence of Christ in the worshiping community in the hymns of the 1780 *Collection*. Wilma Jean Quantrille dealt with the doctrine of the Holy Trinity in the hymns of Charles Wesley in her 1989 dissertation.[57]

So much for the review of the development of Charles Wesley research. A brief look at the works about Charles Wesley produced in the German-speaking world establishes that principal contributions to Wesley research have come primarily from English-speaking countries. Interest in Methodism in German-speaking countries has never been great for a variety of reasons. True, some[58] have been able to highlight specific aspects of John Wesley's life and theology as well as that of developing Methodist communities, but outside Methodist circles little interest in Charles Wesley has been generated. Even among German-speaking Methodists interest in Charles Wesley and his hymns has been quite limited.[59] This neglect is, in large measure, attributable to the influence of nineteenth-century North American revival hymns on the hymnody of German-speaking Methodism, which served to obscure the importance of original Wesleyan hymnody on the movement.[60] The Methodist Bishop John L. Nuelsen's *John Wesley und das deutsche Kirchenlied* [61] (1938, an English translation was published in 1972), and Erika Mayer's dissertation, *Charles Wesleys Hymnen: Eine Untersuchung und literarische Würdigung* (1957), must be cited as exceptions to the general lack of interest in Wesley studies among German-speaking peoples. Nuelsen's study is the first to examine thoroughly the hymns of German Pietism that John Wesley encountered and translated while in North America. Nuelsen's examination of this subject remains a standard reference work. One might also note the contributions of Franz Hildebrandt[62] (a Lutheran who emigrated to England and became a Methodist) and the work of Martin Schmidt, particularly his *Theological Biography of John Wesley* (1953–1966). These authors, at least, suggest a certain interest in Methodism outside Methodist circles.

In 1988, which marked the 250th anniversary of the conversion of the Wesley brothers as well as the 200th anniversary of Charles Wesley's death, an abundance of literature appeared (at least in the English-speaking world). By definition, a significant portion of this literature was "devotional" in nature. After all, a faith community was celebrating the seminal experiences of its founders, without which it would not have been born. To a certain extent serious scholarly projects cannot be planned according to anniversary celebrations. As a result, new scholarly revelations were not necessarily to be expected. In light of the foregoing history of Wesleyan research, it should come as no surprise that even in the year in which Charles Wesley's conversion and death were commemorated, interest in Charles Wesley[63] took second place to interest in his brother, John. Signs, however, emerged indicating an increased interest in Wesleyan hymnody.[64] A subsequent colloquium on Charles Wesley, held in Princeton in October of 1989, led to the establishment of the Charles Wesley Society in October of 1990[65] with its own "The Charles Wesley Society Newsletter."[66] The papers from the 1990 founding meeting of the Society, together with some other papers on Charles Wesley, have meanwhile been edited by S T Kimbrough, Jr. under the title *Charles Wesley: Poet and Theologian* (1992).

This review of Wesleyan studies makes clear that further research into the theological interpretation of the Wesleyan works is warranted. It is apparent that until now the soteriological emphases of the Wesleyan works have received the most attention, and rightly so. But a new and thorough study of the Eucharistic hymns[67] might prove to be as rewarding as an analysis of the poetical texts of Wesley associated with the church year. Above all, an important area for future Charles Wesley research will include work on critical editions of primary literature as well as exhaustive historical/biographical studies.[68] Further research concerns might also include an examination of the traditions assimilated by Charles Wesley in his poetical works from the Holy Scriptures[69] to *Paradise Lost*.[70] Finally, one might also hope that in the wake of the ecumenical overtures churches are making toward one another the research concerns of other traditions might well become the concerns of one's own. *A Rapture of Praise*, edited by H. A. Hodges and A. M. Allchin (1966), is a fine example of ecumenical research on the Wesleys. It provides a collection of Wesleyan poetical texts chosen by both authors along with their commentary from an Anglican perspective. The Roman Catholic priest Francis Frost's article "Biblical Imagery and Religious Experience in the Hymns of the Wesleys" (1980) is also worthy of note. Charles Wesley's works, his sermons, diaries, letters, and poetical texts deserve the attention of scholars from many Christian communities. In order to give researchers access to this Wesleyan work, a critical edition of the complete works of Charles Wesley is sorely needed. It is astounding, considering the above review, how much research has been produced without such a resource.

This overview of Wesleyan research demonstrates, on the one hand, that the question of a "theology in hymns" as a basis for any study continues to be open and relevant. On the other hand, the development of *theological* interpretations of Wesleyan hymns has now provided an important foundation for the study of this question.

B. Characteristics of Wesleyan Hymnody

Before proceeding with a theological interpretation of the hymns contained in *A Collection of Hymns for the Use of the People Called Methodists* of 1780 it is necessary to point out several typical features of the hymns of Charles Wesley. Characteristics found throughout his entire poetical production must be rightly identified here before beginning the discussion of individual theological themes. In both tasks, however, the hymns should be allowed to speak for themselves. I will therefore attempt, by way of several concrete examples to present a few typical features of the Wesleyan poetical corpus. Before beginning, however, we must consider whether the poetical work of Charles Wesley is best characterized as hymns or as poems that were later adapted for the purpose of singing in the society meetings.

1. Hymns or Poems?

In principle any attempt to resolve this question addressing the formal classification of the Wesleyan poetical corpus seems both futile and, at least in the case of *A Collection of Hymns for the Use of the People Called Methodists*, of lesser importance. The *Collection* of 1780 is clearly intended as a hymnbook for Methodist communities. The texts found in it, therefore, at least since their inclusion in the *Collection* function as hymn selections for the community. Such a contextual definition, however, says little about the original intention of the author, especially if that intention was not in agreement with that of the editor of the later collections. Moreover, it must not be forgotten that Methodist hymnbooks (like many others) never served solely as resources for hymn singing in worship but rather were often used as devotional guides for the individual.

Having said this, one must recognize that the designation of the Wesleyan material in *A Collection of Hymns for the Use of the People Called Methodists* as hymns or poems is not easily made. On the one hand, Charles Wesley himself does not always clearly distinguish between the two categories. On the other hand, the use of individual pieces in hymnbooks has often separated them from their original character (in particular see the example below, "Come, O thou Traveller unknown"). Furthermore, after some initial hesitation, Wesley appears to have abandoned any distinction between the two forms in his own vocabulary. In the end he spoke only of "hymns"[71] when referring to his own work. In his first few publications, titles like *Hymns and Sacred Poems* still seem to attempt terminological differentiation even if it was clear that these terms were not mutually exclusive but were rather meant to complement each other. These differentiations are later dropped.

The best example of a hymn in the *Collection* of 1780 originally written as a lyrical poem (some would even say a ballad) is the Wesleyan paraphrase of Genesis 32:24-32. After the death of Charles Wesley, his brother John would refer to this text, "Come, O thou Traveller unknown," as the "poem" that Isaac Watts is said to have suggested overshadowed his own entire work. The text of this poem was first published in *Hymns and Sacred Poems* of 1742. The *Collection* of 1780 contained twelve of the original fourteen stanzas.[72] What follows is the text from the *Collection*:

> Come, O thou Traveller unknown,   (1)
>   Whom still I hold, but cannot see!
> My company before is gone,
>   And I am left alone with thee;

With thee all night I mean to stay,
And wrestle till the break of day.

I need not tell thee who I am, (2)
    My misery or sin declare;
Thyself hast called me by my name,
    Look on thy hands, and read it there.
But who, I ask thee, who art thou?
Tell me thy name, and tell me now.

In vain thou strugglest to get free, (3)
    I never will unloose my hold;
Art thou the Man that died for me?
    The secret of thy love unfold:
Wrestling, I will not let thee go
Till I thy name, thy nature know.

Wilt thou not yet to me reveal (4)
    Thy new, unutterable name?
Tell me, I still beseech thee, tell;
    To know it now resolved I am:
Wrestling, I will not let thee go
Till I thy name, thy nature know.

What though my shrinking flesh complain (5)
    And murmur to contend so long?
I rise superior to my pain:
    When I am weak, then I am strong;
And when my all of strength shall fail
    I shall with the God-man prevail.

Yield to me now—for I am weak, (6)
    But confident in self-despair!
Speak to my heart, in blessings speak,
    Be conquered by my instant prayer:
Speak, or thou never hence shalt move,
And tell me if thy name is LOVE.

'Tis Love! 'Tis Love! Thou diedst for me; (7)
    I hear thy whisper in my heart.
The morning breaks, the shadows flee,
    Pure Universal Love thou art:

To me, to all, thy bowels move—
Thy nature, and thy name, is LOVE.

My prayer hath power with God; the grace   (8)
    Unspeakable I now receive.
Through faith I see thee face to face;
    I see thee face to face, and live!
In vain I have not wept and strove—
Thy nature, and they [!] name, is LOVE.

I know thee, Saviour, who thou art—   (9)
    Jesus, the feeble sinner's friend;
Nor wilt thou with the night depart,
    But stay, and love me to the end:
Thy mercies never shall remove,
Thy nature, and thy name, is LOVE.

The Sun of Righteousness on me   (10)
    Hath rose with healing in his wings;
Withered my nature's strength; from thee
    My soul its life and succour brings;
My help is all laid up above:
Thy nature, and thy name, is LOVE.

Contented now upon my thigh   (11)
    I halt, till life's short journey end;
All helplessness, all weakness, I
    On thee alone for strength depend;
Nor have I power from thee to move:
Thy nature, and thy name, is LOVE.

Lame as I am, I take the prey,   (12)
    Hell, earth, and sin with ease o'ercome;
I leap for joy, pursue my way,
    And as a bounding hart fly home,
Through all eternity to prove,
Thy nature, and thy name, is LOVE.[73]

It comes as no surprise to learn that "Come, O thou Traveller unknown" was not conceived as a hymn to be sung at worship, even though the story of Jacob's struggle on the banks of the river Jabbok was among the favorite biblical texts used by Charles Wesley when preaching. In this poem, entitled "Wrestling Jacob," Charles Wesley uses this Old Testament story of Jacob's struggle with the angel at the river Jabbok as a foil for a completely different "story," one which, however, will be interpreted in light of this Old Testament struggle. Wesley's "story" tells of humankind's encounter with Christ, understood by Charles Wesley, against the backdrop of Jacob's struggle at the river Jabbok, as humankind's struggle to know the name and essence of the one previously unknown: God.

The two stories parallel each other in a variety of ways. Both are situated in the context of a journey: Jacob travels from Haran to the land of Canaan while the "I" of Wesley's poem is on a journey that initially is not identified but is later referred to as "life's short journey." Both travelers are alone ("My company before is gone, And I am left alone"). It is night. The Jacob story and Charles Wesley in depicting the struggle to know the Unknown skillfully set the confrontation of each traveler in the evening only to have the riddle of the Unknown's identity revealed with the coming morning light. Both Jacob and the "I" of the poem seek a blessing. And both depart from the encounter with the Unknown with the marks of struggle.

A detailed interpretation of this poem will demonstrate how effectively Charles Wesley uses Jacob's struggle at the river Jabbok as a foil for the "I's" encounter with Christ. Stanza 1 begins with an exhortation that simultaneously describes the setting for the poem and anticipates its theme. The unknown, unseen Other is addressed: "Come, O thou Traveller unknown." The short phrases of the stanza contain no superfluous information; the reader learns by inference that the speaker is traveling alone at night. The last two lines introduce the theme for the stanzas that follow: "With thee all night I mean to stay, And wrestle till the break of day." Stanza 2 begins with the struggle to know the identity of the unknown Other (which will carry through to the crucial stanza 7) by asking the first direct question of the poem: "who, I ask thee, who art thou?" Even the identity of the poem's "I" is curiously never fully revealed. The reader is provided with riddlelike clues when the poem's "I" suggests that the "unknown Traveller" knows him by the marks in his hands: "Look on thy hands, and read it there." With the second direct question of the poem, stanza 3 focuses on the circumstances surrounding the struggle to know the identity of the Unknown, which now begins to take on a decidedly Christological and soteriological character: "Art thou the Man that died for me?" The nighttime struggle to know the identity of the Unknown, both here and in the stanzas to come, is characterized as the struggle to know the mystery of his name and thus his essence (and his love). The brief reference to the Unknown as "God-man" in stanza 5 further reinforces the Christological allusions.

At the end of the sixth stanza the struggle and questioning reach a climax when the speaker demands of the Unknown: "Speak . . . And tell me if thy name is LOVE." The next stanza lies at the very heart of the poem. Here the identity of the Unknown is revealed. The revelatory character of this situation is underscored through the parallel ending of night and the emergence of the morning light: "The morning breaks, the shadows flee." The revealed identity of the Unknown answers the urgent question of the preceding stanza as well as the questions of other stanzas with the ever-strengthening repeated affirmation: "'Tis Love! 'Tis Love! Thou diedst for me." It is important to note that the speaker of this revelation is the "I" of the preceding stanzas.[74] Precisely this detail suggests the recognition of the identity of the Unknown to be an intrapersonal event, situated in the internal experience of the seeking and struggling "I." Stanza 7 also introduces the refrain, which will conclude henceforth each remaining stanza of the poem: "Thy nature, and thy name, is LOVE." This is the key to the identity of the Unknown.

The stanzas that follow are, in effect, a celebration of the Unknown's revelation and provide an increasingly clear description of the Unknown. Now neither darkness nor shadow obscure visibility. Charles Wesley clearly has the dawn of the new day coincide with a newly awakened faith: "Through faith I see thee face to face . . . I know thee, Saviour, who thou art." Further characterizations of the Unknown now are clearly Christological and soteriological in nature: "Saviour . . . Jesus . . . sinner's friend . . . Sun of Righteousness." As "the Sun of Righteousness" rises at daybreak on the speaker, he continues on his journey (with the assurance that this Sun will not leave him in the coming night). Even the marks of the nighttime struggle with the Unknown ("upon my thigh I halt . . . Lame as I am") present no obstacle to the believing "I" but are rather reminders of the power of God. The last stanza provides a typical Wesleyan eschatological perspective in which the end of life's journey is envisioned and contrasted with the never-ending love of God.

The poem "Wrestling Jacob" describes an event that Wesley repeatedly takes as theme in his poems and hymns: the encounter with Christ, the conversion to new life, the experience of grace, and the day of conversion. "Wrestling Jacob," in this sense, may be characterized as typical of the (religious) work of Charles Wesley. As placed in *A Collection of Hymns for the Use of the People Called Methodists* of 1780, however, it is the best example in that hymnbook of a text for congregational singing that was difficult to use. John Wesley was forced to adopt nearly the entire text so as to not destroy its original meaning. Thus, though included in the *Collection* as a hymn, its many verses inhibited its use for congregational song. Apart from its length, the intricate structure and development of the theme were also likely difficult for a congregation to grasp, although it may have been the case that "Wrestling Jacob" was intended to be read as a private devotion or as a (sung?) presentation in the assembly of the faithful. Finally, the intricate structure and sophisticated vocabulary employed would not necessarily have been well suited to those whom the Methodist renewal movement most wanted to reach. All of these observations together seem to indicate that "Wrestling Jacob" may well have been a part of the Wesleyan corpus best identified as a "sacred poem," which in time (also) came to be used, or as the case may be, understood as a hymn.[75]

So much for determining the nature of the Charles Wesley texts found in *A Collection of Hymns for the Use of the People Called Methodists*. It is clear that this collection contains texts of various types, some of which may be identified as poems ("Come, O thou Traveller unknown"), while others were conceived as hymns for worship from the very beginning. Many texts in the *Collection*, however, are likely to be classified somewhere in between these two categories. To a certain extent, as already mentioned, the literary differences are not that significant since the texts were collected into a single hymnbook.

Another question prompted by the discussion of how to characterize these "hymns" (particularly if the "hymns" actually turn out to be poems) is that of the literary background of the Wesleyan corpus and its connection to the poetical milieu of his day. The following section is devoted to the discussion of this question.

2. The Literary Context

The Wesleyan poetical corpus must be understood within the context of the so-called "Augustan Age" of poetry. Around the end of the seventeenth century, this poetry began to replace the rather ostentatious Baroque poetry and challenge its florid forms by simplicity, order, and distance from the expression of feelings. For the most part, the poetry of the Augustan Age can be understood as the poetical expression of those influenced by the Enlightenment. Perhaps the best example of poetry from this period can be found in Alexander Pope's (1688–1744) satirical poetry, which often sought to teach morality. The parameters for the poetry of the Augustan Age as shaped by Pope were, however, quickly broadened by a newly awakened interest in Renaissance poetry (see, for example, the poetry of Edmund Spenser [1552–1599] and of John Milton [1608–1674]).[76] In particular, the disdain for emotional expression in Augustan poetry now gave way to an increasing interest in matters that transcended dispassionate reason. This broader framework of the Augustan Age was never systematically established in direct contrast to the Augustan poetry, but the poets who encouraged such a broadening are often—and rightly so—identified as those who anticipate Romanticism.

The Wesleyan poetical corpus demonstrates a clear affinity with this pre-Romantic Augustan poetry. However, it does not seem helpful to argue over whether Charles Wesley is rightly identified as belonging to the poets of the Augustan Age proper or to those anticipating Romanticism. In the last analysis, the concern is not so much with the classification of the Wesleyan poetical corpus itself but with the classification of an entire group of poets from the late Augustan Age, who exhibit a tendency to express themselves in the form and vocabulary of early Romanticism. Charles Wesley is but one of these poets and even then not likely the best example one could choose to address this matter.

Charles Wesley's poetical expression belies not only life in the Augustan Age but also a keen desire to make the poetry of this period, which he knew and valued, his own. His choice of words, style, meter, rhyme, and structure all point to the Augustan Age as the fertile soil for the development of his poetry.[77] Similarly, the influence of and reference to the classics of Latin and Greek poetry found in his works are typical of the Augustan Age (Charles Wesley depended more heavily on the classics of *Latin* poetry, especially Virgil and Horace).[78] Wesley's use of Latin phrases has often been pointed out.[79] The influence of many English poets like John Milton, George Herbert, John Dryden, Matthew Prior, and Edward Young can, however, also be recognized.[80] A telling example of this association is noted in the famous Charles Wesley hymn "Love divine, all loves excelling," which, after its initial publication in 1747, was later included by John Wesley in *A Collection of Hymns for the Use of the People Called Methodists* of 1780. Here Charles Wesley borrows quite openly from a text by John Dryden (1631–1700), written for his work *King Arthur*, in which Venus sings this hymn to the honor and glory of Brittania:

> Fairest Isles, all isles excelling,
>   Seat of pleasures, and of loves;
> Venus here will choose her dwelling,
>   And forsake her Cyprian groves.[81]

In taking this text as a blueprint for his work, Charles Wesley creates a hymn that transforms the love and beauty of a particular island dwelling into the love and beauty promised to those who are open to the love of God in Jesus. The love of God is called upon to indwell the heart of every individual believer:

> *Love divine, all loves excelling,*
>   Joy of heaven, to earth come down,
> Fix in us thy humble *dwelling*,
>   All thy faithful mercies crown!
> Jesu, thou art all compassion,
>   Pure, unbounded love thou art;
> Visit us with thy salvation!
>   Enter every trembling heart.
>
> Come, almighty to deliver,
>   Let us all thy grace receive;
> Suddenly return, and never,
>   Never more thy temples leave.
> Thee we would be always blessing,
>   Serve thee as thy hosts above,
> Pray, and praise thee without ceasing,
>   Glory in thy perfect love.

> Finish then thy new creation,
>   Pure and spotless let us be;
> Let us see thy great salvation,
>   Perfectly restored in thee;
> Changed from glory into glory,
>   Till in heaven we take our place,
> Till we cast our crowns before thee,
>   Lost in wonder, love, and praise.[82]

The differing development of each poem suggests that Charles Wesley, in reality, only borrowed from the very beginning of Dryden's text. Though characteristic for Wesleyan poetry, the unabashed borrowing from other poets is seldom of great significance. The occasion for borrowing from another poet seems often random and rarely determines the big picture for any given piece. One literary critic has described this phenomenon in Wesleyan poetry as the "habit of *inconspicuous reference* to previous literature."[83] In this sense "Love divine, all loves excelling" is an excellent example of the manner in which the poetical corpus of Charles Wesley connects with its literary context: Charles Wesley, the poet, was deeply rooted in the (broadened) Augustan poetry of his day, and he freely and openly borrowed from other poetical traditions with which he was familiar. The primary inspiration and resource for his poetry, however, is provided by his evangelical experience and deep commitment to the Methodist renewal movement against which everything else was measured and subordinated. When this is taken into account, it is easy to understand why the poetical corpus of Charles Wesley was influenced more significantly than any of its contemporaries by one text: the Bible. It is this text, the Bible, and not the context of the Augustan Age that provides the primary literary foundation for Wesleyan poetry.

3. The Scriptural Roots

The autobiographical description of John Wesley as a *homo unius libri* may be readily assigned to his brother, Charles, as well.[84] It is after all this single book, the Bible, which grounds the Wesleyan (religious) poetical corpus. The themes, the language used, and the world of the hymns are all formed and nurtured on the fertile soil of biblical story and witness. Methodist admirers of the Wesleys have sometimes taken solace in the notion that if one day the Bible should disappear, its text could nearly be completely reconstructed based on the Wesleyan deposit of hymns alone. Such a thought is helpful even if only to direct one's attention to the fantastic array of references, borrowed phrases, and quotes from the Bible that are found in Wesleyan hymns.[85]

Charles Wesley's familiarity with the biblical text was based on several key elements (beyond his own constant devotional reading) essential to understanding the biblical roots of his poetry. First, as a classicist, Wesley was familiar with Greek and Hebrew and could refer to the original languages when working with Holy Scripture. This can be seen in several of his hymns, where the choice of vocabulary clearly reflects knowledge of Greek and Hebrew and the translation Wesley chooses is at variance with the standard translation of his day.[86] For the most part, however, Wesley's use of biblical language must be understood by way of the standard translation of his day, the so-called *Authorized Version.* It was published in 1611 (under James I and thus also referred to as the King James Version) and reflected a compromise between existing translations produced by both High Church and Puritan interests—an early example of an attempt to produce an "ecumenical" edition of the Bible. The *Authorized Version* was (at least for three hundred years) *the* translation of the Bible in the English-speaking world. In his *Explanatory Notes Upon the New Testament* (1755) John Wesley did offer a few suggestions, however conservative, for alternative translations based on his knowledge of Greek and Hebrew. But, generally, the *Authorized Version* was the recognized authority for the quotation of biblical texts in Wesley's day. Its vocabulary is the mother tongue of the poet Charles Wesley. Only at one point did he consistently deviate from the *Authorized Version.* Whenever he referred to the book of Psalms in his hymns, he would reach for the (older) translation as found in the *Book of Common Prayer.* As a cleric of the Church of England (and thus required to say the Daily Office), this translation of the Psalms would have been more familiar to him.[87] This should not be overlooked. Wesley's command of Greek and Hebrew was sufficient for him to know that the *Authorized Version,* in most cases, offered the better translation. But apparently his familiarity (encouraged by liturgical prayer) with the Psalm translation of the Daily Office was sufficient to overcome the known weaknesses of the translation.

In addition to his knowledge of Greek and Hebrew and his familiarity with the *Authorized Version,* Wesley had at his command the tools of the biblical scholarship of his day of which he made ready use. Three exegetical reference works, in particular, had a lasting influence on him and his poetical corpus:[88] an exegesis of the New Testament by the German Pietist scholar, Johannes Albrecht Bengel (1687–1752), published in 1742 under the title *Gnomon Novi Testamenti* (this work also fascinated John Wesley); an exegesis of the Pentateuch by Robert Gell (1595–1665) published in 1659; and the commentary on both the Old and New Testaments by the Nonconformist, Matthew Henry (1662–1714). This commentary, published between 1708 and 1710 in five volumes under the title *Exposition of the Old and New Testament,* proved to be more influential than all others on the work of Charles Wesley.[89] Wesley's hymns repeatedly exhibit the influence of Matthew Henry's commentary.

Not unlike the exegetical authorities of his day, Wesley's relationship to Holy Scripture was not formed by a historical-critical vision. On the contrary, his deep respect for the Church Fathers and his familiarity with their works led him to appropriate allegory as a particularly suitable tool for the interpretation of Holy Scripture.[90] This allegorical interpretation was accompanied by a decidedly Christological interpretation of the Old Testament. For Wesley (like the Christian tradition that preceded him) everything became a foil for Christ: the leadership of Moses and Joshua, the sacrifice of Isaac, the kingship of David, to name but a few of the most frequently occurring examples. The Old Testament is given a Christocentric reading, as is, naturally, the New Testament. What counts as Christocentric for Wesley is at the same time soteriological. He has little interest in any other aspect of the Bible. In one sense, Wesley wrestles the Good News out of every single text,[91] even when the text does not obviously offer such an interpretation.

The ways in which the Wesleyan poetical corpus is rooted in Holy Scripture are manifold. First, Wesley's religious poetry mines the wealth of ideas and themes contained in Scripture. It was here that Wesley would often seek inspiration for his poetry, at least his religious poetry. Apart from the theme selection, clearly influenced by Holy Scripture, his vocabulary was also thoroughly saturated with the language of the Bible. Wesley, however, did not feel obliged to cite Scripture in every stanza of poetry. The influence of Scripture on his poetry was far more subtle. In some ways, Wesley was as familiar with the language of Scripture as he was with his mother tongue. His poetical thoughts were formed, perhaps often unconsciously, in the literary world of the *Authorized Version.* With this in mind, it is easier to understand how nearly every line of some Wesleyan hymns contains allusions to Scripture that often have little to do with one another and, in most cases, are from completely different books of the Bible. Each hymn became a mosaic of references to Holy Scripture accessible to all who were as familiar with Scripture and the *Authorized Version* as Charles Wesley. (Of course this means that few of these references are recognized and understood today!)

Apart from the often unwitting influence of Holy Scripture on Wesleyan poetry direct references to the Bible are also identifiable. The best example of such references can be found in the collection of 2,349 hymns based on texts of the Bible published in two volumes by Charles Wesley in 1762 with the title *Short Hymns on Select Passages of the Holy Scriptures.* The collection is ordered according to the books of the Bible and contains poetical interpretations of select passages from every book. Its format alone, even in the first edition, unmistakably marked this volume as a devotional guide. Even though the title suggests otherwise, *Short Hymns on Select Passages of the Holy Scriptures* is best understood as an aid for personal meditation on Scripture rather than a hymnbook. In the foreword to this volume Charles Wesley emphasizes his reliance on the already mentioned exegetical reference works of his day.[92]

John Wesley appropriated several of his brother's hymns from this volume for *A Collection of Hymns for the Use of the People Called Methodists* of 1780. An excellent example of the connection between the Wesleyan poetical corpus and the Bible is offered by one of the hymns, which first appeared in the *Short Hymns on Select Passages of the Holy Scriptures* and then again, nearly twenty years later, in the *Collection*:

> O thou who camest from above   (1)
>   The pure celestial fire t'impart,
> Kindle a flame of sacred love
>   On the mean altar of my heart!

There let it for thy glory burn　　　　　　(2)
　　With inextinguishable blaze,
And trembling to its source return
　　In humble love, and fervent praise.

Jesu, confirm my heart's desire　　　　　　(3)
　　To work, and speak, and think for thee;
Still let me guard the holy fire,
　　And still stir up thy gift in me.

Ready for all thy perfect will,　　　　　　(4)
　　My acts of faith and love repeat,
Till death thy endless mercies seal,
　　And make the sacrifice complete.[93]

The biblical text upon which this hymn is based, Leviticus 6:13, is translated by the *Authorized Version* as follows: "The fire shall ever be burning upon the altar; it shall never go out" (KJV). It is clear that Wesley appropriates only the general sense of this cultic commandment from Leviticus. The actual meaning of this priestly charge in the Old Testament is unimportant to him. Wesley's interest in the text is roughly defined by the words *fire, altar,* and *sacrifice.* These words provide the framework in which Wesley's hymn has a believer ask that the inextinguishable fire of Love be kindled within ("on the . . . altar of my heart") so that all of one's whole life might become an acceptable sacrifice before God. A similar interpretation is articulated by Matthew Henry, though not as explicitly or as completely as by Charles Wesley. Matthew Henry, in his exegesis of this text, speaks of the ever-burning "fire of holy love," which must burn in each believer:

> By this law we are taught to keep up in our minds a constant disposition to all *acts of piety and devotion,* an habitual affection to divine things, so as *to be always ready* to every good word and *work.* We must not only not quench the Spirit, but we must *stir up the gift that is in us.* Though we be not always *sacrificing,* yet we must keep *the fire of holy love always burning*; and thus we must pray always.[94]

Henry makes the connection between the "always burning" flame of love and unceasing prayer, while Wesley takes this theme and has it speak of one's entire life as an offering to God. (Interestingly enough, similar themes with similar influences may be found in the poetry of English Classicism, for example, a Richard Blackmore [1654–1729] poem entitled "A Hymn to the Sacred Spirit.")[95] So much for the biblical text upon which Wesley based this hymn. The allusions to Scripture in this hymn have been, however, by no means exhausted with this basic textual dependence. Nearly every line of the hymn could be paired with a corresponding biblical passage, although the diverse nature of usage should be stressed. Some references are direct and clear, for example, 2 Timothy 1:6 is alluded to in the last line of the third stanza. Others can be identified as being based on a common idea (Romans 10:1 and the first line of the third stanza). While still others may be cited as having a certain thematic, if not always linguistic, kinship with specific biblical passages (line 2 of the first stanza refers to Luke 12:49). In one case, the Wesleyan reference to a specific passage of Scripture must be verified by a review of the passage in the original Greek. Wesley links Leviticus 6:13 and 2 Timothy 1:6 in the following line: "Still let me guard the holy fire, And still stir up thy gift in me." The Greek text reveals that Paul is charging Timothy with the task of *rekindling* the gifts of the Holy Spirit. The word that translates as rekindle, ἀναζωπυρεῖν, clearly has the word *fire* as its root (Matthew Henry had noted this in his commentary).[96] When read with Matthew Henry's commentary and the Greek original in mind, Wesley's association of the fire that burns on the altar with the χάρισμα in Timothy, or for that matter in any believer, is easily understood.

So much for the connection between the Wesleyan poetical corpus and the Bible. It is clear that the use of Scripture in the poetry of Charles Wesley is a multifaceted phenomenon, which must be considered as a whole, as a theological, exegetical, and historical nexus, when approaching the task of interpretation. It is, however, also clear that the literary context, otherwise significant in the poetry of Charles Wesley, was not of great influence on his use of Scripture. In the end, it was the Methodist renewal movement itself that encouraged and deepened the connection to Holy Scripture evident in Wesley's work.

4. The Influence of Tradition

Though Wesleyan poetry is primarily characterized by its use of Scripture, Wesley was not given to a puritanical "biblicism" that

105

denigrated other, nonbiblical sources altogether. This can be demonstrated by the manner in which the literary context of his day helped form his work. Furthermore, the integration of theological and ecclesiastical traditions, known to Wesley, into his works would indicate an openness to other influences as well. I mention this knowing full well that *A Collection of Hymns for the Use of the People Called Methodists* of 1780 is not significantly marked by Charles Wesley's knowledge of church tradition. This is due, in part, to the ordering principle (the spiritual journey of the individual) utilized by John Wesley as editor of the volume. This individualistic and soteriological emphasis is not, however, necessarily characteristic of Charles Wesley's *entire* work. It must not be forgotten, for example, that Charles Wesley used a reference work of dogmatic theology on the Holy Trinity[97] for his collection, *Hymns on the Trinity* (1767), and a devotional aid on the Eucharist[98] for his *Hymns on the Lord's Supper* (1745). Neither of these themes were ones typically addressed by the renewal movements of Pietism. Wesley's collections of hymns organized thematically according to the church year must also be mentioned in connection with the above, especially *Hymns for the Nativity of our Lord* (1744), *Hymns for our Lord's Resurrection* (1746), and *Hymns for Ascension Day* (1746).

Wesley also did not hesitate to use his hymns as weapons in a variety of theological skirmishes, which would break out from time to time within the renewal movement. Several hymns in the collection, *Hymns and Sacred Poems*, published in 1739, are directed against the tendency toward Quietism in Moravian circles.[99] A couple of years later Wesley published *Hymns on God's Everlasting Love* (1741) in which he took the supporters of George Whitefield and their understanding of predestination to task. Charles Wesley also used his hymns in the debate over Christian perfection within the Methodist renewal movement (his brother censored a number of these hymns when they did not square with his own understanding).

All of this demonstrates that the poetical corpus of Charles Wesley, even as regards religious matters, was not limited to hymns describing the personal experience of salvation. Dogmatic, theological, and liturgical questions and specific themes were also of interest to him, even though they are not characteristic of the standard hymnal of the Methodist renewal movement, the *Collection* of 1780.

An excellent example of Wesley's use of Patristic writings can be viewed in three different hymns of the *Collection*[100] where he borrows a sentence from Ignatius of Antioch's letter to the Romans, "My love is crucified" (Letter to the Romans 7:20). Wesley's well-known hymn "O Love divine! What hast thou done," published for the first time in *Hymns and Sacred Poems* of 1742, uses this line as a refrain to close each stanza. Below find the first stanza of this hymn:

> O Love divine! What hast thou done!
> Th'immortal God hath died for me!
> The Father's co-eternal Son
> Bore all my sins upon the tree:
> Th'immortal God for me hath died,
> *My Lord, my Love is crucified.*[101]

Other examples of the use of Patristic references (especially Augustine) can also be cited.[102] Further analysis of these references is declined by this study since they seem not to have had as significant an influence on *A Collection of Hymns for the Use of the People Called Methodists* as they did on other Wesleyan hymnbooks.

Thus, the overview of the most important characteristics of the Charles Wesley poetical corpus is brought to a close. The theological interpretation of Wesleyan poetry will assume these characteristics and further illustrate them.

C. The Interpretation of Individual Theological Themes

The preceding overview of the most important characteristics of Charles Wesley's hymns provides the basis upon which the theological interpretation of *A Collection of Hymns for the Use of the People Called Methodists* of 1780 may be made. This interpretation is best begun by addressing the theological themes of the *Collection* one by one. What ought to be avoided is cataloging the hymns by external dogmatic categories. Rather, the themes to be addressed should be prompted and developed by the hymns themselves. As in the preceding sections of this study, I will therefore attempt to allow the hymns to speak for themselves.

If this study is to be determined by the spectrum of individual themes in the hymnody of Charles Wesley as presented in *A Collection of Hymns for the Use of the People Called Methodists* then our starting point is easily determined. The soteriological motif in this hymnbook cannot be overlooked. This soteriological emphasis is the primary characteristic of a "theology in hymns" as found in the *Collection*. The first part of this section on the interpretation of individual theological themes is therefore devoted to this particular characteristic.

1. The Soteriological Emphasis

Heilsgeschichte, as conceived in the hymns of the *Collection*, concentrates on the application of the Christ-event in the life of the individual believer. The activity of God is therefore described almost exclusively in soteriological and Christological categories. This tendency, characteristic not only of Charles Wesley's religious poetry but also of a number of Pietist hymns from this period,[103] is amplified by the ordering principle used by John Wesley as editor of the *Collection*.

By classifying the hymns according to the individual Christian's faith journey, the soteriological emphasis, already apparent in the hymns themselves, is reinforced. Thus, for example, the theme of "creation" is, for the most part, absent in *A Collection of Hymns for the Use of the People Called Methodists*,[104] while the section on "Describing the Goodness of God" contains hymns largely motivated by Christological and soteriological concerns. The theme of creation does not surface at all in this context. Instead, the hymns make constant reference to the life and death of Jesus. Many of the hymns in this section are addressed directly to Christ and use Christ-epithets that are soteriological in orientation: "Saviour," "loving," "all-atoning Lamb," "Lover of souls," "Friend of humankind."[105] The emphasis on God's all-encompassing will to save is particularly important to Charles Wesley (not in the sense of a doctrine of an *apokatastasis panton*, but rather simply in the sense of the universal invitation to salvation) and finds expression in the word *all* used in several of the Christ-epithets: "all-atoning Lamb," "all-redeeming Lord." The hymns also include the corresponding and recurring phrase "for all," highlighted in the following example by literary devices such as anadiplosis, anaphora, and epizeuxis.

O for a trumpet-voice
On all the world to call,
To bid their hearts rejoice

108

> In him who died for all!
> For all my Lord was crucified,
> For all, for all my Saviour died![106]

This is just one example among countless others in *A Collection of Hymns for the Use of the People Called Methodists* that demonstrates Wesley's special emphasis on the universal nature of God's will to salvation. This single example also points to the importance of the phrase "for all" in Wesley's soteriological emphasis. It would be easy to substantiate this statement with an endless list of quotes. Instead it seems more appropriate to analyze in detail *one* example of this central motif in Wesleyan hymnody.

a. "for all": Wesleyan Soteriological Universalism. In the first section of the *Collection,* entitled "Exhorting, and beseeching to return to God," the Wesleyan emphasis on God's will for universal salvation is clearly stated. This is easily explained by way of the following two observations. First, the theme of God's universal invitation to salvation is clearly at the foundation of Wesleyan preaching and the call to conversion. As Charles Wesley notes in his journal entry dated July 12, 1741: "the power and seal of God are never wanting while I declared the two great truths of the everlasting gospel, universal redemption and Christian Perfection."[107] The theme of God's universal invitation to salvation had to be sounded particularly in the introduction of a hymn collection that would trace the journey of the individual to and through faith. The "beseeching to return to God" applies to everyone because God wills that everyone be saved. Thus, the majority of hymns contained in this section of the *Collection* are not addressed to God but to *sinners* who are being called to conversion, to return to God. The hymns are therefore quite clearly hymns of proclamation and preaching. Further emphasis on universal salvation in the first section of this hymnbook can be explained by way of John Wesley's editorial privilege. Most of the hymns in this section were taken from an early collection of his brother, *Hymns on God's Everlasting Love* (published in 1741 and 1742), which had been directed against a particularistic Calvinist view of salvation within the evangelical renewal movement. Many of these hymns were stark and polemical in nature. Many, indeed, used biting irony in rejecting the Calvinistic teaching on predestination.[108] However, John Wesley did, for the most part, use hymns from that collection whose tone was relatively moderate.

The opening hymn "O for a thousand tongues to sing" (certainly the most well-known hymn of this section) is followed by the hymn "Come, sinners to the gospel feast." It brings the Wesleyan emphasis on God's will for universal salvation clearly into focus and thus is chosen for analysis in this study. The text, as it appears in the *Collection*, is considerably abbreviated when compared to the original text published for the first time in *Hymns for those that seek, and those that have Redemption in the Blood of Jesus Christ* (1747). Only nine of the original twenty-four stanzas are retained in the *Collection* of 1780,[109] but John Wesley's editing does not alter the hymn's meaning substantively. Basically, several parallel scenes that occur throughout the hymn have been condensed into a single scene. The hymn is based on the Lukan parable of the Great Dinner (Luke 14:16-24).

> Come, sinners, to the gospel feast;   (1)
>   Let every soul be Jesu's guest;
> Ye need not one be left behind,
>   For God hath bidden all mankind.

> Sent by my Lord, on you I call;   (2)
>   The invitation is to all:
> Come all the world; come, sinner, thou!
>   All things in Christ are ready now.

> Come, all ye souls by sin oppressed.   (3)
>   Ye restless wanderers after rest;
> Ye poor, and maimed, and halt, and blind,
>   In Christ a hearty welcome find.

> Come, and partake the gospel feast,   (4)
>   Be saved from sin, in Jesus rest;
> O taste the goodness of your God,
>   And eat his flesh, and drink his blood.

> Ye vagrant souls, on you I call   (5)
>   (O that my voice could reach you all!):
> Ye all are freely justified,
>   Ye all may live—for Christ hath died.

My message as from God receive: (6)
   Ye all may come to Christ, and live.
O let his love your hearts constrain,
   Nor suffer him to die in vain!

His love is mighty to compel;   (7)
   His conqu'ring love consent to feel,
Yield to his love's resistless power,
   And fight against your God no more.

See him set forth before your eyes,   (8)
   That precious, bleeding sacrifice!
His offered benefits embrace,
   And freely now be saved by grace!

This is the time: no more delay!   (9)
   This is the acceptable day;
Come in, this moment, at his call,
   And live for him who died for all![110]

In this hymn Charles Wesley uses the Lukan parable of the Great Dinner as the backdrop for his own invitation for all to come to the banquet of salvation. The repetition of the imperative *Come*, also the hymn's very beginning, provides the invitation with a certain urgency. The speaker in the hymn is the slave in the parable who has received an assignment from his master ("my all-redeeming Lord")[111] to call to the table all who had been invited to the feast. As those invited decline the invitation, the servant then extends the invitation "to all": "Sent by my Lord, on you I call." "My message as from God receive." The hymn, as it appears in *A Collection of Hymns for the Use of the People Called Methodists,* retains those stanzas that specifically report extending the dinner invitation to everyone, not just the small group initially invited. Those to whom the invitation is addressed are repeatedly named: "sinners," "all the world," "sinner," "thou," "all ye souls by sin oppressed," "Ye vagrant souls." But the call "to all" appears most frequently: "all mankind," "to all," "you all," "Ye all," "for all."[112] With ever-new variations Charles Wesley uses this hymn to proclaim God's desire for universal salvation and God's universal invitation to salvation. As the first stanza indicates: "Ye need not one be left behind, For God hath bidden all mankind."

111

Wesley's soteriological appropriation of the Lukan parable of the Great Dinner in this hymn and others[113] is apparent not only in having the hymn address everyone who is trapped by sin and guilt, but also in the manner in which the poet describes the invitation to the feast, or, as the case may be, the feast itself. It is "the gospel feast,"[114] at which the invited arrive as "Jesu's guest." Everything is prepared: "All things in Christ are ready now." "In Christ a hearty welcome find." The guests are offered nothing less than life itself: "Ye all may come to Christ and live." One of the stanzas not retained in the *Collection* provides an even more precise description. Here it becomes clear how God's desire "for all" to be saved parallels the "all" that is provided for those who believe in Christ: "All, all in Christ is freely given, Pardon, and holiness, and heaven."

Wesley seems to be suggesting in stanza 7 of the hymn (as it appears in the *Collection*) that the grace extended to all cannot be resisted. He describes God's love as a "conqu'ring love" and speaks of "love's resistless power." Other hymns, however, make clear that Wesley's soteriological universalism is limited to God's invitation to salvation alone. Nowhere is it indicated that the acceptance of salvation is or will be universal. On the contrary, the poet continually directs his proclamation to those who have not accepted God's invitation to salvation. He repeatedly asks the following question (based on Ezekiel 18:31) in amazement:

> Sinners, turn, why will you die?
> God, your Saviour asks you why.
> God, who did your souls retrieve,
> Died himself, that you might live.
> Will you let him die in vain?
> Crucify your Lord again?
> Why, ye ransomed sinners, why
> Will you slight his grace, and die?[115]

If we now return to stanza 7 of the hymn in question (as it appears in the *Collection*) and do so within the context of the above cited hymn and others, it becomes clear that this stanza is not born out of a doctrine of *apokatastasis panton,* but instead points to the persuasive demands of the love of God. God turns to everyone, offering God's love without condition, and thus the refusal of this love is all the more mystifying. In his hymn "Come, sinners, to the gospel feast"

Wesley never tires of announcing God's universal offer of salvation as well as God's unconditional love: "Ye all are freely justified," "Freely now be saved by grace," or as it appears in another stanza of this hymn not retained in the *Collection*: "Tell them my grace for all is free."

Stanza 4 specifically offers a Eucharistic interpretation of the salvation banquet. The invitation "O taste the goodness of your God" draws on Psalm 34:8, a reference long appropriated for Eucharistic praxis and understanding. The closing line of this stanza explicitly interprets the salvation banquet as participation in the Eucharistic feast: "eat his flesh and drink his blood." Stanza 4, however, as it appears in this hymn in the *Collection*, is relatively isolated within the hymn as a whole, in spite of the well-established observation that the experience of salvation and the Eucharistic feast are intimately connected for the Wesleys. This hymn makes no other clear reference to the Eucharist save in stanza 8.[116] Another Charles Wesley hymn included in the *Hymns on the Lord's Supper* (1745) demonstrates the connection made by the poet between the Lukan parable of the Great Dinner and the Eucharistic feast:

> COME, to the supper come,
> Sinners, there still is room;
> Every soul may be His guest,
> Jesus gives the general word;
> Share the monumental feast,
> Eat the supper of your Lord.
>
> In this authentic sign
> Behold the stamp Divine:
> Christ revives his sufferings here,
> Still exposes them to view;
> See the Crucified appear,
> Now believe He died for you.[117]

This hymn, like its longer counterpart in the *Collection*, also emphasizes the invitation to all, based on God's universal invitation to salvation: "Every soul may be His guest." At the same time this hymn reveals another central theological motif of the *Collection*—the intensely personal promise of salvation characteristic of Wesleyan hymnody. In the last line, following the emphasis on God's will for universal salvation, the individual is called to a personal experience of salvation: "Now believe He died for you." The longer hymn based on the Lukan parable in the *Collection* also emphasizes a personal invitation to the salvation banquet along with the call to all humankind: "Come all the world; come, sinner, thou!" For Charles Wesley these two, the personal call to faith and the invitation to all humankind, are inseparable: God calls all but each individually. Wesley's hymns reflect this in two parallel expressions: the recurring *for all* and the equally frequent *for me*. Often these two expressions are found side by side within a single stanza. Thus, for example, when referring to everyone who stands guilty before God, Charles Wesley often includes himself specifically: "the heavenly blessing, lost By all mankind, and me."[118] Just as all humankind and thus each individual is guilty, in the same way all humankind and each individual stand as the recipient of God's grace. The following example demonstrates this by way of an antistrophe:

> What shall I do my God to love?
>   My Saviour and the world's to praise?
> Whose bowels of compassion move
>   To me and all the fallen race?
> Whose mercy is divinely free
>   For all the fallen race—and me![119]

Because humankind and each individual stand guilty before God and, at the same time, are the recipients of God's grace, Charles Wesley, based specifically on his personal experience of salvation, is able to announce the universal invitation to salvation: "The arms of love that compass me Would all mankind embrace," as one hymn puts it.[120]

The above cited examples make clear just how closely connected the "for all" and the "for me" are in the hymns of Charles Wesley. It must not be forgotten, however, that the presence of these two expressions in *A Collection of Hymns for the Use of the People Called Methodists* can be traced to two different theological influences. The constant emphasis on God's will for universal salvation originates, in no small measure, by way of negative designs. It is meant to refute, as already mentioned, a particularistic understanding of salvation as embraced by the Calvinist followers of George Whitefield. The "for me" that appears in Wesley's hymns is, on the other hand, a positive appropriation of Pauline and Reformation principles. The theme of the following section is devoted to the discussion of how the latter manifests itself in *A Collection of Hymns for the Use of the People Called Methodists.*

   b. *"for me": The Individual Experience of Salvation.* We know from Charles Wesley's journal how closely the struggle to understand the Lutheran "for me" is linked to his personal conversion experience. In the days preceding his conversion on Pentecost Sunday, 1738, Charles Wesley read Martin Luther's well-known commentary on the Epistle to the Galatians (published in 1535) and struggled to grasp, existentially, the Lutheran emphasis on the "for me" of the saving work of Christ. Luther's interpretation of Galatians 2:20 played a particularly important role in this for Charles Wesley:

> Discamus tantum hoc verbum: "Me," "pro me," ut possimus certa fide concipere et non dubitare: "pro me." Christus enim est laetitia et suavitas cordis pavidi et contribulati, authore Paulo qui eum hic dulcissimo titulo ornat, scilicet "diligentem ME et tradentem se ipsum pro me" . . . Lege igitur cum magna Emphasi has voces: "ME," "PRO ME," et assuefacias te, ut illud, "ME" possis certa fide concipere et applicare tibi, Neque dubites, quin etiam sis ex numero eorum, qui dicuntur (ME).[121]

The impression made on Charles Wesley by this passage from Luther's commentary on the Epistle to the Galatians is reflected in a journal entry written shortly before the decisive Pentecost Sunday in the year 1738. Wesley wrote the following on the Wednesday before Pentecost:

> To-day I first saw Luther on the Galatians, which Mr. Holland had accidentally lit upon. We began, and found him nobly full of faith. My friend, in hearing him, was so affected as to breathe out sighs and groans unutterable. . . . I spent some hours this evening in private with Martin Luther, who was greatly blessed to me, especially his conclusion of the 2nd chapter. I laboured, waited, and prayed to feel "who loved *me*, and gave Himself *for me*."[122]

After his conversion, though later he would put some distance between himself and Martin Luther, Charles Wesley understood the short phrase "for me" to express the personal experience of the saving work of Christ. It is this personal experience of salvation that formed the core of his Pentecost experience in 1738. Both Wesley brothers would later come to use the terms "Formal Religion" and "Inward Religion" when describing their lives before 1738 and their conversion experiences. The differentiation between the two lives was so important to them that two entire sections of *A Collection of Hymns for the Use of the People Called Methodists* were devoted to this distinction.[123] "Formal Religion" was described as the attempt to live a religious life without the personal experience of salvation. For the Wesleys this was an impossibility that they had practiced for years: "A form of godliness was mine—The power I never knew."[124] "Inward Religion," on the other hand, was the grace-filled personal experience of salvation in Christ.

The Methodist renewal movement and its preaching thrived on this distinction. After all, the movement did not primarily reach those who had never heard the gospel of Jesus Christ before, but rather those who stood in some connection with a church (most often the Church of England by way of their baptisms) yet were missing a personal living faith. It is not surprising, in light of this, that the short phrase "for me," understood as denoting the necessity for the individual experience and appropriation of salvation, occurs frequently throughout the entire poetical corpus of Charles Wesley. However, there are two different meanings this short phrase can assume. These two different meanings are born out of two different speech acts, which nevertheless have common theological roots and must be considered together. When Wesley wrote about his own experience of salvation, or as a mouthpiece for members of the Methodist renewal movement who had had similar experiences, he used the words "for me" to emphasize, almost descriptively, the object of Christ's saving work. On the other hand, when he preached with the intent of encouraging his hearers to a personal experience of salvation, the phrase "for me," which bore witness to his own personal experience, was transformed into the kerygmatic exhortation "for you." The common theological foundation shared by these two phrases is easily recognized. More than this, Wesley often used the *descriptive* "for me" *prescriptively*. What the poet bore witness to in his own life, he confessed and recognized as possible for all. Both phrases are required, the "for me" and the "for you," to adequately emphasize the personal experience and acceptance of God's salvation. Both are existential categories, as clearly indicated in Charles Wesley's journal: "I laboured, waited, and prayed *to feel* 'who loved *me*. . .' "[125] Thus, God's universal invitation to salvation, which Wesley never tired of announcing, was also an invitation to a very *personal* experience.

The intensity of an individual's experience of salvation corresponds with the individual's personal awareness of sin. Many of the hymns that take as their theme the personal experience of salvation describe the poet as the "chief of sinners."[126] These same hymns often include dramatic descriptions of the poet's inclination to sin before his conversion (occasionally characterizing, in light of his conversion, even the practice of "formal religion" as sin).[127] These descriptions serve two purposes: first, they allow for a stark contrast between the dark foil of personal sin and the bright experience of salvation, which underlines the emphasis on the wideness of God's love and the complete change of heart that comes with the experience of salvation. Second, this description of Wesley's own sinfulness served to encourage the reception of the Good News by his hearers. The offer of salvation was not limited to those who had committed "insignificant" sins—theologically speaking there is no such thing. The individual experience of salvation was available to all as witnessed by those who had already received the gift of this experience.

It is important to note that for Charles Wesley the emphasis on the personal experience of salvation goes hand in hand with a certain passivity on the part of humankind. The experience of salvation is God's work among humankind. (For the Wesleys, however, the emphasis on humankind's passivity in this experience is limited to the origin and author of this experience of salvation. Otherwise, when the Wesleys spoke out against Quietism they would stress the accountability and responsibility each must assume for the life of faith.) Below I cite an example from *A Collection of Hymns for the Use of the People Called Methodists* where these emphases are apparent:

> Let the world their virtue boast,
>   Their works of righteousness;
> I, a wretch undone and lost,
>   Am freely saved by grace.
> Other title I disclaim,
>   This, only this is all my plea:

117

> I the chief of sinners am,
> But Jesus died for me.[128]

The last two lines of this stanza comprise a refrain that stands at the end of each stanza in this hymn: "I the chief of sinners am, But Jesus died for me." Frequently some Christological title is named as a direct correlation to the anthropological category "chief of sinners." Christ is understood to be the "Friend of sinners" who brings redemption to the "chief of sinners": "Friend of sinners, spotless Lamb, Thy blood was shed for me."[129] The experience of redemption is always a personal experience for Wesley: it is an encounter with Christ. This becomes clear when the basic content of the experiential "for me" is explored. This content, for Charles Wesley, is beyond a shadow of a doubt rooted in the suffering and death of Jesus Christ. His suffering and death "for me" make possible the individual experience of salvation. The subjective experience of salvation in the "for me" thus is rooted in the objective event of Christ's dying "for me."

A Collection of Hymns for the Use of the People Called Methodists contains one hymn of Charles Wesley that reflects, better than any other, the personal, grace-filled experience of salvation in Christ. Not only is the hymn one of the most accomplished of his poetical corpus, it also is directly connected to his conversion experience on May 21, 1738. Below is the text of this hymn, first published in *Hymns and Spiritual Poems* (1739).

> And can it be, that I should gain   (1)
>   An interest in the Saviour's blood?
> Died he for me, who caused his pain?
>   For me? Who him to death pursued?
> Amazing love! How can it be
>   That thou, my God, shouldst die for me?

> 'Tis myst'ry all: th'Immortal dies!   (2)
>   Who can explore his strange design?
> In vain the first-born seraph tries
>   To sound the depths of love divine.
> 'Tis mercy all! Let earth adore!
>   Let angel minds inquire no more.

He left his Father's throne above   (3)
　　(So free, so infinite his grace!),
Emptied himself of all but love,
　　And bled for Adam's helpless race.
'Tis mercy all, immense and free,
　　For, O my God, it found out me!

Long my imprisoned spirit lay,   (4)
　　Fast bound in sin and nature's night.
Thine eye diffused a quick'ning ray;
　　I woke; the dungeon flamed with light.
My chains fell off, my heart was free,
　　I rose, went forth, and followed thee.

No condemnation now I dread,   (5)
　　Jesus, and all in him, is mine.
Alive in him, my living head,
　　And clothed in righteousness divine,
Bold I approach th'eternal throne,
　　And claim the crown, through Christ my own.[130]

The first stanza of this hymn (possibly written immediately after Charles Wesley's conversion experience) is marked by amazement at the personal experience of salvation in Christ.[131] With great skill the poet weaves five questions into the initial stanza. "Can it be" is repeated twice and "for me" is repeated three times, providing the desired emphasis for the stanza's ending (in terms of literary devices, Wesley combines a mesodiplosis and a double epistrophe). The leitmotif of the hymn is captured in the question directed to Christ: "can it be That thou, my God, shouldst die for me?"

Even though the first stanza answers this question in the affirmative, the second stanza denies the possibility of a deeper look into the mystery of God's redeeming love. That the immortal God would die for a sinner cannot be grasped, but only offered up in praise: "Let earth adore!" The next two stanzas are devoted to the description of the personal experience of salvation. In describing his imprisonment Charles Wesley refers to his condition prior to the experience of release in Christ. Again the amazement of stanza 1 over the work of redemption wrought "for me" is echoed: " 'Tis mercy all, immense and free, For, O my God, it found out me!" In the last stanza amazement over the redemption offered in Christ and experienced by the individual is transformed into a poetical confession of faith, which seeks an equal declaration: "Bold I approach th'eternal throne, And claim the crown, through Christ my own."

This hymn provides a consummate expression of Charles Wesley's thoughts on the personal experience of salvation. It makes the logical connection between the objective event of salvation (which takes place "for me") and the subjective experience of that salvation. It portrays this event and experience in Christocentric terms. It assumes humankind's passive posture in the grace-filled reception of salvation, and it stresses the complete transformation of one's existence through the experience of salvation.

Another term from Luther's commentary on the Epistle to the Galatians (2:20) that played an important role in Charles Wesley's conversion experience points to one further central motif in the soteriological emphasis of Wesleyan hymnody. The verb *applicare* appears in that passage from Luther's commentary on the Epistle to the Galatians. For Charles Wesley, it comes to demonstrate the manner in which salvation in Christ is effected for and conveyed to the individual believer: "the blood applied." The next section is devoted to the study of this phrase in Charles Wesley's hymns.

c. "the blood applied": A Formula for Salvation Effected. Charles Wesley's expression "the blood applied" is a metaphor drawn from two spheres of meaning, each of which provides a key to the interpretation of the phrase. The word *blood* is used by Wesley almost exclusively in reference to the blood of Christ and indicates a shorthand formulation for Christ's work of redemption by his suffering and death on the cross. It is hard not to note the influence of the famous "blood-and-wounds theology" of German Pietism, in particular that of Zinzendorf, on the hymns of Charles Wesley. This influence could already be detected in John Wesley's translations of Pietist hymns in which countless references to the blood of Christ are made as shorthand for the work of redemption. In general, Wesley faithfully renders the translation of Zinzendorf's hymns, one of which reads as follows: "I thirst, Thou wounded Lamb of God, To wash me in Thy cleansing blood, To dwell within Thy wounds." [132] The most well known of John Wesley's translations is that of Zinzendorf's "Christi Blut und Gerechtigkeit," which follows the original text judiciously: "Jesu, thy blood and righteousness, My beauty are, my glorious dress . . . Lord, I believe the precious blood which at the mercy-seat of God For ever doth for sinners plead."[133] After the Methodist renewal movement became estranged from German Pietism, John Wesley reacted critically to Charles's continued use (however detached) of the emotional Pietist blood-and-wounds terminology.[134] Nevertheless, John did not exclude all of the hymns that contained this theme from *A Collection of Hymns for the Use of the People Called Methodists*. It is in the context of these hymns that the phrase "the blood applied" frequently appears.

The second building block for this curious phrase is found in the verb *apply*. First, it must be said that this is not a biblical concept. Charles Wesley's love for the turn of a phrase, "the blood applied," looks, in this case, to extrabiblical sources. It is difficult to identify precisely these sources. Lutheran Orthodoxy makes an important connection between soteriology and pneumatology through the doctrinal topic, *de gratia spiritus sancti applicatrice*,[135] which taught that the Holy Spirit was at work in humankind from the call to conversion through the individual's sanctification. The teaching differentiated the stages of an individual's faith journey into a detailed *ordo salutis*. Such an *ordo salutis* can also be found in the thought of both John (though not in any systematic form) and Charles Wesley. Or more precisely, the context of this phrase and its use by Charles Wesley indicates the reception of Lutheran Orthodoxy in German Pietism and its influence on early Methodism.

If Charles Wesley's use of this phrase were to be summarized, then "the blood applied" could be characterized as a short formula for the appropriation and "application" of Christ's saving work in the life of the individual believer. The phrase describes the mediation of salvation. This is clear, first of all, through the use of the word *blood* to refer to the saving work of Christ on the cross.[136] This phrase is used so often in this manner that the word *blood* occasionally is able to stand on its own as an active agent.[137] This is easily recognized in the hymn referenced below, which also contains traces of Wesley's proximity to the Pietist fascination with Christ's blood and wounds. (I cite this hymn at some length to make this point though in the context of this study it is indeed outside the sphere of my interest.) The hymn "With glorious clouds encompassed round," was first published in the 1767 *Hymns for the Use of Families* and later appropriated by John for *A Collection of Hymns for the Use of the People Called Methodists* of 1780.

> In manifested love explain
>> Thy wonderful design:
> What meant the suffering Son of man,
>> The streaming blood divine?

. . . .

> Come then, and to my soul reveal
>> The heights and depths of grace,
> The wounds which all my sorrows heal,
>> That dear disfigured face.

. . . .

> Jehovah in thy person show,
>> Jehovah crucified;
> And then the pard'ning God I know,
>> And feel the blood applied.[138]

By linking the suffering of God's Son with God's blood (stanza 1) and by associating the recognition of God with the application of the blood on the believer (last stanza) this hymn clearly shows the word *blood* as shorthand for Christ's salvific suffering and death. Thus this word is often linked with an adjective to further highlight the meaning. Wesley wrote, for example, of the "purifying" or "precious" blood and of the "sacrificial" or "covenant" blood.[139] Another hymn is yet more explicit: "Th'atonement of thy blood apply"[140] (interestingly, the poet in this hymn places himself next to Christ's wounded side as he makes this petition). Other hymns in *A Collection of Hymns for the Use of the People Called Methodists* point in the same direction. The work of salvation wrought on the cross is applied and appropriated whether in reference to the forgiveness of sin,[141] the individual ("for me") experience of redemption,[142] peace,[143] the recognition of God's love,[144] purification and sanctification,[145] or participation in the Divine nature.[146] Note also, however, that Wesley never suggests that the application and appropriation of salvation is a once-for-all-time event, but rather an event that spans the entire life of each believer.

If one were to ask, "Who is the agent of salvation's application?" the answer, on the one hand, would come clear and simple: the agent of salvation's application is always God. The human being is the recipient in this exchange (thus the use of the word *application* instead of *acquisition*). Wesleyan hymnody does, however, present two views on the agency of God in the application of salvation. The first, and the weaker of the two, sees Christ himself applying the work of salvation to the life of the individual: "Jesu, thy grace bestow; Now thy all-cleansing blood apply."[147] In a very few instances the "blood" itself (again shorthand for the saving work of Christ) becomes the agent of salvation:

> I cannot wash my heart,
>   But by believing thee;
> And waiting for thy blood t'impart
>   The spotless purity.[148]

In most cases, now speaking of the second view of God's agency in the application of salvation, it is the Holy Spirit who applies the saving work of Christ to the life of the individual. Here more than anywhere else the phrase "the blood applied" clearly coincides with the doctrinal topos *de gratia spiritus sancti applicatrice* in Lutheran Orthodoxy. The following hymn from the *Collection* published originally in the 1746 *Hymns of Petition and Thanksgiving* finds the above assertion fully formed:

> Spirit of faith, come down,
>   Reveal the things of God,
> And make to us the Godhead known,
>   And witness with the blood:
> 'Tis thine the blood to apply,
>   And give us eyes to see,
> Who did for every sinner die
>   Hath surely died for me.
>
> No man can truly say
>   That Jesus is the Lord
> Unless thou take the veil away,
>   And breathe the living word;
> Then, only then we feel
>   Our interest in his blood,
> And cry with joy unspeakable,
>   Thou art my Lord, my God!

O that the world might know
   The all-atoning Lamb!
Spirit of faith, descend, and show
   The virtue of his name;
The grace which all may find,
   The saving power impart,
And testify to all mankind,
   And speak in every heart!

Inspire the living faith
   (Which whosoe'er receives,
The witness in himself he hath,
   And consciously believes),
The faith that conquers all,
   And doth the mountain move,
And saves whoe'er on Jesus call
And perfects them in love.[149]

This hymn clearly has the character of an epiclesis, the invoking of the Holy Spirit: "Spirit of faith, come down," "Spirit of faith, descend." The Holy Spirit is called upon to apply the saving work of Christ to the life of the individual. The poetical language nearly trips over itself in the effort to describe the work of the Holy Spirit. The Holy Spirit reveals the essence of God, grants the sinner recognition of redemption ("for me"), "applies the blood," lifts the veil of unknowing from one's eyes, transmits the Living Word, bears witness to the saving work of Jesus, grants saving mercy, and inspires a living faith. With this kind of list, though certainly not formulated with any kind of systematic theology in mind, it is not difficult to rediscover the *ordo salutis* as summarized in the doctrinal topos *de gratia spiritus sancti applicatrice*. Charles Wesley, as did Lutheran Orthodoxy and German Pietism before him, establishes a close connection between soteriology and pneumatology, with an emphasis on the Christocentric foundation of pneumatology. Thus, for example, Christ is petitioned to send the Holy Spirit in the following hymn excerpt:

Lord, we believe the promise sure;
   The purchased Comforter impart!
Apply the blood to make us pure.[150]

124

In summary, the phrase "the blood applied" provides a short formula for soteriological emphasis in the hymns of Charles Wesley. It functions as a catchphrase for Wesley by which the application of the saving work of Christ to the individual believer can be described. One may be able to imagine more profound images, with greater theological detail and poetical beauty. But it must not be forgotten that for Charles Wesley the image of the blood of Christ summarized everything of importance about the saving work of Christ, namely, his life-giving sacrifice for us. Thus Wesley believed that the appropriation of salvation in the life of the individual found apt expression in the phrase "the blood of Christ applied."

d. "to feel—to know—to prove": The Experience and Assurance of Salvation. Recognizing that the conveyance and application of salvation in the life of the individual for Wesley is captured in the phrase "the blood applied," the question still remains, does the phrase have implications for the personal subjective experience of the individual? In other words, how does the individual know that this salvation has been conveyed? This pivotal question was addressed repeatedly by Charles Wesley in the hymns as they are found in A Collection of Hymns for the Use of the People Called Methodists. Of those questions prompted by the soteriological focus of Wesleyan hymnody and the resultant study of its individual themes, this question is the last to be addressed. It is directly related to the Wesleyan understanding of how salvation is conveyed, but the process of salvation as experience for the individual now takes center stage.

In the hymns that address this complex of questions, the terms used most often to describe the personal experience of salvation include the verbs "to feel," "to know," and "to prove." They frequently occur in some combination together linking emotional experience to knowledge ("to feel—to know"), or emotional experience to assurance ("to feel—to prove"), or knowledge to assurance ("to know—to prove"). Even here a proximity of Wesleyan thought to German Pietism is apparent: the Moravians, in particular, emphasized the emotional experience of salvation in the face of a staid and stale Lutheranism. In the same vein, the Wesley brothers' descriptions of their own conversion experiences were marked significantly by their encounter with German Pietism, particularly in regard to the way salvation was experienced. When reading from Luther's commentary on the Epistle to the Galatians, Charles struggled to emotionally and personally grasp the work of redemption: "I laboured, waited, and prayed to feel 'who loved *me*, and gave Himself for *me*.'"[151] The emotional component becomes, in effect, the marker of recognition for the experience and assurance of salvation. Similar emphases are found in the classic description of John Wesley's conversion experience:

> About a quarter before nine, while he was describing the change which God works in the heart through faith in Christ, I felt my heart strangely warmed. I felt I did trust in Christ, Christ alone for my salvation, and an assurance was given me that he had taken away *my* sins, even *mine*, and saved *me* from the law of sin and death.[152]

Both accounts report the inward experience of conversion. Both in the journal of John Wesley and in the hymns of Charles the heart of the individual is constantly referred to as the place where this experience transpires. One hymn states it thusly, "Whisper within, thou love divine, And cheer my drooping heart,"[153] while another in calling to the faithful says, "Go ye forth to meet your Lord, And meet him in your heart."[154] Biblical images of conversion that center on changed hearts of stone or life with a new heart are often echoed in Wesleyan hymnody.[155] These images all point in the same direction: the experience of conversion and the assurance of salvation are personal, subjective experiences in the inner life of the believer, wherein the emotional component becomes the marker of the recognition of the "objective" application of salvation. The frequent linking of "the blood applied" with the verb "to feel" bears out the above assertion. One of many examples of this in *A Collection of Hymns for the Use of the People Called Methodists* is found in the following hymn line: "Nothing I ask or want beside Of all in earth or heaven, But let me feel thy blood applied."[156] The poet, however, speaks to far more than simply the experiential and emotional appropriation of conversion by an individual. Wesley uses these categories to describe the entire life of the believer. Thus, for example, when he asks for the emotional experience of faith he also asks to be made aware of his sins:

> By thy Spirit, Lord, reprove,
>   All mine inmost sins reveal;
> Sins against thy light and love

> Let me see, and let me feel,
> Sins that crucified my God,
> Spilt again thy precious blood.[157]

The individual was, however, not only made aware of her sins in this experiential and emotional appropriation of salvation, she would also know release from them. The forgiveness of sins, the presence of God, and the love of God all are available to each believer and thus attainable.[158] Some might suggest that Charles Wesley is guilty here of hopeless subjectivity. He is not. He knows well objective bases for the personal experience and assurance of salvation. More than this, Wesley never goes so far as to suggest that the inner emotional experience of the individual and the reality of redemption are unconditionally linked such that those who lack the conscious experience of salvation are denied its reality. He does, however, emphasize the personal experience of faith over and against those who would insist on faith primarily as a cognitive assent to revealed truths.

In the end, the foundation for the experience and assurance of salvation was not to be found in the subjective experience of the individual believer but in the *testimonium spiritus sancti internum*. On his deathbed in 1735, Charles Wesley's father spoke of this *testimonium internum* as the most convincing indicator of faith: "The inward witness, son, the inward witness, . . . that is the proof, the strongest proof, of Christianity."[159] Shortly after the beginning of the Methodist renewal movement, the individual assurance of salvation based on the experiential "inner witness" became a central point of contention for (Anglican) opponents of the movement. In the years to come the Wesleys would be accused of uncontrollable emotionalism, private revelations to individual believers, and excessive spiritual self-confidence. The following journal entry was recorded by Charles in 1738 describing a visit to the Bishop of London, who was inquiring into complaints raised against the brothers:

> I waited with my brother on the Bishop of London, to answer the complaints he had heard against us, that we preached an absolute assurance of salvation. Some of his words were, "If by 'assurance' you mean an inward persuasion, whereby a man is conscious in himself, after examining his life by the law of God, and weighing his own sincerity, that he is in a state of salvation, and acceptable to God, I

don't see how any good Christian can be without such an assurance."
"This," we answered, "is what we contend for."[160]

It should also be noted that the Methodist emphasis on the assurance of salvation in the individual believer was primarily about knowing in the present and not about future assurance as hinted at in the Calvinist doctrine of predestination. Charles Wesley is most cautious when it comes to this point. One hymn in *A Collection of Hymns for the Use of the People Called Methodists* clearly speaks out against a *donum perseverantiae*.[161] Furthermore, as stated earlier, the Wesleys did not make the reality of redemption dependent on its emotional experience, even though, most of the time, they believed they belonged together.[162] The brothers also assert a strong pneumatological foundation for the experience and assurance of salvation.[163] In the end, it is the Holy Spirit who conveys salvation and its assurance. This *testimonium spiritus sancti internum* is an event that is experienced emotionally ("to feel"), which conveys—since it is initiated by God—knowledge ("to know"), and which can grant an unshakable certainty ("to prove").

One hymn in *A Collection of Hymns for the Use of the People Called Methodists* provides the quintessential summary of Charles Wesley's thought on the experience and assurance of salvation. Cited below in its entirety, the hymn first appeared in the 1749 *Hymns and Sacred Poems.* When included years later in the *Collection* two crucial pneumatological stanzas were deleted leaving the original intent of the poet somewhat obscured.[164] The context provided by the *Collection* for this hymn, though of secondary importance, may prove helpful in its interpretation. John Wesley included this hymn of his brother in the section devoted to "Describing Inward Religion." Together with three other hymns in this section, it provides a shorthand description of Charles Wesley's thinking on the doctrine of assurance. What follows is the text of the hymn in its original length:

> How can a sinner *know*   (1)
>   His sins on earth forgiven?
> How can my Saviour show
>   *My* name inscribed in heaven?
> What we ourselves have felt, and seen,
>   With confidence we tell,

And publish to the sons of men
    The signs infallible.

We who in Christ believe   (2)
    That He for us hath died,
His unknown peace receive,
    And feel His blood applied:
Exults for joy our rising soul,
    Disburden'd of her load,
And swells, unutterably full
    Of glory, and of God.

His love, surpassing far   (3)
    The love of all beneath,
We find within, and dare
    The pointless darts of death:
Stronger than death, or sin, or hell,
    The mystic power we prove,
And conquerors of the world we dwell
    In heaven, who dwell in love.

The *pledge* of future bliss   (4)
    He now to us imparts,
His gracious Spirit is
    The *earnest* in our hearts:
We antedate the joys above,
    We taste the' [sic] eternal powers,
And *know* that all those heights of love,
    And all those heavens are ours.

Till He our life reveal,   (5)
    We rest in Christ secure:
His Spirit is *the seal*,
    Which made our pardon sure:
Our sins His blood hath blotted out,
    And sign'd our soul's release:
And can we of His favour doubt,
    Whose blood declares us His?

We by His Spirit prove,   (6)
    And know the things of God,
The things which of his love
    He hath on us bestow'd:

Our God to us His Spirit gave,
　　And dwells in us, we *know*,
The witness in ourselves we have,
　　And all His fruits we show.

The meek and lowly heart,　　　　　　(7)
　　Which in our Saviour was,
He doth to us impart,
　　And signs us with His cross:
Our nature's course is turn'd, our mind
　　Transform'd in all its powers,
And both the witnesses are join'd
　　The Spirit of God with ours.

Whate'er our pardoning Lord　　　　　(8)
　　Commands, we gladly do,
And guided by His word
　　We all His steps pursue:
His glory is our sole design,
　　We live our God to please,
And rise with filial fear Divine
　　To perfect holiness.[165]

The hymn's theme is indicated in its very first line: "How can a sinner know His sins on earth forgiven?" The core issue is clearly the possibility of experiencing, of knowing, that guilt is forgiven and redemption assured. The line that immediately follows is a parallel question and serves to focus the personal nature of the quest for individual assurance of redemption. The poet leaves no room for doubt that there are answers to these questions. The third and last question proposed in this hymn (at the end of stanza 5), is thus of a rhetorical nature: "And can we of His favour doubt, Whose blood declares us His?"

The end of stanza 1 already suggests a favorable response to the first two questions. This response points to the "signs infallible" and the language of certainty found throughout the hymn: "With confidence we tell, . . . We rest in Christ secure: His Spirit is the seal, which made our pardon sure." The hymn's focus on answering the opening questions can also be seen in the use of the verbs "to know" and "to prove": "we ourselves have felt, and seen, . . . We by his Spirit prove, And know the things of God." The verb "to know" occurs four times in the hymn and the verb "to prove" occurs twice. Both verbs occupy key positions in the development of the hymn based on their direct connection to the opening questions and thus to the central theme of the hymn.

Wesley answers the opening questions primarily with a reference to the collective experience of redemption by believers ("We who in Christ believe"). In good Johannine fashion Wesley refers to what the witnesses have seen and heard (though, for Wesley, "what is heard" takes a back seat to "what is felt"). The experience of salvation, as he describes it, occurs deep within the believer: "We find within . . . in our hearts . . . in us . . . in ourselves." The experience itself is described in many different ways: as the experience of a heretofore unknown peace, as the "blood of Christ applied" ("feel His blood applied"), as the experience of overwhelming joy, and as victory over the world.

Stanzas 4 through 6 (the first two of which were deleted by John Wesley from the hymn as it appeared in the *Collection*) give voice to the pneumatological dimension of salvation's experience and its assurance. Christ gives the Holy Spirit to believers as a foretaste of the coming glory but also as the present seal of redemption. The inner witness of the Holy Spirit provides the assurance that believers are children of God: "We by His Spirit prove, And know the things of God . . . Our God to us His Spirit gave, And dwells in us, we know, The witness in ourselves we have . . . And both the witnesses are join'd, The Spirit of God with ours." Here Wesley draws on the Pauline teaching that God's Spirit gives our spirit the evidence of redemption. Wesley argues, based on this Pauline teaching and the Johannine concept of "knowing,"[166] for an experience and assurance of salvation rooted in God's work within each believer and not primarily within the subjective feeling of the individual.

So much for the central soteriological themes of the hymns in *A Collection of Hymns for the Use of the People Called Methodists* of 1780. By now it must be clear that we have been dealing with soteriological emphases within a broader soteriological focus. Wesley's attention is fixed on the experience and application of redemption in the life of the individual believer, as effected on the cross. One might go so far as to say that this soteriological emphasis lies at the very heart of the Good News—certainly it does so for Wesley as evidenced by his hymns. In the following section I will address several other themes of the *Collection* and thus of Wesleyan hymnody. Just because these themes have not been dealt with in this section on soteriology does not mean that they are free of soteriological connotations. For Charles Wesley there was no such neutral ground.

2. The Experience of Salvation and the Understanding of Revelation

The linking of the experience of salvation and the understanding of revelation, which is a characteristic of Wesleyan hymnody, presents a theme already addressed, in part, by this study in another context: I chose the text "Wrestling Jacob" to address the question whether the poetical texts of Charles Wesley were hymns or poems.[167] "Wrestling Jacob" is not only an excellent example for discussing the genre of Wesleyan texts, it also provides a key example of Wesley's poetic fascination with the name of God, behind which ultimately lies his understanding of revelation. "Wrestling Jacob" deals specifically with this question and dovetails nicely with the biblical story it tells. Just as Jacob, in his struggle with the angel at the river Jabbok, pleaded: "Tell me, I pray thee, thy name,"[168] so Wesley has the "I" of the hymn ask the Unknown Traveller: "Tell me thy name."[169] Moreover, this plea becomes the refrain repeated at the end of each stanza with little variation: "I will not let thee go Till I thy name, thy nature know." The pursuit of the name of God as a theme in Wesleyan hymnody merits consideration, based not only on its constant repetition as a refrain in this particular hymn, but rather because of the frequency with which it surfaces in the hymns of the *Collection* as a whole. In some places within the *Collection* Charles Wesley explicitly names his search (no doubt with Jacob's struggle at the river Jabbok in mind): "Wrestle with Christ in mighty prayer; Tell him, 'We will not let thee go, Till we thy name, thy nature know.'"[170] In other hymns Wesley depends on a host of different forms and formulations to ask the question with all its hidden implications: "Tell me thy nature, and thy name, And write it on my heart."[171] "Thy mystic name in me reveal,"[172] "Thou wilt in me reveal thy name."[173] These and similar requests are found throughout the hymns of the *Collection*.

What lies hidden behind these pleas? Certainly, in formulating the desire to know the name of God, Wesley seeks more than the simple naming of a "name" for the satisfaction of curiosity. The intensity and pivotal placement of the question in many hymns suggest that there is much more at stake. The answer begins to emerge when yet another term is taken into consideration, one often used by Wesley in connection with the pursuit of God's name: "I will not let thee go Till I thy name, thy nature know." Both in "Wrestling Jacob" and in many other hymns that pursue the same theme, Wesley links "name" and "nature" or, at least, attempts to interpret one with the other. The following stanza demonstrates this connection:

> Answer, O Lord, thy Spirit's groan!
>   O make to me thy nature known,
> Thy hidden name impart
>   (Thy title is with thee the same);
> Tell me thy nature, and thy name,
>   And write it on my heart.[174]

Here, Wesley clearly equates the name and the essence of God ("Thy title is with thee the same"). The poet is supported in such a position by biblical witness, especially that of the Old Testament where a close connection between the name and the essence of a person or thing is stressed. Whenever Wesley has a hymn ask the name of God, he is asking, in effect, to know who God is. These same hymns, however, also assert that the essence of God is an unapproachable mystery: "Thou God unsearchable, unknown, Who still conceal'st thyself from me,"[175] "Thou hidden God, for whom I groan . . . God inaccessible, unknown."[176] Knowledge of God's inaccessible nature and the (paradoxically) pressing desire to know that same nature are interwoven throughout the body of the following hymn and manifested in the phrase, "tell me all thy name," which follows the stanza quoted here:

> With glorious clouds encompassed round,
>   Whom angels dimly see,
> Will the Unsearchable be found,
>   Or God appear to me?[177]

Wesley resolves the tension between the mystery of God's inaccessible nature and the quest to know that mystery with a three-point assertion: God reveals God's self; God reveals God's self in Jesus Christ; and God reveals God's self in Jesus Christ as love. The first point establishes the revelation and recognition of God as the work of God and not of humankind. There is no manner of human struggle through which knowledge of God's essence is attained. God opens God's self to humankind. Wesley makes this clear with the verbs he uses to describe the action of God: God appears, God shows God's self, God reveals. Humankind is the recipient of God's revelation. The form of speech used by Wesley in these hymns, characteristically a petition directed to God, also serves to reinforce this point. God is asked to reveal God's name, implying that God, and only God, can grant revelation.

What about the content of this revelation? For Wesley there is no question that God is revealing not something (as a primarily cognitive understanding of revelation would suggest), rather God is revealing God's very self. For Wesley, the self-revelation of God is Christocentric: God reveals God's self in Jesus Christ. A good example is found in the following hymn, which uses typical Wesleyan terminology. After the petition, "tell me all thy name," the hymn continues:

> Jehovah in thy person show,
>   Jehovah crucified;
> And then the pard'ning God I know,
>   And feel the blood applied.[178]

The text of "Wrestling Jacob" also supplies a Christological answer to the question of the name of God: "I know thee, Saviour, who thou art—Jesus, the feeble sinner's friend." Such citations are countless among Wesley's hymns, so convinced is the poet that the self-revelation of God is God's very self, and more specifically than this, God in the person of Jesus Christ. Thus, the question that seeks to know the "name of God" (though in reality a question seeking to know God's essence) can actually be answered with a *name:* Jesus of Nazareth. The Christological focus of God's self-revelation is the second point of Wesley's three-point assertion in resolving the tension between the mystery of God's inaccessible nature and the quest to know what, or better, who that mystery is.

Wesley's third point looks at the content of God's self-revelation from yet another angle. The text of "Wrestling Jacob" again provides helpful insight here. The hymn contains two complementary refrains. The first refrain urgently seeks to know the name and nature of God while the second provides the answer: "Thy nature, and thy name is LOVE." The refrain's context assures a decidedly Christocentric understanding of this answer. This hymn, like countless others, addresses Jesus Christ directly: "Tell me thy love, thy secret tell, Thy mystic name in me reveal, Reveal thyself in me."[179] According to Wesley, Jesus Christ is God's self-revelation, more specifically a self-revelation of love: "His thoughts, and words, and actions prove—His life and death—that God is love!"[180] "Infinite, unexhausted Love! Jesus and love are one."[181] The revelation of God in the hymns of the *Collection* is most frequently characterized as God's self-revelation in Jesus as love.

Finally, the word *love*, the soteriological connotations of which cannot be overlooked, captures the very essence and name of God that Wesley seeks to know. God reveals God's self as love above all in the incarnation, life, suffering, and crucifixion of Jesus Christ. Thus, Wesley frequently points to Christ's suffering and death as the greatest proof of God's love: "There for me the Saviour stands, Shows his wounds, and spreads his hands! God is love! I know, I feel."[182] Again, "Wrestling Jacob" provides a clear soteriological perspective on the "name" of God:

> 'Tis Love! 'Tis Love! Thou diedst for me;
> > I hear thy whisper in my heart.
> The morning breaks, the shadows flee,
> > Pure Universal Love thou art:
> To me, to all, thy bowels move—
> Thy nature, and thy name, is LOVE.

In locating the place of God's self-revelation within the heart of the individual believer, Charles Wesley presupposes the self-revelation of God in history by affirming Jesus Christ as the central embodiment of this revelation. But Wesley does appear to assume that the historical event of Jesus Christ as God's self-revelation has little meaning if not received and appropriated in the heart of the individual believer. The well-known epigram of the poet and mystic, Angelus Silesius (1624–1677), summarizes Wesley's view ably: "If Christ is born a thousand times in Bethlehem and not in you, you will remain lost." Wesley's hymns concentrate on the personal appropriation of God's self-revelation, which explains the frequent request to have the name of God written on or spoken in the heart

135

of the believer: "Tell me thy nature, and thy name, And write it on my heart."[183] "That name inspoken to my heart, That favourite name of love."[184] Wesley uses phrases like "in me," "my inmost soul," and "my heart" to locate God's revelation in the innermost consciousness of each believer. The appropriation of God's historical self-revelation in the person of Jesus Christ must occur in the heart of each believer.

Another hymn in *A Collection of Hymns for the Use of the People Called Methodists,* besides "Wrestling Jacob," also has as its main theme the pursuit of God's name so characteristic for Charles Wesley. It summarizes well what has been said thus far. The text and interpretation follow:

> Shepherd divine, our wants relieve (1)
>   In this our evil day;
> To all thy tempted followers give
>   The power to watch and pray.
>
> Long as our fiery trials last, (2)
>   Long as the cross we bear,
> O let our souls on thee be cast
>   In never-ceasing prayer!
>
> The spirit of interceding grace (3)
>   Give us in faith to claim,
> To wrestle till we see thy face,
>   And know thy hidden name.
>
> Till thou thy perfect love impart, (4)
>   Till thou thyself bestow,
> Be this the cry of every heart:
>   I will not let thee go.
>
> I will not let thee go, unless (5)
>   Thou tell thy name to me;
> With all thy great salvation bless,
>   And make me all like thee.
>
> Then let me on the mountain top (6)
>   Behold thy open face,
> Where faith in sight is swallowed up,
>   And prayer in endless praise.[185]

This hymn, found in the *Collection* under the heading "For Believers Praying," explores the theme of prayer. Charles Wesley utilizes the biblical story of Jacob's struggle at the river Jabbok as a paradigm for the believers' struggle to know God in prayer—a paradigm also used by Matthew Henry, whose biblical commentary was so often consulted by Wesley.[186] The biblical story itself, however, does not occupy center stage as it does in "Wrestling Jacob." The references to Genesis 32 are indirect ("To wrestle till we see thy face . . . I will not let thee go, unless thou tell thy name to me"). The hymn begins as one long petition for the gift of never-ceasing prayer, a petition that is equated, by the end of stanza 3, with the struggle to know the name of God ("thy hidden name"). The next stanza reveals that the struggle to know God's name is the struggle to know God's love ("thy perfect love"). The one at prayer knows not to pray for God to reveal "something" but rather to reveal God's self: "Till thou thyself bestow." Stanza 4 develops the soteriological connotations of God's self-revelation: God's self-revelation is salvation ("With all thy great salvation bless"), a salvific event that draws the believer into the life of God. The hymn closes with a beautiful image: the poet envisions receiving an answer to his prayer much like Moses encountered YHWH on Mount Sinai. In this encounter, in the final analysis an eschatological event, faith is changed into sight and prayer into praise.

This closes the discussion of the "pursuit of God's name" in Wesleyan hymnody. The next section, while reviewing some of this work again in a different light, will take up some unusual passages of Wesleyan hymnody that seem to attempt a direct identification of "God" with "Heaven." These passages suggest that "Heaven," for Wesley, is more closely related to the vision of a person or a relationship, than that of a "place."

3. The Experience of Salvation as Realized Eschatology?

As mentioned above, many of Charles Wesley's hymns end with an eschatological finale, a tradition often honored in the hymns of Christendom. It is the particular kind of eschatological perspective used in Wesleyan hymns that warrants our consideration, an eschatological perspective, which in theological terms can be described as "realized" eschatology and which in everyday language is best described by the phrase "heaven on earth." The hymns of *A Collection of Hymns for the Use of the People Called Methodists* often end with an eschatological image that seems to locate heaven in the here and now, rather than in a future place beyond the skies. The words "heaven below" are frequently used by Wesley to present this image. This section of my study will focus principally on these words. There is, however, no *one* hymn that can be chosen for the purpose of interpreting the words "heaven below." No single hymn uses these words as its key theme throughout all stanzas. Rather, they occur here and there in many hymns and thus must be interpreted by way of numerous different examples.

When Charles Wesley uses the words "heaven below," he neither denies the existence of a place at the end of time nor does he reduce its existence to the here and now. Wesley is very much bound to traditional images of heaven and never calls them into question. The section in the *Collection*, "Describing Heaven," contains all the traditional images of heaven for which one could ever hope.[187] In fact, Wesley builds the curious phrase "heaven below" precisely on these images, even though "heaven," as used in this phrase, is not primarily a place anymore, nor is it located exclusively in the future. Wesley uses this phrase as a witness to the relationship between Christ and the believer: the experience of salvation for the believer is the beginning of heaven on earth:

> As soon as in him we believe,
>   By faith of his Spirit we take,
> And, freely forgiven, receive
>   The mercy for Jesus's sake;
> We gain a pure drop of his love,
>   The life of eternity know,
> Angelical happiness prove,
>   And witness a heaven below.[188]

For Wesley everything comes together in the experience of salvation: the beginning of eternal life ("The life of eternity"), happiness ("Angelical happiness"), and heaven on earth ("a heaven below"). This identification of "heaven" with the experience of salvation is typical for Wesleyan hymnody and is apparent throughout *A Collection of Hymns for the Use of the People Called Methodists*:

> Happy the souls to Jesus joined,
>   And saved by grace alone;
> Walking in all his ways, they find
>   Their heaven on earth begun.[189]

Such an identification of "heaven" with the experience of salvation allows Wesley to encourage his listeners: "Only believe—and yours is heaven!"[190] In most of the hymns, however, it is not simply the experience of salvation as such that leads Wesley to use this phrase. After all, the experience of salvation has as its foundational reality the personal encounter of a human being with Christ. Thus, it comes as no surprise that the concept of "heaven on earth" for Wesley is not primarily associated with the experience of salvation as such, but rather with its Christological foundation: "heaven on earth" in the final analysis is Jesus. One hymn reads, "My Jesus to know, And feel his blood flow, 'Tis life everlasting, 'tis heaven below!"[191] Another hymn demonstrates even more markedly the association between the person of Jesus Christ and "heaven on earth":

> Thy gifts, alas! cannot suffice,
>   Unless thyself be given;
> Thy presence makes my paradise,
>   And where thou art is heaven![192]

Of course the distinction between soteriological and Christological connotations is somewhat artificial, especially when the Wesleyan poetical corpus as a whole is taken into consideration. What this distinction allows one to stress though is the fact that Wesley's concept of "heaven on earth" is based not on emotional exuberance in the personal experience of salvation but rather on its Christological foundation. The pneumatological characterization of heaven as the indwelling of the Holy Spirit found in some Wesley hymns does not contradict the above: "Come, thou all-inspiring Spirit . . . Present, everlasting heaven, All thou hast, and all thou art!"[193] The Christological foundation even of texts like the one just quoted surfaces as Wesley attempts to describe heaven not only as a present reality but also as a place beyond time: "heaven on earth" and "heaven in heaven" both are personal realities. They are encounters with Christ and as such are to be described as "heaven":

> Jesus, harmonious name!
>   It charms the hosts above;
> They evermore proclaim,
>   And wonder at his love;
> 'Tis all their happiness to gaze,
>   'Tis heaven to see our Jesu's face.[194]

The following hymn also draws on this identification of "Jesus" and "heaven." Here Wesley attempts to demonstrate the unity of the Church Triumphant and the Church Militant:

> The church triumphant in thy love,
>   Their mighty joys we know;
> They sing the Lamb in hymns above:
>   And we in hymns below.
>
> Thee in thy glorious realm they praise,
>   And bow before thy throne!
> We in the kingdom of thy grace:
>   The kingdoms are but one.[195]

These texts make clear why Wesley has no other choice but to describe the life of the believer as "heaven on earth." The encounter with Christ constitutes heaven, which thus is found in the believer's experience of salvation. The parallel use of the words *heaven* and *love* (remembering that "love," for Wesley, is the essence of God's self-revelation in Jesus Christ) further reinforces this line of reasoning: "Anticipate your heaven below, And own that love is heaven . . . Only love to us be given! Lord, we ask no other heaven. For the heaven of heavens is love."[196] Wesley, when defining the essence of heaven in these hymns, makes no distinction between the *visio Dei* and love. They are inseparable. The contemplation of God is the contemplation of love, which is heaven.

Does this remove the eschatological tension between the present life of the believer and the consummation that waits at the end of time? The hymn quoted above in reference to the Church Triumphant and the Church Militant provides the first hint that the tension remains. The hymn's next stanza continues: "The holy to the holiest leads."[197] It is no accident that Wesley refers to "heaven below" at least as many times as "heaven begun": "Find their heaven begun below, . . . Till they gain their full reward, And see thy glorious face!"[198] The phrase "antepast of heaven" also explicitly suggests a fulfillment yet to come.[199]

To suggest therefore that Wesley's concept of "heaven on earth" does away with eschatological tension is to misunderstand the poet altogether. This text from the *Collection* should dispel any doubts:

> My God, I am thine; What a comfort divine,
>   What a blessing to know that my Jesus is mine!
> In the heavenly Lamb Thrice happy I am,
>   And my heart it doth dance at the sound of his name.
>
> True pleasures abound In the rapturous sound;
>   And whoever hath found it hath paradise found.
> My Jesus to know, And feel his blood flow,
>   'Tis life everlasting, 'tis heaven below!
>
> Yet onward I haste To the heavenly feast;
>   That, that is the fullness, but this is the taste;
> And this I shall prove, Till with joy I remove
>   To the heaven of heavens in Jesus's love.[200]

Insofar as this hymn uses two different concepts of "heaven," it places a clear emphasis on the eschatological tension in the life of the believer. Heaven on earth is described as "heaven below" while the heaven to come is described as the "heaven of heavens." Apart from this differentiation, the hymn provides another important indicator for the context of the Wesleyan concept of "heaven on earth." This concept is most frequently used in hymns that take as their theme the experience of salvation and are characterized by a certain emotional exuberance (for example, one also often encounters the word *happiness* in these hymns). This suggests that the concept "heaven on earth" is derivative: Wesley uses this phrase usually connected with the final bliss (at the end of time) to describe the unutterable bliss of salvation experienced in the present. Thus, Wesley assumes a traditional view of heaven but provides it with a unique character when using it as an image for the present experience of salvation. This motif is readily apparent in the references listed above. The concept of "heaven on earth" is inextricably bound to the unspeakable joy of the experience of salvation:

> All fullness of peace, All fullness of joy,
>   And spiritual bliss That never shall cloy;
> To us it is given In Jesus to know
>   A kingdom of heaven, A heaven below.[201]

Other Wesley hymns make the same point. The word *heaven* is used to indicate the unspeakable joy of redemption: "What a mercy is this, what a heaven of bliss, How unspeakably happy am I."[202] Notice here, as mentioned above, how the words *happy* and *happiness* are intimately connected with the concept of "heaven on earth."

Some might suggest that Wesley's concept of "heaven on earth" embraces a triumphalist approach to Christian living and has little to say about the difficulties encountered in the life of the believer. This is not true. But one can hardly expect Wesley to address the difficulties of Christian living within the concept of "heaven on earth." The concept simply does not lend itself to such emphases. "Heaven on earth" is no more suited to address the difficulties of Christian living than is the "recognition of sin" the theological category under which to discuss the positive recognition of works in the faith process. Wesley's recognition of the difficulties of Christian living are best discussed under another heading, namely that of the struggle for Christian perfection. Wesley's frequent use of the words *holiness* and *happiness* in combination clearly suggests a close connection between both his concept of "heaven on earth" and the struggle for Christian perfection.

4. The Struggle for Christian Perfection

This designation, "the struggle for Christian perfection," does not so much amount to a single theological theme as it does to a conglomeration of related images and motifs that do not lend themselves easily to systematic consideration. Here perhaps more than anywhere else the reader is reminded that this study is analyzing a hymnbook and not a systematic theology. In bringing the concerns of systematic theology to a hymnbook, the result can be contrived. The discussion of the "struggle for Christian perfection" as a theological theme in Charles Wesley's hymns is further complicated by the fact that this issue with its varying interpretations appears not to have been settled between John and Charles Wesley, or among the adherents of early Methodism.[203]

No matter what their differences on this subject, one thing is clear: John and Charles Wesley felt compelled to maintain, based on the biblical witness, some notion of Christian perfection as the attainable goal of each believer's earthly existence. Thus, Christian perfection was an important theme of Methodist preaching from the beginning, as was also the case among German Pietists. It is well known that no small number of enthusiastic adherents of early Methodism claimed to have attained Christian perfection in their spiritual lives. Both John and Charles Wesley reported such claims in their journals and letters, though Charles was usually quick to criticize them.

A variety of attacks against members of the Methodist movement who claimed Christian perfection for themselves can be found in the hymns of Charles Wesley. That these Methodists would assume Christian perfection for themselves was indication enough to Charles that they could not possibly have attained the same. Nevertheless Charles continued to maintain that Christian perfection was indeed an attainable goal in each believer's life. Like his brother, he was compelled by the witness of biblical texts. Drawing on 1 Thessalonians 4:3, he wrote in one hymn of *A Collection of Hymns for the Use of the People Called Methodists:* "He wills that I should holy be: What can withstand his will?"[204] Other biblical texts that appear frequently in reference to this theme include Matthew 5:48; John 5:14; 1 John 2:5; and 1 John 3:9. The early hymns of the Wesleyan poetical corpus are considerably more explicit and positive when imagining the possibility of Christian perfection than are those of the later years. Experience had taught Charles Wesley that while the principle apparently must be maintained (again based on the biblical witness), practically speaking it was very difficult to verify in life experience. In fact, its experience was consistently falsified. Thus, in the course of time, Charles Wesley relegated his concept of Christian perfection to eschatological categories and began to associate the attainment of Christian perfection with the death of the believer.

John Wesley held to a concept of Christian perfection less strict in content and thus liked to speak of attaining the same in the here and now (see, for example, his important sermon on "Christian Perfection" written in 1741). The differences between the two brothers on this issue would lead John in some instances to criticize his brother's hymns on Christian perfection, marking them in the margins, even editing out hymn stanzas and lines that did not coincide with his own view.[205]

A Collection of Hymns for the Use of the People Called Methodists contains two large sections of hymns devoted to the struggle for Christian perfection that when taken together comprise a greater number of hymns than any other section. The name and placement of these sections (though of secondary importance and of John's hand) provide hints as to the context in which the struggle to attain Christian perfection has to be seen. The first section, "For Believers Groaning for full Redemption,"[206] is framed by a description of the various stages in the believer's life. The title itself suggests that salvation is a twofold event. "Full" redemption is still awaited even in the life of the believer. But the section that follows it clarifies that the eschatological tension between this age and the next is not to be the focus here. "For Believers Brought to the Birth"[207] suggests that the promised fullness of redemption is to be an experience in this place and time. This "full" redemption is Christian perfection. The vocabulary used here is of particular interest when compared to the *Collection*'s section on conversion entitled "For Mourners brought to the Birth." Wesley in the *Collection* uses the word *birth* in reference to both conversion and sanctification. In short, these hymns of the *Collection* reveal a terminology that identifies two different stages of redemption and classifies them both as (re)birth.

The attainment of Christian perfection or full "sanctification" is, therefore, in the hymns of Charles Wesley, referred to as a (new) birth and on occasion specifically as a "second birth," "second blessing," or "second gift": "Lord . . . the second gift impart";[208] "The graces of my second birth To me shall all be given."[209] Here Charles Wesley obviously divides the process of redemption into two different stages, "justification" and "sanctification," and these two technical terms are not foreign to his hymnody. In the sections devoted to the struggle for Christian perfection, words related to the root word *sanctify* are used over and over again: "sanctified by love divine,"[210] "Thy sanctifying grace,"[211] "the sanctifying word,"[212] "thy sanctifying power."[213] These and other such phrases appear throughout the hymns even though Charles Wesley seems to avoid the *terminus technicus* "sanctification," at least in the hymns of the *Collection*. The reason why the word (re)*birth* is associated with the attainment of perfection (an association that puzzles many commentators) appears to be rather simple. It is based on Wesley's (prehistorical-critical) reading of Scripture. He read, for example, a text like 1 John 3:9 quite literally: "Whosoever is born of God doth not commit sin; for his seed remaineth in him: and he cannot sin, because he is born of God" (KJV). For Wesley, this text clearly indicates that being born of God (new birth) and Christian perfection, understood as sinlessness, are inextricably bound together. Thus, he feels obligated to use the phrase "birth from God" when addressing Christian perfection (even when the image of new birth also serves to describe the conversion experience).[214] The following stanza makes this point:

> Hasten, Lord, the perfect day!
>   Let thy every servant say,
> I have now obtained the power,
>   Born of God, to sin no more.[215]

This, however, only helps to clarify one linguistic peculiarity in the Wesleyan concept of Christian perfection. More important is a review of this concept's content. In this review the reader is confronted by a multitude of images and motifs. I list here several of the most important: Perfection as a new creation, restoration of the *imago Dei* and the reclamation of paradise, a Christological interiorization of these protological images and the corresponding understanding of sin, the importance of the indwelling of God in the believer and the believer's participation in the nature of God, the meaning of the phrase *perfect love*, and the question as to when perfection is attained.

I turn first to the series of themes offered by those images used in forming the parallelism between "creation" and "new creation." Wesley frequently speaks of the struggle for Christian perfection and the believer's new creation in the same context. Thus, for example, in the hymn that opens the *Collection*'s section "For Believers Groaning for full Redemption":

> The thing my God doth hate,
>   That I no more may do,
> Thy creature, Lord, again create,
>   And all my soul renew;
> My soul shall then, like thine,
>   Abhor the thing unclean,

And sanctified by love divine
Forever cease from sin.[216]

This stanza is clear that the attainment of Christian perfection is dependent on God recreating the believer: "Thy creature, Lord, again create." A fundamental aspect of Wesley's doctrine of perfection comes into focus here: Christian perfection, for Charles Wesley, is not about any human struggle for sanctification. Rather, Christian perfection is God-centered. It is focused on God's action with believers, on the creative prerogative of God, which the faithful passively receive—at least this is what the image of perfection as a new creation seems to suggest. As with the image of "birth" used by Wesley, the poet uses an image for Christian perfection that is originally closely associated with redemption (2 Cor. 5:17). The above stanza does not stand alone in addressing this theme within Wesleyan hymnody. Other texts are easily cited, including this text from a hymn in the section "For Believers Groaning for full Redemption": "Come, Lord, and form my soul anew, . . . In love create thou all things new."[217] Another hymn (less attractive poetically) continues:

I shall, a weak and helpless worm,
    Through Jesus strengthening me,
Impossibilities perform,
    And live from sinning free.

For this in steadfast hope I wait;
    Now, Lord, my soul restore,
Now the new heavens and earth create
    And I shall sin no more.[218]

This picture of creation and new creation in Christian perfection is linked with the restoration of the *imago Dei* in humankind. The hymns of the Wesleyan poetical corpus repeatedly plead for the restoration of the *imago Dei* in the believer. One hymn asks, "Let us, to perfect love restored, Thy image here receive,"[219] while another pleads, "stamp thine image on my heart."[220] Yet another hymn looks ahead to the attainment of Christian perfection: "When thou the work of faith hast wrought, I here shall in thine image shine, Nor sin in deed, or word, or thought."[221] This last example is unusual for

Wesley insofar as the images used to describe the new creation and the restoration of the *imago Dei* in humankind customarily are formed by him in the language of petition. This reinforces the notion that Christian perfection is granted by God to humankind and that it is yet to come (nowhere in his hymns does Charles Wesley look back and give thanks for the gift of Christian perfection). This is also true for hymn texts seeking the reclamation of paradise ("paradise" for Charles Wesley refers to life before the Fall, a place that is reclaimed in Christian perfection): "That we our Eden might regain . . .,"[222] "Restored to our unsinning state, To love's sweet paradise."[223] The restoration of the *imago Dei* and the reclamation of "paradise" stand side by side for Wesley. This comes as no surprise since both of these two images come from the biblical creation narrative. The following hymn example provides a good look at the use of these two images and their common origin:

> Father, Son, and Holy Ghost,
> Be to us what Adam lost;
> Let us in thine image rise,
> Give us back our paradise![224]

Another hymn basically inverts this image: the believer is not transferred to a state of paradise as a result of Christian perfection; rather paradise, as a precondition for Christian perfection, is placed in the heart of the believer: "thou plantest in my heart A constant paradise" (again emphasizing the importance of the heart as the seat of Christian experience for Wesley).[225]

This initial series of images used to describe Christian perfection (creation, new creation, restoration of the *imago Dei*, and the reclamation of paradise) forms a coherent picture: Christian perfection is linked to God's first creation of humankind and to God's provision of a perfect environment for humankind. In perfection, the fruits of this first creation are regained. The second series of images is set, in a certain sense, on top of these protological images and reflects two typical elements of Wesleyan thought: the Christological emphasis and the interiorization of soteriological reality in the heart of the believer.

For Charles Wesley, the creation of a new heart is the essence of the "new creation." Wesley's preference for this image of a new heart is a good example of his interiorization of the larger image of the new creation. Those hymns devoted to the theme of Christian perfection repeatedly offer prayers for a new heart as a precondition for the life of perfection:

> O for a heart to praise my God,
>   A heart from sin set free!
> A heart that always feels thy blood,
>   So freely spilt for me!
>
> . . . .
>
> A heart in every thought renewed,
>   And full of love divine,
> Perfect, and right, and pure, and good—
>   A copy, Lord, of thine![226]

This hymn also points to the Christological focus of these protological images: the heart, which longs for re-creation, is to be a copy of the heart of Jesus, and the *imago Dei,* which is to be restored, is the *imago Christi*: "I shall fully be restored To the image of my Lord."[227] The Wesleyan understanding of sin, which stands in opposition to this Christian perfection and thus must be destroyed, also fits neatly into this picture. Charles Wesley rarely thinks in terms of individual sins but rather concentrates, almost exclusively, on the sinful condition of humankind, its predisposition and will to sin. It seems that the ontological perspective of sin is more important for him than individual ethical considerations. Thus hymns on Christian perfection by Charles Wesley that provide appeals for the believer to overcome certain moral shortcomings are hard to find (not to mention the fact that a hymn would hardly be the place for such appeals).

It is God who is repeatedly called upon to lift the predisposition to sin from humankind. The term most often used in Wesleyan hymnody to refer to this predisposition is *inbred sin*. This inbred sin is generally found in the heart of the believer, which is to be made new: "O Jesu, let thy dying cry Pierce the bottom of my heart, . . . Slay the dire root and seed of sin,"[228] "Dry corruption's fountain up, Cut off th'entail of sin," [229] "My inbred malady remove."[230] In one hymn Wesley addresses this indwelling sin directly: in the first three stanzas of the hymn the poet's own inbred sin serves as a dialogue partner[231] (a curious concept for a hymn). It is worth stressing again that all of these petitions (and the list could go on) do not appear in the *Collection*'s section on conversion, but rather in the section that addresses the struggle for Christian perfection in the believer. The image of a new creation of the heart of each believer is, in Wesley's hymns, not to be understood as that which will minimize the occasion of sin. Rather, the image points to life under a completely different set of assumptions: the sheer possibility of sin appears to be gone altogether. With this in mind, it is easy to see why Charles Wesley pushed the attainment of Christian perfection closer and closer to the end of one's earthly existence even though the biblical witness required him to affirm the possibility of perfection (at least theoretically) in this life.

God's indwelling of each believer is the next important image to be considered as a basis for Christian perfection, an image inseparable from that of the creation of a new heart in each believer. The new heart is understood to be the throne or temple of God: "Make, O make my heart thy seat, O set up thy kingdom there!"[232] In the hymns devoted to Christian perfection, Wesley repeatedly prays that God will indwell the heart of each believer. In one hymn God's indwelling is described with gardening imagery:

> When shall I see the welcome hour
>   That plants my God in me!
> Spirit of health, and life, and power,
>   And perfect liberty![233]

This hymn makes clear that the concept of Christian perfection in Wesleyan hymnody cannot be limited to an ethical dimension alone—its mystical dimension is unmistakable. Humankind is made holy by union with the Holy God:

> Thy witness with my spirit bear
>   That God, my God, inhabits there,
> Thou with the Father and the Son
>   Eternal light's coeval beam;
> Be Christ in me, and I in him,
>   Till perfect we are made in one.[234]

This hymn from the *Collection* on the believer's union with Christ is actually addressed to the Holy Spirit as indicated by its opening stanza: "Come, Holy Ghost, all-quick'ning fire." And therein lies yet another characteristic of Wesleyan hymns on Christian perfection. The Holy Spirit is understood to be the agent for the new creation, the restoration of the *imago Dei*, and union with God. The petition for the indwelling of God in the believer is therefore frequently accompanied by pneumatological elements that transform the petition into an epiclesis:

> O come, and dwell in me,
>   Spirit of power within,
> And bring the glorious liberty
>   From sorrow, fear, and sin.
> The seed of sin's disease,
>   Spirit of health, remove,
> Spirit of finished holiness,
>   Spirit of perfect love.[235]

The indwelling of God in the believer in the final analysis does not only imply the gift of a new heart but rather of God's self: "Give me thyself,"[236] "thyself impart."[237] And here the image used is inverted once again: drawing on Galatians 2:20, Wesley speaks not only of Christ's or God's indwelling in the believer but also (perhaps influenced by Mystical Spiritualism) of immersing oneself in God: "lost in an ocean of God,"[238] "lost in Love Divine,"[239] "lost in thy immensity,"[240] "wholly lost in thee."[241] These and other expressions found throughout the hymns on perfection are further indicators that the ethical considerations of Christian perfection are supplemented by, if not subsumed by, its mystical dimension.

Participation in the divine nature, as based on 2 Peter 1:4, is also important to the concept of Christian perfection in Wesleyan hymnody, as it is also of fundamental importance to the adherents of German Pietism.[242] Even though citations of the biblical text 2 Peter 1:4 in the Wesleyan hymns of the *Collection* are not frequent, the notion remains significant, particularly in the hymns on Christian perfection:

> Send us the Spirit of thy Son
>   To make the depths of Godhead known,
> To make us share the life divine;
>   Send him the sprinkled blood t'apply,

Send him our souls to sanctify,
And show and seal us ever thine.[243]

It is obvious from this hymn that for Charles Wesley, the mosaic of Christian perfection also contains the idea of the participation of the believer in "the life divine." But what does participation in the divine nature mean for Wesley? First, this participation is personal and real. For Wesley, it is not so much about partnership with God as it is about union with God:

The promise stands forever sure,
And we shall in thine image shine,
Partakers of a nature pure,
Holy, angelical, divine;
In spirit joined to thee the Son,
As thou art with thy Father one.[244]

Note again how Christian perfection is not purely an ethical concept. Rather, when speaking of participation in the divine nature, Wesley understands union with God to be the sine qua non of Christian perfection. This, in turn, opens the door for understanding what comes as close as anything to a *terminus technicus* for Christian perfection in the hymns of Charles Wesley: *perfect love.*[245] Wesley takes this phrase from the Bible, 1 John 4:17-18, where it appears in three different forms: "love made perfect," "perfect love," and "perfect in love" (cf. also 1 John 2:5). Since Wesley characterizes the essence ("nature") of God as love, it is only logical that his concept of participation in the divine nature should similarly be defined as participation in and communion with love. Christian perfection, as interpreted by the phrase "perfect love," in the final analysis means perfect communion with God. It is thus defined by eminently positive characteristics and not simply negatively as the absence of sin (though this aspect is, of course, present as well). But the phrase "perfect love" resists a primarily negative definition of Christian perfection as sinlessness and embraces instead an eminently positive definition of perfection as the perfect communion with God in love:

Father, Son, and Holy Ghost,
In council join again
To restore thine image, lost
By frail, apostate man;

> O might I thy form express,
>   Through faith begotten from above,
> Stamped with real holiness,
>   And filled with perfect love![246]

As is the case with this hymn, many hymns of the *Collection* contain the phrase "perfect love" in the last stanza and thus are part of the characteristic Wesleyan eschatological perspective. This prompts the question as to when Christian perfection is to be attained. As already mentioned above, Charles Wesley's brother, John, believed that the attainment of Christian perfection could be recognized and located in time. Charles Wesley was much more cautious. His belief that the individual's moment of conversion could be recognized and located in time did not extend to his concept of Christian perfection. Later in life, he was even reluctant to insist upon Christian perfection as a reality in this life. The section in the *Collection* entitled "For Believers Brought to the Birth," though, does not seem consistent with Charles Wesley's thought later in life. After all, the title itself seems to imply that believers have reached this stage of Christian perfection. But the individual hymns of this section are not consistent with its title. Furthermore, there is little to distinguish them from the hymns in the preceding section entitled "For Believers Groaning for full Redemption." In both sections the believer is struggling for Christian perfection. No hymn offers thanks for Christian perfection attained. Instead each hymn looks forward to Christian perfection as a future event.

The hymns of the section "For Believers Groaning for full Redemption" are distinguished from those of the section "For Believers Brought to the Birth" by but two small details: (1) the description of the struggle for Christian perfection is more intensive; and (2) the petition for Christian perfection *now* is emphasized: "Now let me gain perfection's height";[247] "make Me now a creature new";[248] "Now, Saviour, now the power bestow";[249] "Enter now thy poorest home: Now, my utmost Saviour, come";[250] "Jesu, now our hearts inspire . . . Kindle now the heavenly fire."[251] The repetition of the word *now* introduces a certain urgency into these hymns and seems to place Christian perfection within the grasp of the singer. Nevertheless, though Christian perfection may be within reach, it is never actually attained in these hymns. Only once, in the last stanza of the last hymn in the section "For Believers Brought to the Birth," does

Charles Wesley attempt to suggest that the urgent petition for the gift of Christian perfection has been answered:

> 'Tis done! thou dost this moment save,
>   With full salvation bless;
> Redemption through thy blood I have,
>   And spotless love and peace.[252]

But no other hymns in this section embrace this "realized" Christian perfection, and it would be a mistake to interpret this hymn without the benefit of that context. Charles Wesley's reluctance to fix Christian perfection in time should, however, not be understood as a denial of the concept itself. The hymns of both sections discussed above point to Wesley's ongoing struggle for Christian perfection: the hymns themselves capture this struggle. They constantly petition God for the gift of Christian perfection. In this sense they themselves become the struggle.

This final observation on the struggle for Christian perfection in Wesleyan hymnody also applies to *A Collection of Hymns for the Use of the People Called Methodists* as a whole. The *Collection* does not simply contain hymns that address or reflect the experience of salvation and Christian perfection. No, these hymns are the message itself. They celebrate the experience of salvation. They struggle for and anticipate the coming of Christian perfection. They are the praise and proclamation of God's salvific acts. The hymns on the struggle for Christian perfection demonstrate ably how form and performance (the hymn) and substance (its theme) become one.

D. Conclusion

Two issues are prompted by the theological interpretation of individual themes within *A Collection of Hymns for the Use of the People Called Methodists*. First, as long as this kind of interpretation is understood as theological reflection on doxological material there are no problems. Theological reflection is possible on practically any kind of material, and doxological material is no exception. One must, however, be clear to draw the distinction between the theological method and the material to be studied: it needs to be stressed that the theological interpretation of doxological material does not itself become a doxological formulation, nor does doxological material through theological interpretation become a systematic theological formulation.[253]

Second, the application of theological methodology to doxological texts (hymnbooks, for example) is, one could say, "inappropriate." The hymns (whether devotional or liturgical in character) were not written for theological study but for the praise of God. They find their true being in the Christian community's sung praise of God and not as printed words on a page prepared for theological analysis. After all, theological interpretation as text analysis is only made privy to a small part of the act of praise: the written word alone.

Of course, doxology can also be a form of reflection on faith. That, however, is not its primary intention and thus is often implicit rather than explicit. The following section of this study will address the relationship between implicit doxological faith reflection and explicit theological reflection. This section will provide a more detailed description of the characteristics of doxological speech as they relate to theological reflection.

PART III

CHAPTER 4

The Essence of Doxological Speech and Its Relationship to Theological Reflection

The review of discussions on the relationship between doxology and theology in chapter 2 and the study of hymns in *A Collection of Hymns for the Use of the People Called Methodists* in chapter 3 have set the stage for this last part of the study, which will be devoted to describing the distinguishing characteristics of doxological speech and their relationship to theological reflection in light of the preceding.[1] Though the review of other doxological traditions (both hymnic and nonhymnic) would be helpful at this point in the study, the absence of such a review[2] does not inhibit this study of a specific hymnic-doxological tradition from drawing preliminary conclusions about the essence of doxological speech and its relationship to theological reflection. Naturally, observations will be made that apply not only to Wesleyan hymnody but also to all hymnic-doxological traditions. It is hoped that the results of this study will be reviewed, modified, and amplified (but not necessarily refuted) by others.

A. Characteristics of Doxological Speech

Fundamentally, this study asserts that the essence and characteristics of doxology are to be determined by way of an interpretation of doxological speech itself rather than by way of an imposition of prior dogmatic categories, abstracted from doxological speech. Thus, the study of specific doxological material as presented in the previous chapter was necessary to gain an understanding of the unique nature of doxology. Now, in the attempt to identify the essential characteristics of doxological speech, the question might well be asked: what is the specific interpretation of the reality of faith assumed and expressed by doxology? How does doxology qua doxology interpret the reality about which it speaks or sings?[3] The answer to this question will demonstrate that doxological speech assumes a very specific and unmistakable view of the reality of faith, which can only be expressed through the unique medium of doxological speech.[4] Various aspects of the doxological interpretation of reality comprise the essential characteristics of doxological speech.

The most noticeable characteristic of doxology lies in the way it relates itself to God. Doxology is neither *from* nor *about* God; rather it is directed *to* God. This is particularly apparent in the anacletic formulae that often introduce or accompany doxological speech: "My gracious Master and my God," "Maker," "Saviour of Mankind," "O Love divine," "Shepherd of souls," "Saviour," "Prince of Israel's race"—these are just a few of the countless anacletic formulae used by Charles Wesley to begin his hymns. But even where no direct address is used, doxological speech in the final analysis is dialogic in its intent. The implicit or explicit vocative in reference to God is characteristic of all doxological speech, as is most clearly seen in the anacletic formulae noted above. Thus, the "naming of God" in doxological speech is not primarily descriptive but rather ascriptive, even when the grammatical form is descriptive, as is the case in the following stanza:

> Glory to God, and praise, and love
>   Be ever, ever given,
> By saints below, and saints above,
>   The church in earth and heaven.[5]

It is interesting to note a parallel practice developed in late Judaism: when the faithful named God, an expression of praise always immediately followed.[6] Thus, even the descriptive naming of God is placed within an ascriptive-doxological context, thereby suggesting that every naming of God should find, or be grounded in, a doxological orientation. The image of the Divine created and described by this doxological naming of God[7] is of a God to whom one can speak. Doxology, like prayer itself, assumes that God is approachable by humankind. Its content, however, suggests a specific kind of address, namely that of adoration. God is not only approachable by humankind, God is also the only One worthy of humankind's adoration.[8] At the same time doxological speech indicates that the invocation and the adoration of God intended by doxology are never adequate. The choice of doxology as a form of speech already implies this: Doxology typically belongs to the *genus poeticum*, transcending all "objective" speech in hymnic praise, while at the same time challenging the *genus poeticum* to transcend itself, often by breaking into song. Thus, in most cases, doxology finds its fullest expression in song, not in spoken words. Following his conversion, Charles Wesley wrote: "O for a thousand tongues to sing My dear Redeemer's praise."

There is, however, more to doxology than its transcendence of "objective" speech and its constant attempts to transcend all possibilities for human expression.[9] These are not quite the last word in doxology and its overabundant praise of God. Charles Wesley, consistent with the doxological tradition of the church, makes use of another motif best summarized in the Latin short doxology *"tibi silentium laus."*[10] For Charles Wesley, silence emerges as a specific form of praise. In fact, some references in his hymns seem to indicate that he views silence as the highest form of praise. The following stanza provides perhaps the best example of the doxological role of silence:

> The Father shining on his throne,
>   The glorious, coeternal Son,
> The Spirit, one in seven,
>   Conspire our rapture to complete:
> And lo! we fall before his feet,
>   And silence heightens heaven.[11]

Theologically speaking, this silent praise might be characterized as a concluding doxology. It is not the first utterance of believers at worship, but rather it consistently appears at the close of the believers' exuberant praise of God.[12] Silence, as such, is an important indicator of how the explicit and abundant praise of God (and the image it conveys of the One who is adored) is an approach to a mystery that far exceeds human imagination and expression. Thus, the *laus silentii* is no empty silence but an articulate one.[13] The silence itself says something about the One to whom the *laus silentii* is due. Doxology, in this context, clearly continues to push the limits of its own definition. Still, even while continually challenging its own possibilities and boundaries, it is able in this very challenge to say: God is beyond the most exuberant praise afforded God.

A note about paradox as a doxological figure of speech is important here: paradoxical speech in doxology also points to doxology's

159

human limitations in naming God. The following needs to be emphasized about paradox:

> Paradox is not simply used in cases of emergency as an unusual speech form taken up in the meantime because we do not know how to properly express ourselves in the moment. Rather, paradox is the manner in which speech can capture in its fullness both what is and what is beyond human imagination.[14]

This characteristic of paradoxical speech in doxology can be seen as a linguistic indicator that God is beyond our imagination. Thus, to quote but one example, Charles Wesley describes the mystery of the Incarnation in the following short paradox: "Being's Source begins to be And God himself is born!" A doxology such as this may be characterized as paradox, but one which, in the face of mystery, enables praise.

Having reviewed some of the specific characteristics of doxological speech as it pertains to God, let us turn to aspects of doxological speech as it relates to human beings. Though the human being plays a role in the doxological dialogue, the human is not the chief subject of doxology. The bulk of doxological expressions are directed to the One addressed as "you." The "I" fades into the background. As one author puts it rather succinctly "the 'I' is sacrificed in doxology."[15] If that is true, then how does doxology interpret the reality of this "I"? First, the reality of the "I" in doxology is the reality of the one who is speaking. What is of fundamental importance, however, is the fact that the one who is speaking the doxology is *responding* and being called into a dialogue that she did not begin. Thus, doxology is primarily a response, not a decision or action of human prompting. The Hebrew verb ידה typically translated "to praise," makes this clear. Actually it means "to confess" or "to affirm" and always points to some preceding act of God.[16] In this way doxology can be understood as a reaction to the saving acts of God. Doxology assumes and is determined by these saving acts to which it corresponds.[17] "He put a new song in my mouth, a hymn of praise to our God," sings the psalmist (Ps. 40:3). Whether the praise of God for its own sake or as prompted by the saving acts of God is the highest form of doxology does not appear to be important in this context. Both forms of doxology are only imaginable as reactions to the experience of God's saving acts.

In one sense, all Christian speech is a response to the salvific acts of God. Can doxology be set aside as the primary and most suitable (verbal) reaction to these saving acts? It is probably no accident that Morning Prayer begins with the line: "Lord, open my lips; And my mouth shall proclaim your praise." But can the priority of doxology over all other forms of speech about God be asserted? In disputing Gerhard Sauter's thesis that doxology takes priority over theology as the primary language of faith, Dietrich Ritschl suggests that "both the telling of the story with YHWH in early Israel and its retelling in the early church had priority over doxology."[18] He is therefore reluctant to affirm that speech about God begins with speech addressed to God. I agree with Ritschl that the terms under which doxology might be given priority over theology must be better defined. The instances he cites, however, certainly do not indicate a priority of the telling of God's story with humankind over doxology. God's story with humankind told throughout the Old Testament clearly had a cultic context and therefore a doxological *Sitz im Leben*: "If Israel made confession of Jahweh's acts in history, then, especially when this was done in artistic form, it was simply an act of praise."[19] The early church also understood the narrative of God's saving acts as a narrative of praise and thus included it as the high point of praise in its Eucharistic prayer. In a sense, this narrative cannot be told in anything but the language of praise and thus as doxological speech. The "dangerous memory" (Johann Baptist Metz) of God's saving acts is proclaimed by the people of God especially in the liturgical anamnesis, thus having a primarily doxological context (a point often overlooked by the representatives of so-called narrative theology).[20]

Despite this problem in Ritschl's argument I agree with him that the circumstances in which doxology could be given priority (temporal? substantial? theological?) over theology still await clarification. Until then, it should not be forgotten that all Christian speech about God and addressed to God is formed in response to the experience of God's salvific acts. Furthermore, doxology, as praise of God, could then be understood as the most appropriate reaction of humankind to the experience of God's salvific acts since it most clearly corresponds to these acts: "Praise is *the* answer of creation to God's creating and saving action. . . . The praise of God, thus, appears to be fundamental for all believers."[21] In other words, "If the

161

δόξα τοῦ θεοῦ is the goal of all being, then doxology is the one word which sums up humankind's most appropriate response to this goal."[22] Clearly doxology has to be accompanied by a symphony of other speech forms, all of which surface in response to the experience of God's salvific acts (most notably *martyria* and *diakonia*). All this seems to suggest the possibility of granting doxology a certain priority over other human responses to God's saving acts, since doxology comes closest to responding most appropriately to these acts. Proof of a temporal priority of doxology over theology seems more difficult to establish, and in principle unnecessary,[23] once a "priority of appropriateness" seems acceptable.

Here we return to our starting point, aspects of doxological speech as it pertains to humankind. Doxology identifies human beings as beings who praise, and it characterizes their praise as the appropriate response to the experience of salvation. If one assumes the Old Testament's view of death as the end of the praise of God,[24] then the following holds true: "Praise is man's most characteristic mode of existence: praising and not praising stand over against one another like life and death: praise becomes the most elementary 'token of being alive' that exists."[25] As far as doxological speech is concerned, sin and death could then be read as the denial and end of praise, or as the case may be, the praise of other gods. The praise of self might also be included in an understanding of the praise of other gods. In doxology, there is no room for the praise of one's own accomplishments.[26] According to doxology, life in its fullest expression is the praise of God.

From a Christian perspective, of course, death does not mean the end of praise; rather it provides for the transition of earthly existence to that of the heavenly hosts and their praise of God. Doxology, in effect, anticipates the final, unqualified, eschatological appearance of God's *doxa*, that is, God's glory, at the end of time. It therefore serves an anticipatory function:[27] humankind, in offering praise for God's saving acts, anticipates the day when these acts of God will find complete fulfillment.

The previous reflections will have made the following clear: doxology is the bearer of a very specific and unique worldview (or, more concretely, of a particular interpretation of religious existence), which, in the final analysis, only has meaning for those who make doxological speech their own. Specifically, the doxological interpretation of existence has meaning for those who understand and commit themselves to "a sacrifice of praise to God, that is, the fruit of lips that confess his name" (Heb. 13:15). This particular doxological interpretation of religious existence can be summarized as follows: the reality of doxology suggests that all reality is directed towards the *doxa* of God and thus to the very person of God's self. God's saving acts in history are interpreted as an expression of this *doxa*. They draw humankind into a relationship of thanksgiving, confession, adoration, and celebration in which the praise of God's *doxa* anticipates its fulfillment at the end of time. Doxology suggests that the life of faith is not possible outside the realm of this doxological encounter. It also affirms that the encounter of adoration and love between God and God's people is the ultimate goal of salvation history. The most intensive manifestation of this doxological encounter with God will come at the end of time when all humankind will be gathered up into the glory of God. Doxology is the bearer of this particular interpretation of the reality of faith under its own unique operative principles. Thus, the doxological interpretation of reality cannot be achieved in theology, proclamation, or service.[28] Dietrich Ritschl is correct when he writes of the relationship between theology and doxology: "In doxology something is said to be true about God and humanity which could not be expressed in this way in descriptive language."[29] Doxology thus expresses a very specific and unmistakable dimension of religious and human existence.

We must, however, go one step further in order to determine the nature of these operative principles and thus the peculiarities and characteristics of doxology. At the heart of it, doxology is not simply spoken expression but rather a speech event. Our interpretation of Wesleyan hymnody has demonstrated repeatedly that an examination of the texts reveals only part of the hymns' reality. The actual singing of a hymn cannot be taken into account by a study of the text alone. This "doing," however, is fundamental to the understanding of doxological speech. Even when doxology seems to come in the form of a descriptive statement (either about God or humankind), it is not primarily a text; rather "it is a strong, energetic Word . . . a communication not of self-satisfied truths, but rather of reality."[30]

As regards this kind of speech, linguistic analysis has suggested a theory of speech acts (first stated by J. L. Austin and further developed by J. R. Searle) that has bearing on this study. Speech acts do not simply describe a certain reality, but also create and modify reality.[31] Translated for the doxological speech act this would mean that doxology[32] does not primarily convey descriptive statements in which God's majesty is constantly confirmed. Doxology is an event,[33] an encounter between the One adored and the ones who adore. In this encounter, the ones who bring adoration accept and enact the relationship (initiated by God), as is their calling: "to glorify God and enjoy him forever" (see the *Westminster Shorter Catechism* of 1647). Doxology accomplishes that to which it bears witness:[34] the doxological encounter between God and humankind.

This study also wants to suggest at this point (without providing further evidence) that the doxological encounter *par excellence* is found in the liturgy of the church. To follow up this point, the question would have to be asked: to what extent does doxological speech as a speech act assume an "institutional setting" (the community of believers), which an individual can enter without the need for creating anew a doxological community?[35]

The above paragraphs sketch the most important characteristics of doxological speech as determined by doxology itself.[36] However, the fact that doxology suggests a specific and unmistakable interpretation of the reality of faith says little, if anything, about the justification and legitimacy of this interpretation. The next section will pursue this question.

B. Criteria for Legitimacy

In the same way that the essential characteristics of doxological speech were determined by a review of the doxological event itself, the criteria for establishing the legitimacy of doxological speech will have to be gleaned from a careful analysis of that event.

The attempt to establish criteria of legitimacy for doxological speech assumes that doxology is a unique and peculiar speech act. Therefore, doxological speech is justified by its own criteria of legitimacy and their activation.[37] It makes little sense to strip doxology of its own criteria of legitimacy and subject it to criteria for legitimization from elsewhere. The essence and characteristics of doxology would be overlooked, and it would be difficult to develop criteria for legitimacy that would do justice to the specific speech act doxology represents. Based on the above established essential characteristics of doxological speech, the central "function" of doxology could be said to be the facilitation of the doxological encounter between God and humankind. The central criteria for establishing the legitimacy of doxological speech thusly characterized must be found in the answer to these questions: Does doxology accomplish this, does doxology enable this kind of encounter between God and humankind? Does it allow for the exacting of its own specific interpretation of the reality of faith? And does it provide an authentic expression of its own intention?

These criteria for establishing legitimacy, born of doxology's own peculiar characteristics, must be measured by doxological reality itself. In them, the nature of doxology is taken seriously and itself provides the criteria by which it is to be judged.

Doxological speech is not, however, and must never become an "autarchical language game,"[38] (an emphasis of particular importance when one wants to maintain a certain "autonomy" for doxology). Doxology, as one basic form of human response to the saving acts of God, like all other forms of response, is bound to correspond to these acts of God—in its own way.[39] The question of how doxology's response corresponds to the saving acts of God is, however, confronted with the problem of divergent perspectives within doxological speech. This, in turn, prompts the question: what forms of doxology are legitimate and which are not—an acute problem, particularly since doxological speech does not primarily strive for clarity of expression, and doxological statements therefore are rarely unambiguous.

It is obvious, of course, that not every act of praise qua doxology rightly corresponds to the saving acts of God that enable the doxological encounter between God and humankind. After all, God cannot be praised for everything (as some Pentecostal churches and fundamentalist communities would have it): even Jesus died without a *berakah* on his lips. It is therefore only right that many situations of contemporary life have helped with the rediscovery of the ancient prayer form of lamentation. For doxology, the following needs to be stressed: forms of doxology are illegitimate when they violate the essential characteristics of doxology, even though they may formally adhere to the structure of a doxology. Illegitimate forms of doxology deny by their very content any correspondence with the saving acts of God: "God, I thank you that I am not like other people: thieves, rogues, adulterers" (Luke 18:11).[40] "Thanks be to God that I was not born a woman." These classic examples of illegitimate doxologies (one from the Scriptures, one from the traditional prayers of a Jewish male) are missing a critical part of doxological speech and demonstrate why doxology must be subjected to critical theological reflection and study. The critical study of doxology is requisite precisely because doxology is not an autarchical language game but one of several complementary[41] speech acts that respond to the saving acts of God. Doxological speech must be able to justify itself as part of that world. It must not therefore resist the requirements of critical reflection and theological study. This is true for liturgical doxological language but also bears importance for individual devotional speech, as indicated above in the two examples of illegitimate doxologies. The sentence "Prayers must not be analyzed; they must be prayed"[42] may have meaning for the actual performance of prayers, but not in general, especially in light of the manifold dangers encountered by doxological speech (idolatry, magic, self-glorification, and so on).

Critical theological reflection on doxological speech must, however, be guided by the essential characteristics and criteria of legitimacy of doxology itself. Critical theological reflection that imposes its own essential characteristics and criteria of legitimacy on doxology must be rejected. Such reflection would fail to accomplish the initial designs of doxology (a mistake that is possible in doxological speech as well)[43] and adulterate this form of speech altogether. Whenever doxology (or any prayer for that matter) is used as a platform for dogmatic and/or moral instruction this danger is near. An oft-cited example of doxological speech adulterated by the blending of doxology with a compendium of catechetical statements ("prayed dogma") can be found in the old preface of the Eucharistic prayer for Trinity Sunday. Here theological reflection attempts— with considerable effort—to force its own essential characteristics and operative principles onto doxology. The result approaches an unauthentic form of doxology. The basic function of doxology, enabling the encounter of praise between God and humankind, is traded by a self-assured recitation (who is being addressed here?) of dogmatic assertions.

So much for testing the legitimacy of doxological speech. The final section of this study will revisit the relationship between doxology and theological reflection in greater detail. Prior to that, the next section will look at tests of authenticity for doxological speech.

C. Tests of Authenticity

What applies to the interpretation of characteristics of doxological speech and to criteria of legitimacy of such speech also applies to tests of authenticity. If the study of doxological speech is to proceed appropriately it must orient itself according to doxology's own operative principles. Thus, the search for authenticating tests of doxological speech could, for example, begin with a look at the effectiveness of doxology or, more narrowly, the verification of this specific speech event. The bulk of the task at hand, of course, lies in agreeing on such criteria for verification. It has been said that performative speech cannot be subjected to the categories "true or false," rather it either succeeds or fails.[44] Though this distinction may not hold in all cases, it is relevant for the testing of doxology specifically when the practice of doxology is seen to be the encounter of praise with God. Doxology cannot be authenticated as doxology by testing methods and criteria from outside itself (for example, by the question of its informational value, of its correspondence to the "truths" of the natural sciences, its psychologically stabilizing function, or its motivation for action). Doxology must be tested as the event it claims to be: the doxological encounter between God and humankind. Thus, the testing of doxology leads back to its essential characteristics: the claim that doxology is the encounter of praise with God has to be taken at face value.

But how does doxology authenticate itself as the encounter of praise between God and humankind? It does so, not the least of all, by resisting false objects for praise, and by avoiding the ever-present dangers of idolatry and self-glorification. This may sound strange initially, but the significance of these very real dangers (and of resisting them) is readily apparent in the "covenantal grammar" of the Old Testament as expressed in the Decalogue. The first three commandments can be read as a description of doxology as the encounter of praise with God and of its potential shortcomings (liturgical overtones are obvious in the passage):

> I am the LORD your God, who brought you out of the land of Egypt, out of the house of slavery; you shall have no other gods before me.

You shall not make for yourself an idol, whether in the form of anything that is in heaven above, or that is on the earth beneath, or that is in the water under the earth. You shall not bow down to them or worship them; for I the LORD your God am a jealous God, punishing children for the iniquity of parents, to the third and the fourth generation of those who reject me, but showing steadfast love to the thousandth generation of those who love me and keep my commandments.

You shall not make wrongful use of the name of the LORD your God, for the LORD will not acquit anyone who misuses his name. (Exod. 20:2-7)

The speech event of doxology seems, through such negative preconditions (which in the Exodus text are clearly understood as a gift of salvation), to be a protected space where God can be acknowledged and adored and where the people of God experience salvation. That the space for this encounter must be defined and protected suggests that the encounter of praise with God is no magical formulation by which doxology always succeeds and never fails. Doxology must authenticate itself, and it does so by establishing a space for the encounter of praise with God and protecting it against threats from the outside such as magic, idolatry, and self-glorification. Of course, doxology is not primarily utilitarian in nature and therefore not easily authenticated. The determining question asked of utilitarian acts is simply, does it accomplish its agenda? Doxology, in principle,[45] has no agenda and is validated by its own authenticity.

The agenda-free function of doxology also requires an affirmative answer to the question: would God be God without the praise of humankind?[46] The Christian tradition has emphasized an affirmative response by recognizing the angels' (and all of creation's) adoration of God. Doxological speech is agenda-free especially insofar as it does not first have to create the One to be adored. Similarly, doxology does not provide God with anything God lacks but rather acknowledges that which is characteristic of God.[47] But perhaps such questions should not be asked at all. They in no way reflect the reality that God Godself establishes and desires this relationship of adoration. The question as to whether God "needs" this relationship is irrelevant in light of God's loving desire, which called this relationship into being.

168

The reader is again reminded that doxology is not an autarchical language game but rather complements other forms of the language of faith. If in seeking criteria for validation the critical reflection of theological study offers itself to doxology, the question as to authenticating tests moves doxology into the vicinity of the moral life of believers. It would, however, be an oversimplification to make ethical behavior the test for true doxology. In fact, doxology and ethical posture are two different human responses to the saving acts of God, each with its own operative principles. Thus, when testing the authenticity of doxology, ethical posture is a related concern, but it will not be determinative. Doxology has its own authenticating tests to withstand which, in a sense, complement the authenticating tests of ethical posture. Thus, at most the question as to the *correspondence* between these two areas would be seen as legitimate for testing the authenticity of doxology. The service (i.e., worship) of God and the service of humankind are related to each other, but (according to ancient Christological wisdom) they are at the same time inseparable and unconfused. One cannot exist without the other, neither can one replace or neutralize the other. Perhaps this can be taken one step further. In the same way that doxology is able to express more "truths" than theological assertions, so doxology is able to embody more than one's own broken life ever will. We will always evidence only fragmentarily in our words and in our deeds that which doxology anticipates and into which it draws us. In this sense doxology is more like a constant call to and critique of ethical values, rather than ethical values being the measure by which doxological speech is authenticated. It is likely that no *one* specific area of human response to the saving acts of God would provide a balanced test of authenticity for all the others. The authenticating test for all lies in the complementary nature of the various tests.

One more observation needs to be made as regards the truth of doxological speech: even if one accepts as an authenticating criterion the question of whether doxology succeeds or fails, and denies categories of "true and false," the question of the authenticity of doxology points in the final analysis to God. God Godself is the authentication of the truth expressed by doxology,[48] for God creates the relationship that doxology embodies and celebrates. In other words, it is the very Spirit of God at prayer in us,[49] the *testimonium sancti spiritus internum*, that authenticates this prayer. This is cer-

169

tainly the witness of the early church as encountered in the New Testament. This church understood its prayer, praise, and song as inspired by the Holy Spirit, and therefore primarily as the work of God and not of humankind. Adoration of God occurs in spirit and in truth (John 4:23): "be filled with the Spirit, as you sing psalms and hymns and spiritual songs among yourselves, singing and making melody to the Lord in your hearts" (Eph. 5:18-19); "Let the word of Christ dwell in you richly; teach and admonish one another in all wisdom; and with gratitude in your hearts sing psalms, hymns and spiritual songs to God" (Col. 3:16).

Doxology as the pneumatic, transfigured, anticipatory "last" word therefore in one sense distances itself from the tests of authenticity and from verification of other speech events. For the believer, however, who embraces doxological speech as the embodiment of the encounter of praise with God, doxology is validated precisely by its ability to approach the holy and mysterious One with the language of transcendence and transfiguration. At the same time, while doxology is authenticated by the mystery it embodies, its own authentication of that mystery is never complete. In this sense perhaps one is justified in seeking an "eschatological authentication and verification" of doxology. As the *doxa* of God shines forth in doxology—in fullness at the end of time—so doxology is authenticated. This shining forth of the praise of God is the very substance, value, and honor of doxology: it is a space for the presence of God and the encounter of God's being. "You [God] are holy, enthroned on the praises of Israel," sings the psalmist (Ps. 22:3). Believers and their community of faith, the church, for that reason can never forsake doxology. It is, after all, an explicit encounter—in praise—with their God.

D. "Audemus dicere . . . ": *Doxological Speech and Theological Reflection*

Thus far, this study has attempted, in light of a review of the scholarly discussion (part 1) and the special study of early Methodism's hymnody (part 2) to identify the essential characteristics, criteria for legitimacy, and tests of authenticity for doxological speech. The question remains, given our assumed description of doxology: what is the relationship of doxological speech to theological reflection? The final section of this study is devoted to the discussion of this question. A criteriology of doxological speech will not be developed here; this study was not designed for such. Other studies of other doxological traditions must be undertaken before such a criteriology could be developed.

This study has assumed the constitutive multilingual nature of faith or of the faithful in which doxological speech and theological reflection are seen as two basic forms of human response to the saving acts of God. The whole of faith, however, will only find expression in the blending of all the different forms of faithful response to God's history with humankind. Such a characterization of this study's starting point already suggests certain similarities and differences between doxological speech and theological reflection. A close connection between doxological speech and theological reflection can be asserted when the larger context in which they exist is observed. Both doxology and theology are statements of faith that assume faithful response to the saving acts of God. Both find in the saving acts of God the address to which they respond. They share, however, not only this common point of reference but also a common "speaker," namely, the people of God called upon to respond to God. After all, it is not that one part of the believing community distances itself from prayer for the purpose of theological reflection while the other prays (without reflection). Both activities are owned by the entire people of God, though obviously with differing intensity.

Whether or not it can be said that doxology and theology have a common goal depends on the context in which such a unity might be posited. Certainly the direct intention of doxology and theology would suggest that each has a goal distinct from the other. Doxology as the agenda-free praise of God is clearly distinguished from theology as the constructive and critical reflection on the history of God with humankind. A broader context might suggest, however, a certain unity between these two, indeed between all forms of faithful response to God. Without falling prey to doxological fundamentalism, this broader context seems to be indicated by the Letter to the Ephesians: "so that that we . . . might live for the praise of his glory" (Eph. 1:12; cf. also 1:6, 14). From this vantage point, "that we might live for the praise of his glory," the goals of doxology and theology coincide. More specifically, it could be asserted, in this context, that theological reflection is *subsumed* by doxology. The eschatological vision for the end of time in the Christian tradition has consistently

171

maintained that all of creation will join in the unceasing adoration of God (see the image of the New Jerusalem, depicted in the Revelation to John, as a place of constant worship; cf. Rev. 4–5; 11:15-19; 15; 19). This context also allows for a (better) understanding of Peter Brunner's statement in which he characterizes hymns as "the eternal and final *Gestalt* of *theologia*."[50] This broader context, which goes beyond the apparent and immediate intention of both speech forms, allows for a common end of both doxology and theology insofar as doxology becomes the overriding goal of all theology.[51] It must be added, however, that this broader context has indeed moved beyond the specific intention of each speech form.

The shared qualities of doxology and theology as forms of faithful response to the saving acts of God indicate important concurrences between the two.[52] There are many examples of the interdependence of doxology/liturgy and theology as encountered through the history of the church and the development of dogma: the importance of doxological formulae in the Christological debates, the influence of the battle over semi-Pelagianism on several prayers in the Roman liturgy, and the traces of the Adoptionist controversy in the Mozarabic liturgy. These examples (and the list could go on) demonstrate that doxology and theology stand side by side in this broader context so that developments that affect one necessarily have implications for the other. The concurrence between these two is particularly clear when they are held up against assertions taken from other language games; for example, when doxological and theological statements are compared with those of the natural sciences.

This close connection between doxological speech and theological reflection must be maintained, but not at the expense of the characteristics unique to each. Doxology, as a specific response to the saving acts and presence of God, has its own operative principles distinguished from those of theological reflection. This difference must not be overlooked. In my opinion, it limits the "use" of doxological speech for theology and forbids the direct distillation of dogmatic assertions from doxological speech. In this sense, doxology is hardly a *locus theologicus* and certainly not "prayed dogma." Neither, in this sense, does a "theology in hymns" exist. It should not be forgotten, in this context, that theological reflection on doxology is typically geared to doxological *texts*. This means, however, that the theologian is never confronted by the actual event of doxology. She typically confronts the text, which functions as an aid, a relic, and little more in the doxological event itself. The theologian could be led to believe that the doxological speech event reflected in the text might be appropriated with little difficulty. But like the musicologist who assumes she understands the entire symphony based on a single musician's score, she is mistaken. The doxological text is but a small part of the doxological event, and it is impossible to study the nature of doxology based on texts alone.[53] This kind of theological approach to doxology is limited and reductionist in nature.

Some may argue that theological reflection can be brought to bear on the doxological event as such and thus, in fact, finds its primary orientation in the event and not the text. But, since theology, in the strict sense of the word, is suspended within the actual doxological event,[54] the *genus* "doxology" is violated when the encounter of praise with God is transformed into a theological question-and-answer session. Does this mean that all scholarly theological analysis of doxology is impossible? Of course not, and I hope this study makes that clear! I do not mean to suggest that doxology and doxological texts have no theological implications,[55] or that they might not be analyzed for their theological content. Such theological analyses of doxological material are absolutely appropriate and necessary, and I have pursued such an analysis of Wesleyan hymnody in this study. Dietrich Ritschl's term "implicit theology" may be helpful here to describe the sense in which doxology might be said to be theological, as long as the reader is reminded that this term does not suggest that the *genus* "theological reflection" applies to doxological statements. The differentiation between the theological understanding of particular material and the material itself must be maintained. Theological reflection on doxological texts that appreciates this differentiation is certainly possible. But the theological study of doxological material does not turn the theological study itself into a doxology (as suggested in the term "doxological theology"), nor does it change the doxology into a theology (as suggested in the term "prayed dogma"). The proposed material for any given study and the manner of study have to be clearly distinguished from each other, even when the material makes certain demands on (and thus influences) the nature of the study.

Still little has been said thus far about the specific relationship of theology to doxology. After all, almost anything in the world can be subjected to theological reflection. But can theology actually appropriate doxology as a *locus theologicus?* That is a very different matter. Theological interpretation, the subject matter considered, and its appropriateness as a *locus theologicus* are three distinctly different categories that should not be confused. Still, the possible appropriateness of doxology as a source for theology does not have to be denied altogether. Doxology as the encounter of praise with God is also an encounter with truth—although under doxology's own operative principles. This is particularly true for doxology as a theologically responsible speech act in the liturgy ("liturgical speech" as opposed to "the language of devotion"), which is, after all, an important part of the church's tradition. However, even here theology must bear in mind the peculiar character of doxology and approach it as such.

Doxology cannot become a source for theology by being stripped of its essential and defining characteristics and operative principles but rather only by radically bringing these to light. If this is not done, the theological demands on doxology become inappropriate (read: doxology is not treated as doxology), and theological mistakes become inevitable. Edmund Schlink cites an example of such a failure that he attributes to "structural changes" between doxology and theology as they pertain to the doctrine of predestination: "Instead of a thankful recognition of the abundance of God's grace (which alone can save), and instead of God's eternal loving decree, we are confronted with the problem of determinism, in the face of whose awful logic, the voice of doxology is put to silence. This is what happens when expressions of doxology are isolated and incorporated into the structure of theoretical instruction."[56] Other examples of theological failure with respect to doxology are easily found.

If, however, the essential characteristics and operative principles of doxology are honored and taken seriously, then doxology may readily be characterized as a *locus theologicus,* as the source and goal of all theology, or as the "'margin' of theology."[57] Still such designations should be made cautiously at this point. Similarly, any discussion of doxology as *theologia prima,* or of the call for a "poetical"[58] and "doxological theology," as well as any talk of a "kneeling theology" [59] must very carefully define on which level they locate

174

commonalities between these two basic forms of faithful response to the saving acts of God.

Clearly this relationship between doxological speech and theological reflection has developed with varying intensity throughout the history of the church and the different denominations. Dangers persist when doxology pulls away from theological reflection altogether or when theology no longer recognizes that it speaks of the God whom doxology praises[60] (a danger not always successfully avoided by Western theology). Whenever aberrant developments (theological or doxological) separate doxology from theology, the two must be brought together again. This is also a liturgical and ecumenical question that should be carefully considered, particularly inasmuch as it might challenge the methodology of much recent ecumenical dialogue—but this is for another study. The ecumenical relevance of my study is readily apparent and suggests that perhaps the time has come to question the focus on the dogmatic traditions of the churches as it characterizes many ecumenical dialogues. The concentration on the dogmatic problem is not able to appropriate the ecumenial potential of the multilingual nature of faith—simply note the "hidden ecumenicity" in the hymnbook traditions of the church. Moreover, the danger exists, that ecumenical consensus (based primarily on doctrinal concurrence) will be isolated within a multilingual faith community and therefore will not survive. Recognizing this danger, several of the new ecumenical consensus documents rely significantly on the liturgical-doxological traditions of the churches (and not simply the liturgical texts but the liturgical event as a whole) for theological reflection.

Much study, however, remains to be done, in my opinion, on the doxological traditions of the divided churches particularly in view of the relationship of liturgy to ecumenism, or, as the case may be, of liturgiology to ecumenical theology. The results of this study indicate that the ecumenical struggle cannot focus primarily on the dogmatic texts of the divided churches. The scope must be broadened to include prayer books and hymnbooks, even the actual event of the people of God at worship preserved in and guided by these texts.

The closing words of this study are taken from the liturgy, the communal doxology of the people of God throughout the centuries. These words are found in the Eucharistic liturgy as the introduction to the fundamental prayer of all Christians and capture decisive aspects of both doxological *and* theological speech. The assembly, in the Roman Catholic liturgy, is invited as follows to pray the Lord's Prayer: "Jesus taught us to call God our Father, and so we have the courage to pray [Latin: *audemus dicere*]: Our Father." The Lord's Prayer then follows. This short formulation invites the assembled people of God to risk doxological *and* theological speech. While both must be *risked* (and we would do well never to take one up without the other), it is not a risk in vain: After all, it is the Spirit of Jesus Christ who invites us to risk speech to and about God. Thus, both theology and doxology can be prefixed by this Eucharistic claim: *audemus dicere*, we are bold to say.

Notes

PART I

Chapter 1: Definition of the Theme

1. A. Stenzel, "Liturgie als theologischer Ort," in *Mysterium Salutis. Vol. 1: Die Grundlagen heilsgeschichtlicher Dogmatik*, ed. J. Feiner and M. Löhrer (Einsiedeln: Benziger, 1965), 614, n. 16.

2. M. B. Merz, "Gebetsformen der Liturgie," in *Gottesdienst der Kirche: Handbuch der Liturgiewissenschaft. Vol. 3: Gestalt des Gottesdienstes*, ed. H. B. Meyer et al. (Regensburg: Pustet, 1987) 107; cf. J. A. Jungmann, "Doxologie," in *Lexikon für Theologie und Kirche*, 3 (1959, 2d ed.), 534: "short hymn-like phrases of praise at the close of any confession of faith or prayer."

3. See A. Stuiber, "Doxologie," *Reallexikon für Antike und Christentum* 4 (1959):210.

4. See R. Deichgräber, "Formeln, liturgische II. Neues Testament und Alte Kirche," *Theologische Realenzyklopädie* 11 (1983):258.

5. On the choice of the word *speech* (German: *Rede*) see B. Welte, "Religiöse Sprache," *Archiv für Liturgiewissenschaft* 15 (1973):7-20.

6. D. Ritschl, *Memory and Hope: An Inquiry Concerning the Presence of Christ* (New York: Macmillan; London: Collier-MacMillan, 1967), 169. Marquardt takes this even further in his "Theologie des Gotteslobs," in *Theologie des Gotteslobs*, ed. M. Weyer (Stuttgart: Christliches Verlagshaus, 1991), 7: "We understand 'the praise of God' to include all of those expressions through which the faithful honor God."

7. Both of these terms have been formed under the influence of Romano Guardini's distinction between *Kultbild* and *Andachtsbild*; see his brief work *Kultbild und Andachtsbild: Brief an einen Kunsthistoriker* (Würzburg: Werkbund-Verlag, n.d.). The kind of distinctions made by Guardini in this work with respect to *Kultbild* and *Andachtsbild*, however, do not seem to be helpful for the distinction I have made between "cultic speech" and the "language of devotion."

8. See Merz, "Gebetsformen der Liturgie," 109; C. Mohrmann, "Sakralsprache und Umgangssprache," *Archiv für Liturgiewissenschaft* 10 (1968):344-54.

9. See H. Becker, "Einleitung," in *Liturgie und Dichtung. Ein interdisziplinäres Kompendium. Vol. 1: Historische Präsentation*, ed. H. Becker and R. Kaczynski (St. Ottilien: EOS, 1983), 3.

10. See J. Pascher, "Theologische Erkenntnis aus der Liturgie," in *Einsicht und Glaube (Festschrift for G. Söhngen)*, ed. J. Ratzinger and H. Fries (Freiburg i. B.: Herder, 1962), 247.

11. See, for example, the book *Theologie in Hymnen: Theologische Perspektiven der byzantinischen Liturgie* (Trier: Paulinus-Verlag, 1973) by Julius Tyciak, which is dedicated to a theological interpretation of the Byzantine liturgy. S T Kimbrough, Jr. postulates, in his article "Hymns are Theology," *Theology Today* 42 (1985):59-68, an even closer relationship between theology and hymns than suggested by the title of Tyciak's book.

12. Important material on this point is to be found in M. Seckler's "Theologie als Glaubenswissenschaft," in *Handbuch der Fundamentaltheologie. Vol. 4: Traktat Theologische Erkenntnislehre*, ed. W. Kern et al. (Freiburg i.B.: Herder, 1988), 180-241.

13. The first three reports of the Joint Commission (Denver Report 1971, Dublin Report 1976, Honolulu Report 1981) were published in *Growth in Agreement: Reports and Agreed Statements of Ecumenical Conversations on a World Level,* ed. H. Meyer and L. Vischer (New York: Paulist Press; Geneva: WCC, 1984); for my point, see especially 310, 321, 325, 352, and 354. The fourth (1986) and fifth (1991) reports were published separately.

14. *Growth in Agreement,* 309; Marquardt concurs on the theology of John and Charles Wesley in "Theologie des Gotteslobs," 9.

15. *Growth in Agreement,* 309. (The published text seems to include a printing error. The word *only* appears where the word *soul* should be.)

16. See *Growth in Agreement,* 309, 401.

17. E. Schlink, "Die Struktur der dogmatischen Aussage als ökumenisches Problem," *Kerygma und Dogma* 3 (1957):251-306. (Reprinted in *Der kommende Christus und die kirchlichen Traditionen: Beiträge zum Gespräch zwischen den getrennten Kirchen,* 24-79.) English translation: "The Structure of Dogmatic Statements as an Ecumenical Problem," in *The Coming Christ and the Coming Church* (Edinburgh: Oliver & Boyd, 1967), 16.

18. M. Jenny, "'Vocibus unitis': Auch ein Weg zur Einheit," in *Liturgie und Dichtung. Ein interdisziplinäres Kompendium, Vol. 2: Interdisziplinäre Reflexion,* ed. H. Becker and R. Kaczynski (St. Ottilien: EOS, 1983), 173.

19. For greater detail see my "Lex orandi—lex credendi—lex agendi. Auf dem Weg zu einer ökumenisch konsensfähigen Verhältnisbestimmug von Liturgie, Theologie und Ethik," *Archiv für Liturgiewissenschaft* 27 (1985):425-32.

20. This three-fold formula also finds expression in Geoffrey Wainwright's systematic theology, *Doxology. The Praise of God in Worship, Doctrine and Life: A Systematic Theology* (London: Oxford University Press; New York: Oxford University Press, 1980), as "doctrine, worship, and life"; and in the systematic theology of Frans Jozef van Beeck, *God Encountered: A Contemporary Catholic Systematic Theology,* vol. 1 (San Francisco: Harper & Row, 1989), as "cult, conduct, and creed."

Chapter 2: Doxology and Theology

1. For an overview with quite different emphases from mine, see K. W. Irwin, *Liturgical Theology: A Primer* (Collegeville, Minn.: Liturgical Press, 1990), 18-63.

2. This phrase, composed by Tiro Prosper of Aquitaine under the influence of Augustine's writing, is found in the "Indiculus de Gratia Dei" 8 (*Patrologia Latina* 51, 209f) also referred to as *Capitula Coelestini* (according to the supposed author Pope Celestin I).

3. For a more detailed account of Augustine's position, see J. A. Vinel, "L'argument liturgique opposé par Saint Augustin aux Pélagiens," *Questions Liturgiques* 68 (1987):209-41, and for a look at the early Church Fathers in general see B. Capelle, "Autorité de la liturgie chez les Pères," *Recherches de théologie ancienne et médievale* 21 (1954):5-22.

4. See George Tyrrell's books *Lex Orandi, or Prayer and Creed* (the last of Tyrrell's books to appear with an imprimatur) and *Lex Credendi, a Sequel to Lex Orandi.*

5. Now found in: G. Tyrrell, *Through Scylla and Charybdis, or: the Old Theology and the New* (London: Longmans, Green and Co., 1907), 85-105, under the title "Lex Orandi, Lex Credendi."

6. See H. A. P. Schmidt, "Lex orandi lex credendi in recentioribus documentis pontificiis," *Periodica de re morali canonica liturgica* 40 (1951):5-28.

7. Pius XII, "Mediator Dei," *Acta Apostolicae Sedis* 39 (1947):521-600, 541.

8. See W. Dürig, "Zur Interpretation des Axioms 'Legem credendi lex statuat supplicandi,'" *Veritati catholicae (Festschrift for L. Scheffczyk)*, ed. A. Ziegenaus et al. (Aschaffenburg: Pattloch, 1985), 226-36.

9. See J. Brinktrine, "Die Liturgie als dogmatische Erkenntnisquelle," *Ephemerides liturgicae* 43 (1929):44-51; similarly see J. Brinktrine, "Der dogmatische Beweis aus der Liturgie," *Scientia sacra (Festschrift for K. J. Schulte)* (Köln: J. P. Bachem; Düsseldorf: L. Schwann, 1935), 231-51.

10. For example see K. Adam, "Die dogmatischen Grundlagen der christlichen Liturgie," *Wissenschaft und Weisheit* 4 (1937):43-54; M. Cappuyns, "Liturgie et théologie," *Questions liturgiques et paroissiales* 19 (1934):249-72; A. Eguiluz, "Lex orandi, lex credendi," *Verdad y Vida* 6 (1948):45-67; J. de Castro Engler, "Lex Orandi, Lex Credendi," *Revista eclesiástica brasileira* 11 (1951):23-43; P. Oppenheim, "Liturgie und Dogma," *Theologie und Glaube* 27 (1935):559-68, for greater detail see his book, *Principia theologiae liturgicae* (Turin: Marietti, 1947); M. Pinto, *O valor teológico da liturgia* (Braga: Cruz, 1952); T. Vaquero, "Valor Dogmatico da Liturgia ou Relações Entre Liturgia e Fé," *Revista eclesiástica brasileira* 9 (1949):346-63; A. Vonier, "The Doctrinal Power of the Liturgy in the Catholic Church," *Clergy Review* 9 (1935):1-8; W. de Vries, "Lex supplicandi - lex credendi," *Ephemerides liturgicae* 47 (1933):48-58.

11. This catchphrase seems to have been met with approval in the high church movement of the Lutheran Church as well. See F. O. Schöfer, "Die Liturgie als gebetetes Dogma," *Eine Heilige Kirche* 17 (1935):111-15; similarly see P. Schorlemmer, "Der liturgische Charakter der dogmatischen Theologie," *Eine Heilige Kirche* 17 (1935):115-21.

12. This statement has been transmitted orally—see K. Lehmann, "Gottesdienst als Ausdruck des Glaubens. Plädoyer für ein neues Gespräch zwischen Liturgiewissenschaft und dogmatischer Theologie," *Liturgisches Jahrbuch* 30 (1980):197-214, 199. See also C. Vagaggini, *Theological Dimensions of the Liturgy: A General Treatise on the Theology of the Liturgy* (Collegeville, Minn.: Liturgical Press, 1976); from the Fourth Italian Edition, revised and augmented by the author, 512-41.

13. See J. B. Umberg, "Liturgischer Stil und Dogmatik," *Scholastik* 1 (1926):481-503.

14. See J. Pascher, "Theologische Erkenntnis aus der Liturgie," 246.

15. For example see I.-H. Dalmais, "La liturgie comme lieu théologique," in *La Maison-Dieu* 78 (1964):97-105; and I.-H. Dalmais, "The Liturgy and the Deposit of Faith," vol. 1 of *The Church at Prayer*, ed. A. G. Martimort (New York: Desclée Co., 1968), 212-19; A. Stenzel, "Liturgie als theologischer Ort," 606-20; G. Lukken, "La liturgie comme lieu théologique irremplaçable," *Questions liturgiques et paroissiales* 56 (1975):97-112; see also his more recent article, "Plaidoyer pour une approche intégrale de la liturgie comme lieu théologique: Un défi à toute la théologie," *Questions liturgiques et paroissiales* 68 (1987):242-55; D. N. Power, "Two Expressions of Faith: Worship and Theology," *Liturgical Experience of Faith*, Concilium Series, vol. 82 (New York: Herder and Herder, 1973), 95-106.

16. Note especially the studies of Karl Federer, *Liturgie und Glaube: "Legem credendi lex statuat supplicandi": Eine theologiegeschichtliche Untersuchung* (Freiburg i. d. S.: Paulusverlag, 1950). See also G. Schückler, "Legem credendi lex statuat supplicandi: Ursprung und Sinn des Liturgiebeweises," *Catholica* 10 (1955):26-41; and P. de Clerk, "'Lex orandi, lex credendi': Sens originel et avatars historiques d'un adage équivoque," *Questions liturgiques et paroissiales* 59 (1978):193-212; who build on but also deepen Federer's conclusions with respect to the nature and use of Prosper's axiom.

17. See Arno Schilson's study of Odo Casel's *Mysterientheologie: Theologie als Sakramententheologie: Die Mysterientheologie Odo Casels* (Mainz: Matthias-Grünewald-Verlag, 1982); see also B. Neunheuser, "Der Beitrag der Liturgie zur theologischen Erneuerung," *Gregorianum* 50 (1969):589-614.

18. For example, see E. Schillebeeckx, "The Liturgy and Theology," in *Revelation and Theology* (New York: Sheed and Ward, 1967), 1:218-22. See also the lecture of the dogmatic theologian, Winfred Gruber, *Der Beitrag der Dogmatik zur Liturgischen Bewegung* (Graz: Akademische Druck- und Verlagsanstalt, 1959). Thematically similar in content is C. Davis, *Liturgy and Doctrine: The Doctrinal Basis of the Liturgical Movement* (New York: Sheed and Ward, 1960), 25-120.

19. K. Lehmann, "Gottesdienst als Ausdruck des Glaubens. Plädoyer für ein neues Gespräch zwischen Liturgiewissenschaft und dogmatischer Theologie," 197-214.

20. For example see W. Kasper, "Die Wissenschaftspraxis der Theologie," in *Handbuch der Fundamentaltheologie. Vol. 1: Traktat Theologische Erkenntnislehre*, ed. W. Kern et al. (Freiburg i. B.: Herder, 1988), 244: "Theologie als gedachte Liturgie." Arno Schilson, in his recent article "'Gedachte Liturgie' als Mystagogie. Überlegungen zum Verhältnis von Dogmatik und Liturgie," in *Dogma und Glaube. Bausteine für eine theologische Erkenntnislehre (Festschrift for W. Kasper)*, ed. E. Schockenhoff and P. Walter (Mainz: Matthias-Grünewald-Verlag, 1982), 213-34, looks critically at this phrase coined by Walter Kasper.

21. For a detailed review of this book see T. Maas-Ewerd, "Die Liturgie in der Theologie: Zur letzten Festgabe für Emil Joseph Lengeling (18.6. 1986)," *Liturgisches Jahrbuch* 38 (1988):173-89.

22. H. Vorgrimler, "Liturgie als Thema der Dogmatik," in *Liturgie - ein vergessenes Thema der Theologie?* ed. K. Richter (Freiburg i. B.: Herder, 1987, [2d ed.]), 118.

23. Vorgrimler, "Liturgie als Thema der Dogmatik," 125.

24. K. Richter, "Die Liturgie - zentrales Thema der Theologie," in *Liturgie - ein vergessenes Thema der Theologie?* 9-27.

25. M.-J. Krahe, "'Psalmen, Hymnen und Lieder, wie der Geist sie eingibt': Doxologie als Ursprung und Ziel aller Theologie," in *Liturgie und Dichtung: Ein interdisziplinäres Kompendium. Vol. 2: Interdisziplinäre Reflexion*, ed. H. Becker and R. Kaczynski (St. Ottilien: EOS, 1983), 940.

26. A. Kavanagh, *On Liturgical Theology* (New York: Pueblo, 1985), 75. Similar statements from the perspective of liturgiology are surfacing more frequently in recent times; for example see A. M. Triacca, "Le sens théologique de la liturgie et/ou le sens liturgique de la théologie: Esquisse initiale pour une synthèse" in *La Liturgie, son sens, son ésprit, sa méthode: Liturgie et théologie*, ed. A. Pistoia and A. M. Triacca (Rome: CLV Edizioni liturgiche, 1982), 330-34.

27. Kavanagh, *On Liturgical Theology*, 126.

28. Kavanagh, *On Liturgical Theology*, 146.

29. L. Lies, "Theologie als eulogisches Handeln," *Zeitschrift für Katholische Theologie* 107 (1985):76-91.

30. E. J. Kilmartin, *Systematic Theology of Liturgy*, vol. 1 of *Christian Liturgy: Theology and Practice* (Kansas City: Sheed and Ward, 1988), 97.

31. C. M. LaCugna, "Can Liturgy ever again become a Source for Theology?" *Studia Liturgica* 19 (1989):1-13; see especially page 3.

32. See also the volume published by Herman Schmidt and David Power, *Liturgical Experience of Faith*, Concilium Series, vol. 82 (1975).

33. R. Schaeffler, *Religionsphilosophie* (Freiburg i. B.: K. Alber, 1983), 161. Note Schaeffler's presentation of Wainwright's position, 191-96.

34. See G. Ebeling, *Dogmatik des christlichen Glaubens. Vol. 1: Prolegomena, Teil 1* (Tübingen: Mohr, 1979), 44-49. Also note Ebeling's essay, "Die Notwendigkeit des christlichen Gottesdienstes," *Zeitschrift für Theologie und Kirche* 67 (1970):232-49.

35. See Ebeling, *Dogmatik des christlichen Glaubens*, 193.

36. See F. Merkel, "Liturgie - ein vergessenes Thema evangelischer Theologie?" in *Liturgie - ein vergessenes Thema der Theologie?*, 33-41. On Brunner, Prenter, and Vajta see D. W. Fagerberg, *What Is Liturgical Theology? A Study in Methodology* (Collegeville, Minn.: Liturgical Press, 1992), 33-41 and 76-102.

37. The German Lutheran, Erhard Griese, indicated a similar direction in his 1969 article, "Perspektiven einer liturgischen Theologie," *Una Sancta* 24 (1969):102-13.

38. For additional contributions of Geoffrey Wainwright see the bibliography at the end of this study.

39. However, Power (see "Doxology: The Praise of God in Worship, Doctrine and Life," *Worship* 55 [1981]: 64) accuses Wainwright of granting the *theolgia secunda* priority over the *theologia prima*.

40. See Wainwright, *Doxology. The Praise of God in Worship, Doctrine and Life: A Systematic Theology*, 240-45.

41. G. Sauter, "Reden von Gott im Gebet," in *Gott nennen: Phänomenologische Zugänge*, ed. B. Casper (Freiburg i. B.: Alber, 1981), 237. Similarly, G. Sauter, "Das Gebet als Wurzel des Redens von Gott," *glaube und lernen* 1 (1986):21-38.

42. On Pannenberg's definition of doxology see J. Drumm, *Doxologie und Dogma: Die Bedeutung der Doxologie für die Wiedergewinnung theologischer Rede in der evangelischen Theologie* (Paderborn: Ferdinand Schöningh, 1991), 191-292. See also the dissertations of Barbara D. Alpern, *The Logic of Doxological Language: A Reinterpretation of Aquinas and Pannenberg on Analogy and Doxology* (Ph. D. thesis, University of Pittsburgh, 1980) and of Elizabeth A. Johnson, *Analogy/Doxology and their Connection with Christology in the Thought of Wolfhart Pannenberg* (Ph.D. thesis, Catholic University, 1981).

43. D. W. Hardy/D. Ford, *Jubilate: Theology in Praise* (London: Darton, Longman & Todd, 1984). North American edition: *Praising and Knowing God* (Philadelphia: Westminster Press, 1985), 108.

44. Many pages of the book cry out for supplemental liturgical material and explanation, especially the sections dealing with the development of the early church's doctrine of the Trinity and Christology, 53-57, 132-34.

45. Hardy/Ford, *Praising and Knowing God*, 168.

46. D. Ritschl, *Memory and Hope: An Inquiry Concerning the Presence of Christ*, (New York: Macmillan; London: Collier-MacMillan, 1967), 169.

47. See G. Müller, "Gebet. VIII. Dogmatische Probleme gegenwärtiger Gebetstheologie," in *Theologische Realenzyklopädie* 12 (1983):84-94. See also the recent work by the Lutheran Gordon W. Lathrop, *Holy Things: A Liturgical Theology* (Minneapolis: Fortress Press, 1993).

48. See the subtitle of R. Mössinger's book, *Zur Lehre des christlichen Gebets: Gedanken über ein vernachlässigtes Thema evangelischer Theologie* (Göttingen: Vandenhoeck & Ruprecht, 1987). Along the same lines see C. Klein, "Das Gebet in der Begegnung zwischen westlicher und ostkirchlicher Theologie und Frömmigkeit," *Kerygma und Dogma* 34 (1988):232-50.

49. G. van der Leeuw, *Sakramentales Denken: Erscheinungsformen und Wesen der außerchristlichen und christlichen Sakramente* (Kassel: J. Stauda, 1959), 175.

50. E. Schlink, *Ökumenische Dogmatik: Grundzüge* (Göttingen: Vandenhoeck & Ruprecht, 1983), 175; similarly Prenter, "Liturgie et dogme," *Revue d'histoire et de*

philosophie religieuses 38 (1958):115-28, and R. Prenter, "Liturgy and Theology," in *Theologie und Gottesdienst: Gesammelte Aufsätze* (Arhus: Aros; Göttingen: Vandenhoeck & Ruprecht, 1977), 139-51.

51. D. Ritschl, *Zur Logik der Theologie: Kurze Darstellung der Zusammenhänge theologischer Grundgedanken* (München: Chr. Kaiser, 1984). English edition: *The Logic of Theology: a Brief Account of the Relationship between Basic Concepts in Theology* (Philadelphia: Fortress Press, 1987), 101.

52. D. E. Saliers, "Theology and Prayer: Some Conceptual Reminders," *Worship* 48 (1974):230. See also his new book *Worship as Theology: Foretaste of Glory Divine* (Nashville: Abingdon Press, 1994).

53. D. B. Stevick, "The Language of Prayer," *Worship* 52 (1978):557; similarly Stevick, "Toward a Phenomenology of Praise," in *Worship Points the Way (Festschrift for M. H. Shepherd)*, ed. M. C. Burson (New York: Seabury Press, 1981), 153.

54. L. L. Mitchell, "The Liturgical Roots of Theology," in *Time and Community (Festschrift for T. J. Talley)*, ed. J. N. Alexander (Washington, D.C.: Pastoral Press, 1990), 253.

55. In addition to the works cited in this paragraph see C. Andronikof, "Dogme et liturgie," in *La Liturgie: Expression de la foi. Conférences Saint-Sèrge, XXVe Semaine D'Etudes Liturgiques, Paris 1978*, ed. A. M. Triacca and A. Pistoia (Rome: CLV Edizioni liturgiche, 1979), 13-27; E. Braniste, "Le culte byzantin comme expression de la foi orthodoxe," in *La Liturgie: Expression de la foi. Conférences Saint-Sèrge, XXVe Semaine d'Etudes Liturgiques, Paris 1978*, 75-88; N. Nissiotis, "La théologie en tant que science et en tant que doxologie," *Irénikon* 33 (1960):291-310; N. Nissiotis, "Österliche Freude als doxologischer Ausdruck des Glaubens," in *Gottes Zukunft - Zukunft der Welt (Festschrift für J. Moltmann)*, ed. H. Deuser (München: Chr. Kaiser, 1986), 78-88; E. Theodorou, "Theologie und Liturgie," in *La théologie dans l'Eglise et dans le monde* (Chambésy: Centre orthodoxe du Patriarcat oecuménique, 1984), 343-60.

56. A. Kallis, "Theologie als Doxologie: Der Stellenwert der Liturgie in der orthodoxen Kirche und Theologie," in *Liturgie - ein vergessenes Thema der Theologie?* 50.

57. See M. M. Garijo-Guembe, "Überlegungen für einen Dialog zwischen Orthodoxie und Katholizismus im Hinblick auf den Satz 'Lex orandi - lex credendi,'" in *Liturgie - ein vergessenes Thema der Theologie?* 136f.

58. See Julius Tyciak, *Theologie in Hymnen: Theologische Perspektiven der byzantinischen Liturgie* (1973).

59. A. Schmemann, "Theology and Liturgical Tradition," in *Worship in Scripture and Tradition*, ed. M. H. Shepherd (New York: Oxford University Press, 1963), 165-78. Reprinted in: *Liturgy and Tradition: Theological Reflections of Alexander Schmemann*, 18; also see A. Schmemann, *Introduction to Liturgical Theology* (Portland, Maine: American Orthodox Press, 1966), 140. See Fagerberg, *What Is Liturgical Theology? A Study in Methodology*, 143-80.

60. Alexander Schmemann's book, *Introduction to Liturgical Theology* and his posthumously published collection of essays, *Liturgy and Tradition* are important works to reference on this point.

61. A. Kallis, "Theologie als Doxologie: Der Stellenwert der Liturgie in der orthodoxen Kirche und Theologie," 51.

62. See, for example, the work of Julie Kirchberg on the dialogue with Judaism, *Theologie in der Anrede als Weg zur Verständigung zwischen Juden und Christen* (Innsbruck: Tyrolia, 1991). The author attempts to point out, in the core prayers of the synagogue liturgy, "speech about God" in the "speech to God," which enables a certain understanding between Jewish theology and Christian theology.

63. For a more complete reference see T. Berger, "Unity in and through Doxology? Reflections on Worship Studies in the World Council of Churches," *Studia Liturgica* 16 (1986–1987):1-12.

64. *Ways of Worship. The Report of a Theological Commission of Faith and Order*, ed. P. Edwall et al. (London: SCM Press, 1951), 23.

65. *Ways of Worship*, 22, 24.

66. "Worship and the Oneness of Christ's Church," in *The Fourth World Conference on Faith and Order. The Report from Montreal 1963*, ed. P. C. Rodger and L. Vischer (London: SCM Press, 1964), 69.

67. "Worship and the Oneness of Christ's Church," 70.

68. *The Mandate from the Fourth World Conference on Faith and Order at Montreal* (Geneva: WCC, 1963), 25.

69. Supporting references found in Berger, "Unity in and through Doxology? Reflections on Worship Studies in the World Council of Churches," 7-9.

70. See P. Lønning, "'Die eucharistische Vision'—eine neue Zusammenschau von Gottesdienst- und Bekenntnisgemeinschaft?" *Una Sancta* 39 (1984):232f.

71. Schlink, "The Structure of Dogmatic Statements as an Ecumenical Problem," 16.

72. For Schlink's justification for the use of this terminology see Schlink, "The Structure of Dogmatic Statements as an Ecumenical Problem," 32. For more on Schlink's definition of doxology see the thorough presentation by J. Drumm, *Doxologie und Dogma: Die Bedeutung der Doxologie für die Wiedergewinnung theologischer Rede in der evangelischen Theologie*, 123-90.

73. Schlink, *Ökumenische Dogmatik: Grundzüge*, vi.

74. See E. Schlink, "Changes in Protestant Thinking about the Eastern Church," in *The Coming Christ and the Coming Church*, 269-84.

75. See E. Schlink, "Law and Gospel as a Controversial Theological Problem," in *The Coming Christ and the Coming Church*, 164-85.

76. Schlink, "The Structure of Dogmatic Statements as an Ecumenical Problem," 42.

77. Schlink, *Ökumenische Dogmatik: Grundzüge*, vi; see E. Chr. Suttner, "Glaubensverkündigung durch Lobpreis: Zur Interpretation der byzantinischen gottesdienstlichen Hymnen," in *Unser ganzes Leben Christus unserm Gott überantworten: Studien zur ostkirchlichen Spiritualität (Festschrift for F. von Lilienfeld)*, ed. P. Hauptmann (Göttingen: Vandenhoeck & Ruprecht, 1982), 79.

78. E. Schlink, "Die Aufgaben einer ökumenischen Dogmatik," in *Zur Auferbauung des Leibes Christi (Festschrift for P. Brunner)*, ed. E. Schlink and A. Peters (Kassel: J. Stauda, 1965), 93; see also E. Schlink, "Die Methode des dogmatischen ökumenischen Dialogs," *Kerygma und Dogma* 12 (1966):209f.

79. E. Schlink, "Die Aufgaben einer ökumenischen Dogmatik," in *Zur Auferbauung des Leibes Christi (Festschrift for P. Brunner)*, 87.

80. See, for example, M. Jenny, "'Vocibus unitis': Auch ein Weg zur Einheit," 174f.

81. See Wainwright, *Doxology. The Praise of God in Worship, Doctrine and Life: A Systematic Theology*, 303-8.

82. H.-J. Schulz, *Ökumenische Glaubenseinheit aus eucharistischer Überlieferung* (Paderborn: Verlag Bonifacius-Druckerei, 1976) 8, n. 6. When referencing Schlink, Schulz notes, at the same time, the influence of Eucharistic ecclesiology in his own thinking.

83. This is easily demonstrated by way of recent ecumenical consensus documents, which, generally, accord the liturgical traditions increasing attention; see

T. Berger, "Die Liturgie im Gespräch der Kirchen. Ein Überblick über neue ökumenische Dialoge auf Weltebene," in *Christus Spes (Festschrift for S. Kraft)*, ed. A. Berlis and K. D. Gerth (Frankfurt: Peter Lang, 1994), 39-45.

84. H. Oliphant Old, *Themes and Variations for a Christian Doxology: Some Thoughts on the Theology of Worship* (Grand Rapids: W. B. Eerdmans, 1992), 15.

PART II

Chapter 3: Theology in Hymns?

1. See J. L. Nuelsen, *John Wesley and the German Hymn: A Detailed Study of John Wesley's Translations of thirty-three German Hymns* (Keighley: Mantissa Press, 1972).

2. *A Collection of Hymns for the Use of the People Called Methodists*, ed. Franz Hildebrandt and Oliver A. Beckerlegge with James Dale, vol. 7 of *The Works of John Wesley* (New York: Oxford University Press, 1983; Nashville: Abingdon Press, 1989), hereafter referred to as *Collection*, 231:1.

3. Nuelsen, *John Wesley and the German Hymn*, 108. (I have adapted the spelling to more contemporary German.)

4. The importance of this experience is unclear in the writings of John Wesley and even less so in the secondary literature. Whether the experience of May 1738 is to be interpreted as the main event or as but a part of an ongoing chain of religious "conversions," one thing is certain—it was not until the so-called Aldersgate experience of John (May 24, 1738) and the Pentecost Day experience of Charles (May 21, 1738) that the Wesleys became the leaders of a rapidly growing renewal movement.

5. *The Journal of the Rev. Charles Wesley: The Early Journal, 1736–1739*, ed. J. Telford (London: Culley, 1910; reprint ed., Taylors, S.C.: The Methodist Reprint Society, 1977), 149.

6. See M. Schmidt, "Luthers Vorrede zum Römerbrief im Pietismus," in *Wiedergeburt und neuer Mensch: Gesammelte Studien zur Geschichte des Pietismus* (Witten: Luther-Verlag, 1969), 299-330.

7. John Wesley, *Journal and Diaries I*, vol. 18 of *The Works of John Wesley*, ed. W. R. Ward and R. P. Heitzenrater (Nashville: Abingdon Press, 1988), 249f.

8. *Collection*, 29:1.

9. *Collection*, 193:1. A third hymn, "Hymn for Whitsunday," appears to be directly connected with the conversion of Charles Wesley. The text is reproduced in *Charles Wesley: A Reader*, ed. John R. Tyson (New York: Oxford University Press, 1989), 104f.

10. On this see the small book by Ulrich F. Damm, *Die Deutschlandreise John Wesleys: Grund - Orte - Begegnungen* (Stuttgart: Christliches Verlagshaus, 1984). For more on the relationship between Pietism and early Methodism see K. Zehrer, "The Relationship between Pietism in Halle and early Methodism," *Methodist History* 17 (1979):211-24.

11. See R. P. Heitzenrater, "The Quest for the First Methodist: Oxford Methodism Reconsidered," in *Mirror and Memory: Reflections on Early Methodism* (Nashville: Kingswood/Abingdon, 1989), 69-73 and 179f.

12. The best-known example is the hymn "Behold, the Saviour of mankind," written by Samuel Wesley, Sr. and included by John Wesley in the *Collection* of 1780 albeit without the original stanzas 2 and 6:

Behold the Saviour of mankind
   Nail'd to the shameful tree!
How vast the love that Him inclined
   To bleed and die for thee!

Though far unequal our low praise
   To Thy vast sufferings prove,
O Lamb of God, thus all our days
   Thus will be grieve and love.

Hark, how He groans! while nature shakes,
   And earth's strong pillars bend;
The temple's veil in sunder breaks;
   The solid marbles rend.

'Tis done! the precious ransom's paid;
   "Receive my soul," He cries:
See where He bows His sacred head!
   He bows His head and dies!

But soon he'll break death's envious chain,
   and in full glory shine:
O Lamb of God! was ever pain,
   Was ever love like Thine!

Thy loss our ruins did repair,
   Death, by Thy death, is slain;
Thou wilt at length exalt us where
   Thou dost in glory reign.

In L. Tyerman, *The Life and Times of the Rev. Samuel Wesley, Rector of Epworth and Father of the Revs. John and Charles Wesley, the Founders of the Methodists* (London: Simpkin, Marshall, 1866), 328f; see also *Collection,* 22.

13. See O. A. Beckerlegge, "Charles Wesley's Poetical Corpus," in *Charles Wesley: Poet and Theologian,* ed. S T Kimbrough, Jr. (Nashville: Kingswood/Abingdon, 1992), 30-44.

14. See F. Baker, *Charles Wesley's Verse: An Introduction* (London: Epworth Press, 1964 [1st ed.], 1988 [2d ed.]), 5f.

15. See the list of diary entries on Charles Wesley's preaching activity in Tyson's, *Charles Wesley's Theology of the Cross: An Examination of the Theology and Method of Charles Wesley as Seen in His Doctrine of the Atonement* (Ph.D. thesis, Drew University: Madison, N.J., 1983), Appendix A, and the list of his preferred preaching texts in *Charles Wesley Reader,* 487-90. See also W. L. Doughty, "Charles Wesley, Preacher," *London Quarterly and Holborn Review* 182 (1957):263-67.

16. *Charles Wesley Reader,* 481.

17. Thus quoted in *Charles Wesley Reader,* 483.

18. *Collection,* p. 73.

19. See R. Stevenson, "John Wesley's first Hymnbook," *Review of Religion* 14 (1950):140-60, and M. W. England, "The First Wesley Hymn Book," *Bulletin of the New York Public Library* 68 (1964):225-38.

20. For the period before Wesley see L. F. Benson, *The English Hymn: Its Development and Use in Worship* (New York: Hodder & Stoughton, George H. Doran Co., 1915), 73-218.

21. These include among others: "O God, thou bottomless abyss" (Ernst Lange, "O Gott, du Tiefe sondern Grund"); "Jesu, to thee my heart I bow" (Nikolaus Ludwig Graf von Zinzendorf, "Reiner Bräutigam meiner Seelen"); "O Jesu, source of calm repose" (Johann Anastasius Freylinghausen, "Wer ist wohl wie Du"); "Thou Lamb of God, thou Prince of Peace" (Christian Friedrich Richter, "Stilles Lamm und Friedensfürst"); "My soul before thee prostrate lies" (Christian Friedrich Richter, "Hier legt mein Sinn sich vor dir nieder").

22. See O. A. Beckerlegge, "The Development of the 'Collection,'" *Collection*, pp. 22-30 and O. A. Beckerlegge, "The Sources of the 'Collection,'" *Collection*, pp. 31-38 for details.

23. The title indicates the strong ecumenical orientation of the nascent Methodist movement, likely attributable, in no small measure, to the influences of German Pietism.

24. *Collection*, pp. 73f. Wesley's foreword indicates a certain kinship in several places to Freylinghausen's foreword to his *Neues Geistreiches Gesang-Buch* (Halle: Verlegung des Waysenhauses, 1714), a hymnbook Wesley encountered during his travels to Georgia. The German Pietist wrote in his foreword: "Die Ursach, so mich zu dergleichen Arbeit abermal bewogen, ist insgemein, weil Christliche und geistreiche Lieder eines der allerbequemsten Mittel sind, die Erkäntnis Göttlicher Wahrheit und daraus herfliessende wahre Gottseligkeit unter den Menschen zu befordern . . . sowohl aus der Schrift als der Erfahrung."

25. B. Manning, *The Hymns of Wesley and Watts: Five informal Papers* (London: Epworth Press, 1948 [2d ed.]), 14.

26. *Collection*, p. 74. See also John Newton's foreword to the *Olney Hymns*: "I hope most of these hymns, being the fruit and expression of my own experiene, will coincide with the views of real Christians of all denominations" (*Olney Hymns, in Three Books*. [London: W. Oliver, 1779], viii).

27. See Beckerlegge, "John Wesley as Hymn-book Editor," in the *Collection*, p. 58.

28. Included in the *Olney Hymns* were two other sections: "On select Texts of Scripture" and "On occasional Subjects." John Newton wrote the following in his foreword: "The third Book (i.e., section) is miscellaneous, comprising a variety of subjects relative to a life of faith in the Son of GOD, which have no express reference either to a single text of Scripture, or to any determinate season or incident," *Olney Hymns*, xi. See also D. E. Demaray, *The Innovation of John Newton (1725–1807): Synergism of Word and Music in Eighteenth Century Evangelism* (Lewiston, Queenston: E. Mellen Press, 1988), 225-42.

29. See E. Röbbelen, *Theologie und Frömmigkeit im deutschen evangelisch-lutherischen Gesangbuch des 17. und 18. Jahrhunderts* (Göttingen: Vandenhoeck & Ruprecht, 1957), 40-45.

30. *Neues Geistreiches Gesang-Buch*, foreword, n.p. A similar formulation can be found in the so-called *Berliner Gesangbuch* (1708), written by Johann Porst (1668–1728), a Spener Pietist: "according to the order of salvation"; Freylinghausen's *Geistreiches Gesang-Buch* of 1704 claims as its ordering principle that which is "required and produced by the economy of our salvation," thus quoted in A. Völker, "Gesangbuch," in *Theologische Realenzyklopädie* 12 (1984):553f.

31. See Röbbelen, *Theologie und Frömmigkeit im deutschen evangelisch-lutherischen Gesangbuch des 17. und 18. Jahrhunderts*, 286-90.

32. *The Poetical Works of John and Charles Wesley. Reprinted from the Originals, with the Last Corrections of the Authors; together with the Poems of Charles Wesley not before Published,* vol. 1, ed. G. Osborn (London: Wesleyan Methodist Conference Office, 1868–1872), 299-301; cf. *Charles Wesley Reader,* 108f.

33. For example, see the doxological lines at the beginning of the following hymns: "Glory, and praise, and love to Thee," *The Poetical Works of John and Charles Wesley,* vol. 1, 240; "Glory, and thanks, and praise," *The Poetical Works of John and Charles Wesley,* vol. 5, 128; "Glory, honour, thanks, and praise," *The Poetical Works of John and Charles Wesley,* vol. 5, 390. The examples are endless.

34. Nuelsen, *John Wesley and the German Hymn,* 32, refers to the hymn by Johann Mentzer "O daß ich tausend Zungen hätte," in the Moravian hymnbook but disavows any connection with this stanza of Charles Wesley because of the lack of evidence suggesting Wesley had any knowledge of this hymn. This reasoning seems weak. The similarity of the formulations alone could provide a basis on which to explore such a connection, particularly since the Wesleys would have had access to the Moravian hymnbook during their journey to Georgia. On the other hand, the legends that surround the person of Charles Wesley suggest that the hymn's inspiration can be traced to the words of the Moravian, Peter Böhler, who is said to have told Wesley: "If I had a thousand tongues I would use them all to praise God." Naturally, it is also possible that these words of Böhler were an indirect quote of Mentzer's hymn. Such connections will, in all likelihood, never be established beyond doubt.

35. W. F. Lofthouse, "Charles Wesley," in *A History of the Methodist Church in Great Britain. Vol. 1,* ed. R. E. Davies and G. Rupp (London: Epworth Press, 1965), 134.

36. The *Collection* retained the following stanzas of the original: 7-10, 12-14, and 17-18.

37. *The Poetical Works of John and Charles Wesley,* vol. 1, 259f. I cite the first stanza, which ably demonstrates the emotional quality of the entire hymn:

> Jesu, Lover of my soul,
>   Let me to Thy bosom fly,
> While the nearer waters roll,
>   While the tempest still is high:
>
> Hide me, O my Saviour, hide,
>   Till the storm of life is past;
> Safe into the haven guide;
>   O, receive my soul at last.

38. See M. F. Marshall and J. Todd, *English Congregational Hymns in the Eighteenth Century* (Lexington: University Press of Kentucky, 1982), 62: "An unconfident singer learns by example the joys of salvation, while a happy convert is reminded of his or her joyful certainty."

39. This section has been reworked from Berger, "Charles Wesley: A Literary Overview," in *Charles Wesley: Poet and Theologian,* 21-29.

40. One seldom finds works that attempt to deal with both brothers simultaneously. The following should be cited as exceptions: Mabel Richmond Brailsford, *A Tale of Two Brothers: John and Charles Wesley* (1954), where the author operates primarily from a historical perspective; Samuel J. Rogal, *John and Charles Wesley* (1983), which is dedicated to the literary production of the brothers; and, theologi-

cally the most important, the collection edited by Frank Whaling, *John and Charles Wesley: Selected Prayers, Hymns, Journal Notes, Sermons, Letters and Treatises* (1981). One bibliography is available: Betty M. Jarboe, *John and Charles Wesley: A Bibliography* (Metuchen, N.J.: Scarecrow Press, 1987).

41. The mammoth project with its thirty-five planned volumes was begun in 1975 by Oxford University Press under the title *The Oxford Edition of the Works of John Wesley*. Frank Baker functioned as editor-in-chief. Since 1984 the project has been entrusted to Abingdon Press (Nashville, Tennessee) as *The Bicentennial Edition of the Works of John Wesley*. Richard P. Heitzenrater is editor-in-chief. A two-volume interpretive bibliography of the complete works of John Wesley is planned as a part of this series.

42. See the research overview on John Wesley in V. Schneeberger, *Theologische Wurzeln des sozialen Akzents bei John Wesley* (Zürich: Gotthelf-Verlag, 1974), 18. F. E. Maser, "Charles Wesley and His Biographers," *Methodist History* 21 (1990):47 reads the evidence differently.

43. See for example, the first biography of Charles Wesley written by John Whitehead (1793), who was the physician to John Wesley, and the biography by John Telford (1886).

44. The volumes include roughly 4,600 published individual pieces of both Wesleys and approximately 3,000 of the, until then, unpublished texts of Charles Wesley, which, however, did not represent his entire legacy. Also, certain texts published by Osborn were abridged without being identified as having been shortened.

45. This edition of the journal was not complete. Some sixty years later appeared *The Journal of the Rev. Charles Wesley: The Early Journal, 1736–1739*, edited by John Telford. Actually, a three-volume edition of the journal was planned of which only the first volume ever appeared. In 1977 this volume was reprinted under the same title by The Methodist Reprint Society in Taylors, South Carolina.

46. Thus, for example, Franklin Wilder, *The Methodist Riots: The Testing of Charles Wesley* (Great Neck: Todd & Honeywell, 1981). The author concentrates on the struggles of the nascent Methodist movement between the years 1739 and 1756.

47. A. A. Dallimore, *A Heart Set Free: The Life of Charles Wesley* (Westchester, Ill.: Crossway Books, 1988), 73.

48. Wesley's hymns had, of course, received considerable attention in work done on Methodist hymnbooks. See for example, David Creamer's book, *Methodist Hymnology; Comprehending Notices of the Poetical Works of John and Charles Wesley* (New York: Joseph Longking, 1848).

49. See H. Bett, *The Hymns of Methodism* (London: Epworth Press, 1945 [3rd ed., revised]), 2.

50. See Bett, *The Hymns of Methodism*, 129-35.

51. Frank Baker's preliminary work for an edition of the letters of Charles Wesley is also important; see his *Charles Wesley as Revealed by His Letters* (London: Epworth Press, 1948), and "Charles Wesley's Letters," in *Charles Wesley: Poet and Theologian*, 72-84. Some letters are now published in: *Wesley-Langshaw Correspondence: Charles Wesley, his Sons and the Lancaster Organists*, ed. A. W. Wainright (Atlanta: Scholars Press for Emory University, 1993).

52. Among others, see especially Donald Davie and James Dale for this debate. Frederick C. Gill, *The Romantic Movement and Methodism: A Study of English Romanticism and the Evangelical Revival* (London: Epworth Press, 1937 [1st ed.], 1957 [2d ed.]) makes the case for the connection with Romanticism, still more for the influence of Methodism on emerging Romanticism. See also Mark A. Noll, "Roman-

ticism and the Hymns of Charles Wesley," *Evangelical Quarterly* 46 (1974):195-223. See also the chapter "The carnality of Charles Wesley" in Davie's more recent book *The Eighteenth-Century Hymn in England* (Cambridge: Cambridge University Press, 1993), 57-70.

53. See also J. Dale, "Some Echoes of Charles Wesley's Hymns in His Journal," *London Quarterly and Holborn Review* 184 (1992):336-44.

54. A summary is offered by J. R. Tyson, "Charles Wesley's Theology of Redemption: A Study in Structure and Method," *Wesleyan Theological Journal* 20 (1985):7-28.

55. See the (largely critical) review of this book by S T Kimbrough, Jr. in: *Methodist History* 29 (1990):54-58.

56. Also see his article on the influence of Charles Wesley's hymns on *The United Methodist Hymnal:* "Tradition Meets Revision: The Impact of the Wesley Hymn Corpus on the New United Methodist Hymnal," *Quarterly Review* 9 (1989):64-79.

57. Cf. B. E. Bryant, "Trinity and Hymnody: The Doctrine of the Trinity in the Hymns of Charles Wesley," *Wesleyan Theological Journal* 25:2 (1990):64-73. The article gives no indication of the author's awareness of Quantrille's 1989 dissertation.

58. See especially the publications in the series "Beiträge zur Geschichte des Methodismus" and "Beiträge zur Geschichte der Evangelisch-Methodistischen Kirche." In 1992, Charles Wesley's diary for the year 1738 was published in a German translation by Martin Brose.

59. The only German biography of Charles Wesley known to me comes from Karl G. Eißele, *Karl Wesley, Sänger des Methodismus* (Bremen: Anker-Verlag, 1932). To Eißele's credit, he includes in this biography translations of a few chosen Charles Wesley hymns. See also H. Bett, "German Books on Wesley's Hymns," *Proceedings of the Wesley Historical Society* 21 (1938):180-81, which contains a discussion of the books of Eißele and Nuelsen.

60. See Dahn, "Die Hymnologie im deutschsprachigen Methodismus," in *Der Methodismus,* ed. C. E. Sommer (Stuttgart: Evangelisches Verlagswerk, 1968), 166-84.

61. On this theme see also O. A. Beckerlegge, "John Wesley and the German Hymns," *London Quarterly and Holborn Review* 193 (1940):430-39; and H. Bett, "John Wesley's Translations of German Hymns," *London Quarterly and Holborn Review* 165 (1940):288-94. For Charles Wesley, see J. R. Tyson, "Charles Wesley and the German Hymns," *The Hymn* 35 (1984):153-57, where additional literature is listed.

62. See F. Hildebrandt's *From Luther to Wesley* (London: Lutterworth Press, 1951), also his *Christianity According to the Wesleys* (London: Epworth Press, 1956), and the *Wesley Hymn Book* (London: A. Weekes and Co., 1958 [1st ed.], 1960 [2d ed.]), which Hildebrandt edited.

63. At least one article from the abundance of literature in 1988 should be noted here: Frank Baker's "Charles Wesley's Productivity as a Religious Poet," *Proceedings of the Wesley Historical Society* 47 (1989):1-12.

64. See, for example, S T Kimbrough, Jr., *Lost in Wonder. Charles Wesley: The Meaning of His Hymns Today* (Nashville: Upper Room Books, 1987); and Timothy Dudley-Smith's edition, *A Flame of Love: A Personal Choice of Charles Wesley's Verse* (London: Triangle, 1987). J. Alan Kay's, *Wesley's Prayers and Praises* (London: Epworth Press, 1958) is representative of earlier anthologies in this style.

65. See S T Kimbrough, Jr., "Charles Wesley Society," *Methodist History* 29 (1991):251-62.

66. The Society is also in charge of a number of facsimile reprints of hymn collections of Charles Wesley, such as the *Hymns for the Nativity of our Lord,* and the *Hymns for our Lord's Resurrection.*

67. However, see Richard L. Fleming's thesis, *The Concept of Sacrifice in the Eucharistic Hymns of John and Charles Wesley* (D. Min. thesis, Southern Methodist University: Dallas, 1980). As to the latter theme, see also Kathryn Nichols, "Charles Wesley's Eucharistic Hymns: Their Relationship to the Book of Common Prayer," *The Hymn* 39 (1988):13-21. See also the thematic issue devoted to Charles Wesley in *Methodist History* 29 (1991): No. 4.

68. Important here are the non-Wesleyan sources from the early stages of the Methodist renewal movement, e.g., journal entries about Charles Wesley. See Geoffrey F. Nuttall, "Charles Wesley in 1739. By Joseph William of Kidderminster," *Proceedings of the Wesley Historical Society* 42 (1980):181-85.

69. See S T Kimbrough, Jr., "Charles Wesley and Biblical Interpretation," in *Charles Wesley: Poet and Theologian*, 106-36. The short book published by John W. Waterhouse, *The Bible in Charles Wesley's Hymns* (London: Epworth Press, 1954), is not an adequate appraisal of the subject.

70. See the thesis by Elizabeth [Hannon] Hart, *The Influence of Paradise Lost on the Hymns of Charles Wesley* (M.A. thesis, University of British Columbia, 1985).

71. See Baker, *Charles Wesley's Verse*, 90-92.

72. The two stanzas omitted here, stanzas 5 and 7, fall in the midst of the long description of the struggle with the "unknown traveller." The absence of these two stanzas does not detract from the poem's fundamental meaning. For the full poem in its original length see *The Poetical Works of John and Charles Wesley*, vol. 2, 173-76.

73. *Collection*, 136.

74. G. Clark, "Charles Wesley's Greatest Poem," *Methodist History* 26 (1988):166, identifies the entire text as a "dramatic monologue."

75. To suggest that "Wrestling Jacob" never gained popularity as a congregational hymn is at best an assumption. The emphases and nature of its editing (occasionally leaving as few as four stanzas) in later Methodist hymnbooks seems, however, to give credence to such an assumption.

76. In the foreword to the *Collection* (p. 74) John Wesley cites both (along with Shakespeare) as important poets for his day.

77. For a detailed exposition on this matter see Baker, *Charles Wesley's Verse*, 9-12, 19-87; see also O. A. Beckerlegge, "An Attempt at a Classification of Charles Wesley's Metres," *London Quarterly and Holborn Review* 169 (1944):219-27; and O. A. Beckerlegge, "Charles Wesley's Vocabulary," *London Quarterly and Holborn Review* 193 (1968):152-61.

78. See Bett, *Hymns of Methodism*, 70f.

79. See for example, Baker, *Charles Wesley's Verse*, 19-25.

80. See Bett, *Hymns of Methodism*, 73-85; Tyson, "Wesley and Edward Young," *Methodist History* 27 (1988):110-18.

81. John Dryden, King Arthur (1691) as cited in the *Collection*, 545.

82. *Collection*, 374 (added emphasis mine). The publishers of the critical edition note that the original comma at the end of the first line (later replaced by a semicolon) likely suggests a confession of faith rather than a call upon God. For the hymn in its entirety see *The Poetical Works of John and Charles Wesley*, vol. 4, 219f.; Tyson, *Charles Wesley Reader*, 225f. The second stanza, missing by the editorial hand of John Wesley (likely for theological reasons), reads as follows:

> Breathe, O breathe Thy loving Spirit,
>   Into every troubled breast,
> Let us all in Thee inherit,
>   Let us find that second rest:

> Take away our power of sinning,
> Alpha and Omega be,
> End of faith and its Beginning,
> Set our hearts at liberty.

83. D. Davie, *Purity of Diction in English Verse* (New York: Oxford University Press, 1953), 75 (added emphasis mine).

84. See O. A. Beckerlegge, "A Man of One Book: Charles Wesley and the Scriptures," *Epworth Review* 15 (1988):44.

85. *Collection*, p. 5, n. 4 provides a list of the most frequently recurring instances of biblical citations. On Charles Wesley's interpretation of Holy Scripture see Kimbrough, "Charles Wesley and Biblical Interpretation," 106-36.

86. See Bett, *Hymns of Methodism*, 21-32, for examples.

87. See Bett, *Hymns of Methodism*, 17-20, for examples.

88. Charles Wesley names these works in the foreword to his *Short Hymns on Select Passages of the Holy Scriptures*, 2 vols. (Bristol: Farley, 1762).

89. For more detail on this point see A. K. Lloyd, "Wesley's Debt to Matthew Henry," *London Quarterly and Holborn Review* 171 (1944):330-37; E. Routley, "Wesley and Matthew Henry," *The Congregational Quarterly* 33 (1955):345-51. The most explicit example of Matthew Henry's influence on the work of Charles Wesley can be found in hymn no. 309 of the *Collection*, where Wesley paraphrases a section of Henry's commentary.

90. See J. Dale, *The Theological and Literary Qualities of the Poetry of Charles Wesley in Relation to the Standards of his Age* (Ph.D. thesis, Cambridge University, 1960), 64-78, even though his analysis suffers from an unnecessarily negative polemic against allegorical exegesis.

91. See Tyson, *Charles Wesley's Theology of the Cross*, 803.

92. See Wesley, *Short Hymns on Select Passages of Scripture*, vol. 1, Preface, n.p. The second volume of *The Unpublished Poetry of Charles Wesley* contains more biblical passages addressed by Wesleyan poetry, i.e., texts from the four Gospels, the Acts of the Apostles, and other selected biblical texts.

93. *Collection*, 318. The editors of the critical edition of the *Collection* list (p. 733) their estimation of biblical references contained in this hymn. (One correction: the reference to Ecclesiastes 2:7 should read Ecclesiastes 12:7).

94. M. Henry, *An Exposition of the Old and New Testament: Wherein Each Chapter is Summed up in its Contents; Each Sacred Text Inserted at large, in Distinct Paragraphs; Each Paragraph Reduced to its Proper Heads: the Sense Given, and Largely Illustrated; with Practical Remarks and Observances* [1708–1710], 4 vols. (New York: Fleming H. Revell Company, new ed., n.d.), n.p. The words I have underlined have direct counterparts in the Wesleyan hymn.

95. This example and others are cited in the *Collection*, p. 473. Blackmore describes the indwelling of the Holy Spirit in the following manner:

> Vile Man becomes, when purified by grace,
>   Thy living temple, and abiding place.
> His heart is made thy altar, whence
>   To heav'n arise pure flames of holy fire;
> . . . .
> To the blest seats above aspire,
> Winged with celestial love, and strong desire.

191

96. Bett, *The Hymns of Methodism*, 30, assumes that Wesley is working from the Greek text. It appears to me, however, that the reference in Henry's commentary to these two passages is significant. Henry distinctly makes a connection between these two passages.

97. I refer to the work of the High Church theologian, William Jones [of Nayland] (1726–1800), *The Catholic Doctrine of a [sic] Trinity*, published in 1756.

98. I refer to a work by the Anglican theologian, Daniel Brevint (1616–1695), *The Christian Sacrament and Sacrifice*, published for the first time in 1673.

99. See also the wide open attacks against Zinzendorf: "the German Tempter . . . The German Pope . . . O German Witchcraft! . . . the German Wolf," in *The Unpublished Poetry of Charles Wesley, Vol. 1*, 173, 175, 180, 186.

100. See *Collection*, 25:6, 26:2, and 27's refrain.

101. *Collection*, 27:1 (added emphasis mine). In this refrain Charles Wesley owns a Christological interpretation of the Ignatian reference, traditional since the time of Origen. Upon closer examination it becomes clear that Ignatius is in all likelihood not speaking of the Crucified Christ but rather of his own love of the world which has been put to death.

The use of this sentence, word for word, is also found in the translation of a German hymn by John Wesley. See Nuelsen, *John Wesley and the German Hymn*, 147. The sentence is nowhere to be found in the German original. Wesley's translation is cited below:

> Hence our hearts melt, our eyes o'erflow,
> Our words are lost: nor will we know,
> Nor will we think of aught, beside
> "My Lord, my Love is crucified."

102. See Bett, *The Hymns of Methodism*, 39-52; and J. Dale, "Charles Wesley, the Odyssey, and Clement of Alexandria," *Methodist History* 30 (1992):100-103.

103. See W. Bettermann, *Theologie und Sprache bei Zinzendorf* (Gotha: L. Klotz, 1953), 65-75.

104. See G. S. Wakefield, "Charles Wesley's Spirituality and Its Meaning for Today," *The Charles Wesley Society Newsletter* 3/2 (1993):17. Occasionally, the theme of "creation" can be recognized in the Psalm paraphrases of the *Collection*, see *Collection*, 215-17. These are, however, the hymns of Isaac Watts and not Charles Wesley. For more on this subject see also E. Mayer, *Charles Wesleys Hymnen. Eine Untersuchung und literarische Würdigung* (Ph.D. thesis, University of Tübingen, 1957), 44-48.

105. See T. Berger, "'Theologie, die man singen kann.': Christologische Titel im methodistischen Gesangbuch von 1780," *Una Sancta* 47 (1992):125-28; *Charles Wesley Reader*, 491.

106. *Collection*, 33:7.

107. *The Journal of the Rev. Charles Wesley. To which are Appended Selections from his Correspondence and Poetry*, vol. 1, ed. T. Jackson (London: John Mason, 1849), 286.

108. See H. Davies, "Charles Wesley and the Calvinist Tradition," in *Charles Wesley: Poet and Theologian*, 186-96.

109. The original text can be found in *The Poetical Works of John and Charles Wesley*, vol. 4, 274-77 (see also *Charles Wesley Reader*, 228-31, a version transcribed from a manuscript containing spelling variants). John Wesley retained stanzas 1, 2, 12, 14, 19-22, and 24) in the *Collection*.

110. *Collection*, 2.

111. This characteristic designation is found in stanza 15 of the original, which was not retained in the version of the hymn that appears in the *Collection*.

112. Stanza 18 of the original is most explicit: "Tell every creature under heaven."

113. See for example, the hymn "Sinners, obey the gospel word" (*Collection*, 9) where Charles Wesley also uses the Lukan parable of the great dinner as a backdrop.

114. The phrase "gospel feast" appears in Matthew Henry's exegetical commentary on Luke 14:16-24; see Henry, *An Exposition of the Old and New Testament*, Vol. V, n.p. It is possible that Charles Wesley first encountered this term here.

115. *Collection*, 6:2. On the same theme see *Collection*, 7 and 8, and also the translation of one of the German hymns by John Wesley where this same rhetorical question emerges (though with no equivalent in the German text): "Why, sinner, wilt thou perish, why?" in Nuelsen, *Wesley and the German Hymn*, 156.

116. Stanza 23 of the original implicitly refers to the Eucharist but was not retained in the *Collection*:

> Ye who believe His record true
> Shall sup with Him, and He with you:
> Come to the feast; be saved from sin,
> For Jesus waits to take you in.

117. *The Poetical Works of John and Charles Wesley*, vol. 3, 221; *Charles Wesley Reader*, 227.

118. *Collection*, 243:1.

119. *Collection*, 367:1.

120. See *Collection*, 36:4.

121. M. Luther, *D. Martin Luthers Werke: Kritische Gesamtausgabe. Weimarer Ausgabe*, vol. 40, 1 (Weimar: Hermann Böhlaus Nachfolger, 1911), 299.

122. *Early Journal of Charles Wesley*, 142f. For John Wesley's later critique of Luther's commentary on the Galatians see M. Schmidt, *John Wesley. Vol. 2: Das Lebenswerk John Wesleys* (Zürich: Gotthelf-Verlag, 1966), 55f. This critique is part of the "stillness controversy" and the related separation from the Moravians.

123. See *Collection*, 88-91 and 92-95.

124. *Collection*, 88:2.

125. *Early Journal of Charles Wesley*, 143 (I have italicized the words "to feel" for emphasis).

126. For example see *Collection*, 111.

127. See for example *Collection*, 88:6, 90:2-6, 91:1-4.

128. *Collection*, 111:1. Similarly see the hymn "Let others of their virtue boast," in *Charles Wesley Reader*, 456.

129. *Collection*, 168. This is the refrain for all five stanzas.

130. *Collection*, 193. The hymn in its original form can be found in *The Poetical Works of John and Charles Wesley*, vol. 1, 105f. The *Collection* is only missing one stanza, the original stanza 5. Nothing of significance is lost by its deletion:

> Still the small inward voice I hear,
> That whispers all my sins forgiven;
> Still the atoning blood is near,
> That quench'd the wrath of hostile Heaven:
> I feel the life His wounds impart;
> I feel my Saviour in my heart.

Bett attributes the entire hymn to John Wesley instead of Charles but most scholars do not agree with him on this point. I find the similarities between the last verse of this hymn and one of John's translations of a German hymn puzzling. One stanza of that hymn ends as follows (two lines are practically identical to lines 1 and 3 in the last stanza of the hymn cited above!):

> No condemnation now I dread;
>   I taste salvation in Thy name,
> Alive in thee my living Head!
> (Nuelsen, *John Wesley and the German Hymn*, 127)

It is difficult to know what to do with these similarities. On the one hand, scholarship is no longer clear that John (and not his brother, Charles) actually translated all of these hymns, while on the other hand Charles would make ready use of borrowed phrases from other poetry. Thus, conclusions as to authorship cannot be drawn based on the similarity of formulation alone. At this point, I simply want to note the puzzling similarities between the two hymns.

131. See also *Collection*, 27:1.

> O Love divine! What hast thou done!
>   Th'immortal God hath died for me!
> The Father's co-eternal Son
>   Bore all my sins upon the tree:
> Th'immortal God for me hath died.
> My Lord, my Love is crucified.

132. Nuelsen, *Wesley and the German Hymn*, 146. This hymn is also found in the *Collection*, 25.

133. Nuelsen, *Wesley and the German Hymn*, 153. This hymn is also found in the *Collection*, 183.

134. Charles, however, also strongly criticizes the Moravian fascination with this terminology: "What is it that in all their meetings sounds? 'Wounds, wounds, & wound holes, nothing else but wounds,'" in *The Unpublished Poetry of Charles Wesley*. Vol. 1, 192.

135. See W. Elert, *Morphologie des Luthertums. Vol. 1: Theologie und Weltanschauung des Luthertums hauptsächlich im 16. und 17. Jahrhundert* (München: Beck, 1952 [2d ed.]), 124-54.

136. For more detail see Tyson, *Charles Wesley's Theology of the Cross*, 133-96; and Morris, *Imagery in the Hymns*, 230-35.

137. For references see Morris, *Imagery in the Hymns*, 133.

138. *Collection*, 124:3, 5, 7. For the influence of the Pietist blood-and-wound theology on Charles Wesley see, for example, also *Collection*, 29:6, 7:

> His bleeding heart shall make you room,
>   His open side shall take you in.
> . . . .
> For you the purple current flowed
>   In pardons from his wounded side.

139. See Tyson, *Charles Wesley's Theology of the Cross*, 140-59.

140. *Collection*, 337:4.

141. See *Collection*, 121:6; 124; 144:8; 244:3.

142. See *Collection*, 34:8; 83:1.

143. See *Collection*, 93:2; 144:8; 353:3.

144. See *Collection*, 83:1; 124:7; 244:2.

145. See *Collection*, 246:4; 337:2; 398:5f; 508:2; 509:6.

146. See *Collection*, 366:2.

147. *Collection*, 398:6; see *Collection*, 34:8; 144:8; 337:4; 509:6.

148. *Collection*, 398:5.

149. *Collection*, 83. John Wesley excluded only one stanza of the original hymn from the *Collection*, quite possibly on account of its proximity to the Pietist blood-and-wounds theology:

> I know my Saviour lives,
>   He lives, who died for me,
> My inmost soul His voice receives
>   Who hangs on yonder tree:
> Set forth before my eye
>   Even now I see him bleed,
> And hear his mortal groans, and cries,
>   While suffering in my stead.

In *The Poetical Works of John and Charles Wesley*, vol. 4, 197.

150. *Collection*, 246:4.

151. *Early Journal of Charles Wesley*, 143.

152. Wesley, *Journal and Diaries I*, 249f.

153. *Collection*, 177:3.

154. *Collection*, 53:1.

155. Ezekiel 11:19 is one of the biblical texts often utilized in Wesleyan hymnody; see, for example, *Collection*, 9:3; 26:2; 34:5; 98:1; 100:3; 106:4; 113:3; and other places as well.

156. *Collection*, 121:6. See also *Collection*, 27:2: "Come, feel with me his blood applied."

157. *Collection*, 98:2; see also, for example, 97:2.

158. See *Collection*, 29:2; 33:5; 53:2; 83:2; 84:5; 97:2; 121:6; 127:1.

159. Quoted from a letter of John Wesley dated 3.22.1748, in *Letters II*, vol. 26 of *The Works of John Wesley*, ed. F. Baker (Oxford: Oxford University Press, 1982), 289.

160. *Early Journal of Charles Wesley*, 208; see also the correspondence from the same year, for example, *Letters I*, vol. 25 of *The Works of John Wesley*, ed. F. Baker (Oxford: Oxford University Press, 1980), 562-66; John Wesley, *Letters II*, especially 244-52, 254f, 287-94.

161. See *Collection*, 308.

162. See John Wesley's letter dated 7.31.1747 to his brother, Charles, in John Wesley, *Letters II*, 254f.

163. See T. Smith, "The Holy Spirit in the Hymns of the Wesleys," *Wesleyan Theological Journal* 16, 1 (1981):20-48. For more detail on the assurance of salvation see J. A. Townsend, *Feelings Related to Assurance in Charles Wesley's Hymns* (Ph.D. thesis, Fuller Theological Seminary, Pasadena, Calif., 1979), 135-76.

164. See *Collection*, 93; the original stanzas 4 and 5 were omitted. John Wesley also changed the meter of the poem without, however, thereby altering the theological content of the hymn.

165. *The Poetical Works of John and Charles Wesley*, vol. 5, 363-65.

166. The passages to which Charles Wesley referred most often are found in 1 John, especially 1 John 1:3; 4:16; 3:24; 4:13; 5:10; 5:2.

167. See chapter 3 under the subheading B:1 of this study.

168. Genesis 32:29, in the King James translation of the Bible with which Wesley would have worked.

169. The complete text of this hymn is found under the subheading B:1 of this study. "Wrestling Jacob" in an abbreviated form was included in the *Collection* as No. 136.

170. *Collection*, 369:5.

171. *Collection*, 138:4.

172. *Collection*, 138:5.

173. *Collection*, 144:6.

174. *Collection*, 138:4.

175. *Collection*, 126:1.

176. *Collection*, 144:1.

177. *Collection*, 124:1.

178. *Collection*, 124:7.

179. *Collection*, 138:5. Along these same lines see Tyson, *Charles Wesley's Theology of the Cross*, 196-204.

180. *Collection*, 30:1.

181. *Collection*, 207:1.

182. *Collection*, 162:8.

183. *Collection*, 138:4.

184. *Collection*, 240:4.

185. *Collection*, 288.

186. See Henry, *An Exposition of the Old and New Testament*, Vol. 1, n.p. Wesley uses the image in other places as well, see, for example, *Collection*, 516:4.

187. See *Collection*, 65-77. This section is followed by a section on "Describing Hell," which only contains one hymn (78). This hymn may well be the least beautiful of the entire *Collection*. It was originally published in the 1763 volume *Hymns for Children* (!) and describes the reality of hell as imagined in Wesley's day.

188. *Collection*, 77:2.

189. *Collection*, 15:1.

190. *Collection*, 29:7. See also, for example, 20:3 where his listeners are challenged:

> Ye may now be happy too,
> Find on earth the life of heaven;
> Live the life of heaven above,
> All the life of glorious love.

191. *Collection*, 197:2.

192. *Collection*, 403:5. Note that 344:5 is even more explicit when referring to Christ as "My heaven on earth, my heaven above."

193. *Collection*, 516:1, 4.

194. *Collection*, 33:3. The hymn ends with the following line: "The life of heaven on earth I live."

195. *Collection*, 15:2f. Interestingly, this hymn is taken from *Hymns on the Lord's Supper* where it is listed under the heading "The Sacrament as a Pledge of Heaven."

196. For this and other references to the use of the word *heaven* in the hymns of Charles Wesley see G. H. Findlay, *Christ's Standard Bearer: A Study in the*

Hymns of Charles Wesley as They are Contained in the Last Edition (1876) of A Collection of Hymns for the Use of the People Called Methodists by the Rev. John Wesley, M. A. (London: Epworth Press, 1956), 72. The author devotes a short chapter to this subject (67-74). Another hymn in the *Collection* (368:5) that speaks of God's love uses equally strong imagery: "My precious pearl, my present heaven."

197. *Collection*, 15:4.

198. *Collection*, 316:5.

199. For more on this phrase in the hymns of Charles Wesley see Beckerlegge, "Charles Wesley's Vocabulary," 153.

200. *Collection*, 197:1-3.

201. *Collection*, 19:3.

202. *Collection*, 221:6.

203. For more detail about the background and development of this discussion, as well as the differences between John and Charles Wesley see Townsend, *Feelings Related to Assurance in Charles Wesley's Hymns*, 232-53. Townsend provides a brief but solid discussion of this theme in the hymns of Charles Wesley. The same cannot be said about J. C. Ekrut, *Universal Redemption, Assurance of Salvation, and Christian Perfection in the Hymns of Charles Wesley, With Poetic Analyses and Tune Examples* (M. Mus. thesis, Southwestern Baptist Theological Seminary, Fort Worth, Tex., 1978), 66-93. See also R. S. Nicholson, "The Holiness Emphasis in Wesley's Hymns," *Wesleyan Theological Journal* 5 (1970):49-61.

204. *Collection*, 373:3.

205. For more detail see Tyson, *Charles Wesley's Theology of the Cross*, 659-61.

206. *Collection*, 331-79.

207. *Collection*, 380-405.

208. *Collection*, 344:3.

209. *Collection*, 347:8.

210. *Collection*, 331:1.

211. *Collection*, 344:2.

212. *Collection*, 372:3.

213. *Collection*, 384:6.

214. For an opposing point of view see Hodges/Allchin, editors of *A Rapture of Praise* (London: Hodder & Stoughton, 1986), 21, who maintain that Wesley uses the image of new birth strictly in reference to salvation.

215. *Collection*, 388:8; similarly 341:1; 365:4.

216. *Collection*, 331:1; see also 478:4.

217. *Collection*, 341:2.

218. *Collection*, 346:9f.

219. *Collection*, 333:2; see also Tyson, *Charles Wesley's Theology of the Cross*, 631f.

220. *Collection*, 383:6.

221. *Collection*, 389:4.

222. *Collection*, 369:6.

223. *Collection*, 378:1.

224. *Collection*, 500:4; see also 501:6:

> Rise eternal in our heart!
>   Thou our long sought Eden art:
> Father, Son, and Holy Ghost,
>   Be to us what Adam lost!

225. *Collection*, 393:5.

226. *Collection*, 334:1, 4.

227. *Collection*, 345:13.

228. *Collection*, 332:1f.

229. *Collection*, 344:4.

230. *Collection*, 353:4.

231. See *Collection*, 371. In particular, see stanza 1: "O great mountain, who art thou, Immense, immovable? . . . Thou art indwelling sin."

232. *Collection*, 342:3; see also 338:4f.

233. *Collection*, 351:3.

234. *Collection*, 341:2.

235. *Collection*, 356:1.

236. *Collection*, 355:7.

237. *Collection*, 346:7.

238. *Collection*, 76:2.

239. *Collection*, 357:1.

240. *Collection*, 363:3.

241. *Collection*, 377:3.

242. See M. Schmidt, "Teilnahme an der göttlichen Natur. 2 Petr 1,4 in der theologischen Exegese des Pietismus und der lutherischen Orthodoxie," in *Wiedergeburt und neuer Mensch: Gesammelte Studien zur Geschichte des Pietismus* (Witten: Luther-Verlag, 1969), 238-98. Pietists were interested in this topic by way of Mystical Spiritualism. Albert Outler, in his well-known and influential book on John Wesley, published in 1964, attempts to trace John's interest in Christian perfection to the writings of the early Greek Church Fathers. Even though such evidence does exist, the influence of German Pietists and Mystical Spiritualism would seem to provide a far more direct connection.

243. *Collection*, 366:2.

244. *Collection*, 369:8.

245. For more on this term see Findlay, *Christ's Standard Bearer*, 52-59; Tyson, *Charles Wesley's Theology of the Cross*, 204-12.

246. *Collection*, 357:4.

247. *Collection*, 381:4.

248. *Collection*, 390:2.

249. *Collection*, 391:3.

250. *Collection*, 399:2.

251. *Collection*, 402:2.

252. *Collection*, 405:6.

253. But see also Langford, "Charles Wesley as Theologian," in *Charles Wesley: Poet and Theologian*, 97-105, who attempts to interpret the hymns of Charles Wesley through the category "theology-as-hymn."

PART III

Chapter 4: The Essence of Doxological Speech

1. I am indebted to the work of and correspondence with Richard Schaeffler (Tübingen) for insight provided regarding this final section. I cite three of his works in particular: "Kultus als Weltauslegung," in *Kult in der säkularisierten Welt*, ed. B. Fischer et al. (Regensburg: Pustet, 1975), 9-62; "Kultisches Handeln. Die Frage nach Proben seiner Bewährung und nach Kriterien seiner Legitimation," in *Ankunft Gottes und Handeln des Menschen: Thesen über Kult und Sakrament*, ed. P. Hünermann

and R. Schaeffler (Freiburg i. B.: Herder, 1977), 5-90; and *Kleine Sprachlehre des Gebets* (Einsiedeln: Johannes Verlag, 1988). Anyone who knows these works will recognize their influence on this section (including the order in which characteristics are addressed). I thank Richard Schaeffler also for his helpful correspondence.

2. It is not that doxological traditions have not and are not serving as the objects of theological study, but rather that these studies typically do not take into account the essential characteristics of doxology and its relationship to theological reflection.

3. W. Brueggemann, in *Israel's Praise: Doxology Against Idolatry and Ideology* (Philadelphia: Fortress Press, 1988), 1-28, assumes that doxology itself "constitutes" reality.

4. See T. W. Jennings, "On Ritual Knowledge," *The Journal of Religion* 62 (1982):111-27.

5. Charles Wesley, see chapter 3 under the subheading A.4 of this study.

6. See A. Stuiber, "Doxologie," in *Reallexikon für Antike und Christentum* 4 (1959):212.

7. See A. A. Häußling, "Liturgical Language," in *Sacramentum Mundi: An Encyclopedia of Theology*, vol. 3, ed. K. Rahner (New York: Herder and Herder, 1969), 331-33 and M. Steinheimer, *Die Doxa tou Theou in der römischen Liturgie* (München: K. Zink, 1951), 100-107. The latter tries to analyze the use of the concept of *doxa* in the Roman liturgy.

8. See G. Wainwright, "Adoration," in *The Westminster Dictionary of Christian Theology*, ed. A. Richardson and J. Bowden (Philadelphia: Westminster Press, 1983), 6.

9. Henkys speaks of the "Grenzverletzungen" of doxological speech, see J. Henkys, *Dietrich Bonhoeffers Gefängnisgedichte: Beiträge zu ihrer Interpretation* (München: Chr. Kaiser, 1986), 76.

10. For the history and meaning of this phrase see I. Cecchetti, "Tibi silentium laus," in *Miscellanea Liturgica. Vol. 2 (Festschrift for C. Mohlberg)* (Rome: Edizioni liturgiche, 1949), 521-70.

11. *Collection*, 324:6.

12. For a different perspective see B. Welte, *Religionsphilosophie* (Freiburg i. B.: Herder, 1978), 18, who sees silence as the "mother of all speech about God." His observation and mine are not necessarily inconsistent with one another. Silence could easily be viewed as the mother of all speech *about* God when speech about God has its origin in speech addressed to God.

13. For more see B. Casper, *Sprache und Theologie: Eine philosophische Hinführung* (Freiburg i. B.: Herder, 1975), 162.

14. Casper, *Sprache und Theologie*, 172.

15. Schlink, "The Structure of Dogmatic Statements as an Ecumenical Problem," 82.

16. See G. von Rad, *Old Testament Theology. Vol. 1: The Theology of Israel's Historical Traditions* (New York: Harper & Row, 1962), 357.

17. See Welte, *Religionsphilosophie*, 188.

18. Ritschl, *The Logic of Theology*, 284. Similarly, Casper, *Sprache und Theologie: Eine philosophische Hinführung*, 185f. A different position is taken by A. E. McGrath, "Geschichte, Überlieferung und Erzählung," *Kerygma und Dogma* 32 (1986):234-36.

19. von Rad, *Theology of Israel's Historical Traditions*, 357.

20. See A. A. Häußling, "Liturgiewissenschaft zwei Jahrzehnte nach Konzilsbeginn," *Archiv für Liturgiewissenschaft* 24 (1982):1-18.

21. O. Lang, "Vom Opfer des Lobes," in *Gott feiern. Theologische Anregung und geistliche Vertiefung zur Feier von Messe und Stundengebet (Festschrift for Th. Schnitzler),* ed. J. G. Plöger (Freiburg i. B.: Herder, 1980 [2d ed.]), 342f.

22. Krahe, "'Psalmen, Hymnen und Lieder, wie der Geist sie eingibt:' Doxologie als Ursprung und Ziel aller Theologie," 939.

23. See also D. N. Power, "Cult to Culture: The Liturgical Foundation of Theology," *Worship* 54 (1980):489.

24. See P. Miller, "'Enthroned on the Praises of Israel': The Praise of God in Old Testament Theology," *Interpretation* 39 (1985):5-19; D. Zeller, "Gott nennen an einem Beispiel aus dem Psalter," in *Gott nennen: Phänomenologische Zugänge,* ed. B. Casper (Freiburg i. B.: Alber, 1981), 13-34.

25. von Rad, *Theology of Israel's Historical Traditions,* 369f.

26. See A. Adam, "Vom Rühmen des Herrn," in *Gott feiern. Theologische Anregung und geistliche Vertiefung zur Feier von Messe und Stundengebet (Festschrift for Th. Schnitzler),* ed. J. G. Plöger (Freiburg i. B.: Herder, 1980, 2d ed.), 85, where he states this emphatically.

27. See Ritschl, *The Logic of Theology,* 283f, and Brueggemann, *Israel's Praise: Doxology Against Idolatry and Ideology,* 52: "Thus the doxology is an act of hope. It promises and anticipates a hoped-for world that is beyond present reality."

28. See also Schaeffler, "Kultus als Weltauslegung," 48.

29. Ritschl, *The Logic of Theology,* 279; also Stenzel, "Liturgie als theologischer Ort," 616 in reference to the liturgy.

30. Stenzel, "Liturgie als theologischer Ort," 616.

31. See Casper, *Sprache und Theologie: Eine philosophische Hinführung,* 43.

32. For more on the liturgical speech act see J. Ladrière, "The Performativity of Liturgical Language," in *Liturgical Experience of Faith,* Concilium Series, vol. 82, 50-61; M. B. Merz, "Gebetsformen der Liturgie," in *Gottesdienst der Kirche: Handbuch der Liturgiewissenschaft. Vol. 3: Gestalt des Gottesdienstes,* ed. H. B. Meyer et al. (Regensburg: Pustet, 1987), 100-115; and A. Schermann, *Sprache im Gottesdienst* (Innsbruck: Tyrolia, 1987).

33. See I. Werlen, *Ritual und Sprache: Zum Verhältnis von Sprechen und Handeln in Ritualen* (Tübingen: G. Narr, 1984), 210. Werlen identifies "to adore" as a performative verb.

34. This is true also for the language of faith in general. See J. Ladrière, *Language and Belief* (Notre Dame: University Press, 1972), 188-90.

35. See also *Theorie der Sprachhandlungen und heutige Ekklesiologie* (1987), especially page 8f; and M. M. Olivetti, "Sich in seinem Namen versammeln: Kirche als Gottesnennung," in *Gott nennen: Phänomenologische Zugänge,* ed. B. Casper (Freiburg i. B.: Alber, 1981), 189-217.

36. See also the analysis of the basic structure of "ursprüngliche Theologie," (i.e., doxology) in Krahe, "'Psalmen, Hymnen und Lieder, wie der Geist sie eingibt:' Doxologie als Ursprung und Ziel aller Theologie," 927f.

37. See for the liturgy Schaeffler, "Kultisches Handeln," 9-11, 38.

38. The term "autonomous language game" fostered in linguistic analysis is not helpful for my purposes since I am, in fact, arguing for doxology as an autonomous speech event. The term *autarchical* is borrowed from Schaeffler, *Das Gebet und das Argument, zwei Weisen des Sprechens von Gott: Eine Einführung in die Theorie der religiösen Sprache* (Düsseldorf: Patmos, 1989), 212-330.

39. For more on this question of correspondence see Ritschl, *The Logic of Theology,* 77, 246f.

40. See A. A. Häußling, "Kosmische Dimension und gesellschaftliche Wirklichkeit: Zu einem Erfahrungswandel in der Liturgie," *Archiv für Liturgiewissenschaft* 25 (1983):6: "The Pharisee uses, strictly speaking, a *berakah:* he properly recognizes God as the Lord of his zealously faithful life."

41. See Schaeffler, "Kultus als Weltauslegung," 55.

42. Ritschl, *Memory and Hope: An Inquiry Concerning the Presence of Christ*, 169.

43. For more on the mistaken forms of "prayer" see Merz, "Gebetsformen der Liturgie," 127f.

44. See (under the influence of J. L. Austin) Casper, *Sprache und Theologie: Eine philosophische Hinführung*, 44.

45. For more about this as it pertains to hymnic doxology see P. Brunner, "Zur Lehre vom Gottesdienst der im Namen Jesu versammelten Gemeinde," in *Leiturgia: Handbuch des evangelischen Gottesdienstes*. Vol. 1, ed. K. F. Müller and W. Blankenburg (Kassel: J. Stauda, 1954), 264.

46. See Ritschl, *The Logic of Theology*, 280.

47. See G. Kittel/G. von Rad, "δοξα," in *Theological Dictionary of the New Testament*. Vol. 2 (Grand Rapids: W. B. Eerdmans, 1985), 248, 251.

48. See Ritschl, *The Logic of Theology*, 98f.

49. See M. Plathow, "Geist und Gebet," *Kerygma und Dogma* 29 (1983):47-65.

50. Brunner, "Zur Lehre vom Gottesdienst der im Namen Jesu versammelten Gemeinde," 264.

51. See W. Kasper, "Wissenschaftspraxis der Theologie," in *Handbuch der Fundamentaltheologie. Vol. 1: Traktat Theologische Erkenntnislehre*, ed. W. Kern et al. (Freiburg i. B.: Herder, 1988), 244, 275. Kasper speaks of the "doxological dimension" of theology and of how theology "must be anchored in the liturgy all the while again and again becoming doxology." See also Schilson, "Gedachte Liturgie," 215-18, and J. Driscoll, "Liturgy and Fundamental Theology: Frameworks for a Dialogue," *Ecclesia Orans* 11 (1994):69-99.

52. See also J. Macquarrie, "Prayer and Theological Reflection," in *The Study of Spirituality*, ed. C. Jones et al. (New York: Oxford University Press, 1986), 584-87.

53. Two important new studies begin to address the deficiencies of focus on the text alone: Merz, *Liturgisches Gebet als Geschehen*, 95, 139, 142; L. A. Hoffman, *Beyond the Text: A Holistic Approach to Liturgy* (Bloomington: Indiana University Press, 1987), 172-82.

54. See Ritschl, *The Logic of Theology*, 101.

55. See Lehmann, "Gottesdienst als Ausdruck des Glaubens. Plädoyer für ein neues Gespräch zwischen Liturgiewissenschaft und dogmatischer Theologie," 207.

56. Schlink, "The Structure of Dogmatic Statements as an Ecumenical Problem," 42.

57. See Ritschl, *The Logic of Theology*, 285.

58. See A. Stock, "Zur poetischen Theologie von Huub Oosterhuis," *Theologische Quartalschrift* 167 (1987):45-55.

59. A. Grabner-Haider, *Glaubenssprache: Ihre Struktur und Anwendbarkeit in Verkündigung und Theologie* (Wien: Herder, 1975), 54.

60. See A. A. Häußling, "Die kritische Funktion der Liturgiewissenschaft," in *Liturgie und Gesellschaft*, ed. H. B. Meyer (Innsbruck: Tyrolia-Verlag, 1970), 103-30.

Bibliography

I. Doxology and Theology

Adam, A. "Vom Rühmen des Herrn." In *Gott feiern. Theologische Anregung und geistliche Vertiefung zur Feier von Messe und Stundengebet [Festschrift for Th. Schnitzler].* Ed. J. G. Plöger. Freiburg i.B.: Herder, 1980 (2d ed.), 85-93.

Adam, K. "Die dogmatischen Grundlagen der christlichen Liturgie." *Wissenschaft und Weisheit* 4 (1937):43-54.

Alpern, B. D. *The Logic of Doxological Language: A Reinterpretation of Aquinas and Pannenberg on Analogy and Doxology.* Ph.D. dissertation, University of Pittsburgh, 1980.

Andronikof, C. "Dogme et liturgie." In *La Liturgie: Expression de la foi. Conférences Saint-Serge, XXVe Semaine d'Etudes Liturgiques,* Paris 1978. Ed. A. M. Triacca and A. Pistoia. Rome: CLV Edizioni liturgiche, 1979, 13-27.

Becker, H. "Einleitung." In *Liturgie und Dichtung. Ein interdisziplinäres Kompendium.* Vol. 1: *Historische Präsentation.* Ed. H. Becker and R. Kaczynski. St. Ottilien: EOS, 1983, 1-3.

Beeck, F. J. van. *God Encountered: A Contemporary Catholic Systematic Theology.* Vol. 1, *Understanding the Christian Faith.* San Francisco: Harper & Row, 1989.

Berger, T. "Die Liturgie im Gespräch der Kirchen. Ein Überblick über neue ökumenische Dialoge auf Weltebene." In *Christus Spes [Festschrift for S. Kraft].* Ed. A. Berlis and K. D. Gerth. Frankfurt: Peter Lang, 1994, 39-45.

————. "Lex orandi—lex credendi—lex agendi. Auf dem Weg zu einer ökumenisch konsensfähigen Verhältnisbestimmung von Liturgie, Theologie und Ethik." *Archiv für Liturgiewissenschaft* 27 (1985):425-32.

————. "Unity in and through Doxology? Reflections on Worship Studies in the World Council of Churches." *Studia Liturgica* 16 (1986/1987):1-12.

Braniste, E. "Le culte byzantin comme expression de la foi orthodoxe." In *La Liturgie: Expression de la foi. Conférences Saint-Serge, XXVe Semaine d'Etudes Liturgiques, Paris 1978.* Ed. A. M. Triacca and A. Pistoia. Rome: CLV Edizioni liturgiche, 1979, 75-88.

Brinktrine, J. "Der dogmatische Beweis aus der Liturgie." In *Scientia sacra [Festschrift for K. J. Schulte].* Köln: J. P. Bachem; Düsseldorf: L. Schwann, 1935, 231-51.

————. "Die Liturgie als dogmatische Erkenntnisquelle." *Ephemerides liturgicae* 43 (1929):44-51.

Brueggemann, W. *Israel's Praise: Doxology Against Idolatry and Ideology.* Philadelphia: Fortress Press, 1988.

Brunner, P. "Zur Lehre vom Gottesdienst der im Namen Jesu versammelten Gemeinde." In *Leiturgia: Handbuch des evangelischen Gottesdienstes.* Vol. 1. Ed. K. F. Müller and W. Blankenburg. Kassel: J. Stauda, 1954, 83-364.

Capelle, B. "Autorité de la liturgie chez les Pères." *Recherches de théologie ancienne et médievale* 21 (1954):5-22.

Cappuyns, M. "Liturgie et théologie." *Questions liturgiques et paroissiales* 19 (1934):249-72.

Casper, B. *Sprache und Theologie: Eine philosophische Hinführung.* Freiburg i.B.: Herder, 1975.

Castro Engler, J. de. "Lex Orandi, Lex Credendi." *Revista eclesiástica brasileira* 11 (1951):23-43.

Cecchetti, I. "Tibi silentium laus." In *Miscellanea Liturgica. [Festschrift for C. Mohlberg].* Vol. 2. Rome: Edizioni liturgiche, 1949, 521-70.

Clerck, P. de. "'Lex orandi, lex credendi': Sens originel et avatars historiques d'un adage équivoque." *Questions liturgiques et paroissiales* 59 (1978):193-212. English translation: "'Lex orandi, lex credendi': The Original Sense and Historical Avatars of an Equivocal Adage." *Studia Liturgica* 24 (1994):178-200.

Dalmais, I.-H. "La liturgie comme lieu théologique." *La Maison-Dieu* 78 (1964):97-105.

———. "The Liturgy and the Deposit of Faith." In *The Church at Prayer.* Vol. 1. Ed. A. G. Martimort. New York: Desclée Co., 1968, 212-19.

Davis, C. *Liturgy and Doctrine: The Doctrinal Basis of the Liturgical Movement.* New York: Sheed and Ward, 1960.

Deichgräber, R. "Formeln, liturgische II. Neues Testament und Alte Kirche." In *Theologische Realenzyklopädie* 11 (1983):252-71.

Driscoll, J. "Liturgy and Fundamental Theology: Frameworks for a Dialogue." *Ecclesia Orans* 11 (1994):69-99.

Drumm, J. *Doxologie und Dogma: Die Bedeutung der Doxologie für die Wiedergewinnung theologischer Rede in der evangelischen Theologie.* Paderborn: Ferdinand Schöningh, 1991.

Dürig, W. "Zur Interpretation des Axioms 'Legem credendi lex statuat supplicandi.'" In *Veritati catholicae [Festschrift for L. Scheffczyk].* Ed. A. Ziegenaus et al. Aschaffenburg: Pattloch, 1985, 226-36.

Ebeling, G. *Dogmatik des christlichen Glaubens.* Vol. 1, *Prolegomena, Teil 1.* Tübingen: Mohr, 1979.

———. "Die Notwendigkeit des christlichen Gottesdienstes." *Zeitschrift für Theologie und Kirche* 67 (1970):232-49.

Eguiluz, A. "Lex orandi, lex credendi." *Verdad y Vida* 6 (1948):45-67.

Fagerberg, D. W. *What Is Liturgical Theology? A Study in Methodology.* Collegeville, Minn.: Liturgical Press, 1992.

Federer, K. *Liturgie und Glaube: "Legem credendi lex statuat supplicandi": Eine theologiegeschichtliche Untersuchung.* Freiburg i.d.S.: Paulusverlag, 1950.

Garijo-Guembe, M. M. "Überlegungen für einen Dialog zwischen Orthodoxie und Katholizismus im Hinblick auf den Satz 'Lex orandi—lex credendi.'" In *Liturgie—ein vergessenes Thema der Theologie?* Ed. K. Richter. Freiburg i.B.: Herder, 1987 (2d ed.), 128-52.

Grabner-Haider, A. *Glaubenssprache: Ihre Struktur und Anwendbarkeit in Verkündigung und Theologie.* Wien: Herder, 1975.

Griese, E. "Perspektiven einer liturgischen Theologie." *Una Sancta* 24 (1969):102-13.

Growth in Agreement: Reports and Agreed Statements of Ecumenical Conversations on a World Level. Ed. H. Meyer and L. Vischer. New York: Paulist Press; Geneva: WCC, 1984.

Gruber, W. *Der Beitrag der Dogmatik zur Liturgischen Bewegung.* Graz: Akademische Druck- und Verlagsanstalt, 1959.

Guardini, R. *Kultbild und Andachtsbild: Brief an einen Kunsthistoriker.* Würzburg: Werkbund Verlag, n.d.

Häußling, A. A. "Kosmische Dimension und gesellschaftliche Wirklichkeit: Zu einem Erfahrungswandel in der Liturgie." *Archiv für Liturgiewissenschaft* 25 (1983):1-8.

———. "Die kritische Funktion der Liturgiewissenschaft." In *Liturgie und Gesellschaft.* Ed. H. B. Meyer. Innsbruck: Tyrolia Verlag, 1970, 103-30.

———. "Liturgical Language." In *Sacramentum Mundi: An Encyclopedia of Theology.* Vol. 3. Ed. K. Rahner. New York: Herder and Herder, 1969, 331-33.

———. "Liturgiewissenschaft zwei Jahrzehnte nach Konzilsbeginn." *Archiv für Liturgiewissenschaft* 24 (1982):1-18.

Hardy, D. W. and Ford, D. *Jubilate: Theology in Praise.* London: Darton, Longman & Todd, 1984. North American edition: *Praising and Knowing God.* Philadelphia: Westminster Press, 1985.

Henkys, J. *Dietrich Bonhoeffers Gefängnisgedichte: Beiträge zu ihrer Interpretation.* München: Chr. Kaiser, 1986.

Hoffman, L. A. *Beyond the Text: A Holistic Approach to Liturgy.* Bloomington: Indiana University Press, 1987.

Irwin, K. W. *Liturgical Theology: A Primer.* Collegeville, Minn.: Liturgical Press, 1990.

Jennings, T. W. "On Ritual Knowledge." *The Journal of Religion* 62 (1982):111-27.

Jenny, M. "'Vocibus unitis': Auch ein Weg zur Einheit." In *Liturgie und Dichtung. Ein interdisziplinäres Kompendium.* Vol. 2, *Interdisziplinäre Reflexion.* Ed. H. Becker and R. Kaczynski. St. Ottilien: EOS, 1983, 173-205.

Johnson, E. A. *Analogy/Doxology and Their Connection with Christology in the Thought of Wolfhart Pannenberg.* Ph.D. dissertation, Catholic University of America, 1981.

Jungmann, J. A. "Doxologie." In *Lexikon für Theologie und Kirche* 3 (1959 [2d ed.]):534-36.

Kallis, A. "Theologie als Doxologie: Der Stellenwert der Liturgie in der orthodoxen Kirche und Theologie." In *Liturgie—ein vergessenes Thema der Theologie?* Ed. K. Richter. Freiburg i.B.: Herder 1987 (2d ed.), 42-53.

Kasper, W. "Die Wissenschaftspraxis der Theologie." In *Handbuch der Fundamentaltheologie.* Vol. 1, *Traktat Theologische Erkenntnislehre.* Ed. W. Kern et al. Freiburg i.B.: Herder, 1988, 242-76.

Kavanagh, A. *On Liturgical Theology.* New York: Pueblo, 1985.

Kilmartin, E. J. *Christian Liturgy: Theology and Practice.* Vol. 1, *Systematic Theology of Liturgy.* Kansas City: Sheed and Ward, 1988.

Kimbrough, S T, Jr. "Hymns are Theology." *Theology Today* 42 (1985):59-68.

Kirchberg, J. *Theologie in der Anrede als Weg zur Verständigung zwischen Juden und Christen.* Innsbruck: Tyrolia, 1991.

Kittel, G. and Rad, G. von. "δόξα." In *Theological Dictionary of the New Testament.* Vol. 2. Grand Rapids: W. B. Eerdmans, 1985, 233-53.

Klein, C. "Das Gebet in der Begegnung zwischen westlicher und ostkirchlicher Theologie und Frömmigkeit." *Kerygma und Dogma* 34 (1988):232-50.

Krahe, M.-J. "'Psalmen, Hymnen und Lieder, wie der Geist sie eingibt': Doxologie als Ursprung und Ziel aller Theologie." In *Liturgie und Dichtung: Ein interdisziplinäres Kompendium.* Vol. 2, *Interdisziplinäre Reflexion.* Ed. H. Becker and R. Kaczynski. St. Ottilien: EOS, 1983, 923-57.

LaCugna, C. M. "Can Liturgy ever again become a Source for Theology?" *Studia Liturgica* 19 (1989):1-13.

Ladrière, J. *Language and Belief.* Notre Dame: University Press, 1972.

———. "The Performativity of Liturgical Language." In *Liturgical Experience of Faith.* Concilium series. Vol. 82. Ed. H. Schmidt and D. Power. New York: Herder and Herder, 1973, 50-61.

Lang, O. "Vom Opfer des Lobes." In *Gott feiern. Theologische Anregung und geistliche Vertiefung zur Feier von Messe und Stundengebet [Festschrift for Th. Schnitzler].* Ed. J. G. Plöger. Freiburg i.B.: Herder, 1980 (2d ed.), 340-49.

Lathrop, G. W. *Holy Things: A Liturgical Theology*. Minneapolis: Fortress Press, 1993.

Leeuw, G. van der. *Sakramentales Denken: Erscheinungsformen und Wesen der außerchristlichen und christlichen Sakramente*. Kassel: J. Stauda, 1959.

Lehmann, K. "Gottesdienst als Ausdruck des Glaubens. Plädoyer für ein neues Gespräch zwischen Liturgiewissenschaft und dogmatischer Theologie." *Liturgisches Jahrbuch* 30 (1980):197-214.

Lies, L. "Theologie als eulogisches Handeln." *Zeitschrift für Katholische Theologie* 107 (1985):76-91.

Liturgical Experience of Faith. Concilium series. Vol. 82. Ed. H. Schmidt and D. Power. New York: Herder and Herder, 1973.

La Liturgie: Expression de la foi. Conférences Saint-Serge, XXVe Semaine d'Etudes Liturgiques, Paris 1978. Ed. A. M. Triacca and A. Pistoia. Rome: CLV Edizioni liturgiche, 1979.

Liturgie—vergessenes Thema der Theologie? Ed. K. Richter. Freiburg i.B.: Herder, 1987 (2d ed.).

Lønning, P. "'Die eucharistische Vision'—eine neue Zusammenschau von Gottesdienst und Bekenntnisgemeinschaft?" *Una Sancta* 39 (1984):224-33.

Lukken, G. "La liturgie comme lieu théologique irremplaçable." *Questions liturgiques et paroissiales* 56 (1975):97-112.

———. "Plaidoyer pour une approche intégrale de la liturgie comme lieu théologique: Un défi à toute la théologie." *Questions Liturgiques* 68 (1987) 242-55.

Maas-Ewerd, Th. "Die Liturgie in der Theologie: Zur letzten Festgabe für Emil Joseph Lengeling (18.6.1986)." *Liturgisches Jahrbuch* 38 (1988):173-89.

Macquarrie, J. "Prayer and Theological Reflection." In *The Study of Spirituality*. Ed. C. Jones et al. New York: Oxford University Press, 1986, 584-87.

The Mandate from the Fourth World Conference on Faith and Order at Montreal. Geneva: WCC, 1963.

Marquardt, M. "Theologie des Gotteslobs." In *Theologie des Gotteslobs*. Ed. M. Weyer. Stuttgart: Christliches Verlagshaus, 1991, 7-23.

McGrath, A. E. "Geschichte, Überlieferung und Erzählung." *Kerygma und Dogma* 32 (1986):234-53.

Merkel, F. "Liturgie—ein vergessenes Thema evangelischer Theologie?" In *Liturgie—ein vergessenes Thema der Theologie?* Ed. K. Richter. Freiburg i.B.: Herder, 1987 (2d ed.), 33-41.

Merz, M. B. "Gebetsformen der Liturgie." In *Gottesdienst der Kirche: Handbuch der Liturgiewissenschaft*. Vol. 3, *Gestalt des Gottesdienstes*. Ed. H. B. Meyer et al. Regensburg: Pustet, 1987, 97-130.

————. *Liturgisches Gebet als Geschehen: Liturgiewissenschaftlich-linguistische Studie anhand der Gebetsgattung Eucharistisches Hochgebet.* Münster: Aschendorff, 1988.

Miller, P. "'Enthroned on the Praises of Israel': The Praise of God in Old Testament Theology." *Interpretation* 39 (1985):5-19.

Mitchell, L. L. "The Liturgical Roots of Theology." In *Time and Community [Festschrift for T. J. Talley].* Ed. J. N. Alexander. Washington, D.C.: Pastoral Press, 1990, 243-54.

Mössinger, R. *Zur Lehre des christlichen Gebets: Gedanken über ein vernachlässigtes Thema evangelischer Theologie.* Göttingen: Vandenhoeck & Ruprecht, 1987.

Mohrmann, C. "Sakralsprache und Umgangssprache." *Archiv für Liturgiewissenschaft* 10 (1968):344-54.

Müller, G. "Gebet. VIII. Dogmatische Probleme gegenwärtiger Gebetstheologie." In *Theologische Realenzyklopädie* 12 (1983):84-94.

The Myth of God Incarnate. Ed. J. H. Hick. London: SCM Press, 1977.

Neunheuser, B. "Der Beitrag der Liturgie zur theologischen Erneuerung." *Gregorianum* 50 (1969):589-614.

Nissiotis, N. "Österliche Freude als doxologischer Ausdruck des Glaubens." In *Gottes Zukunft—Zukunft der Welt [Festschrift for J. Moltmann].* Ed. H. Deuser. München: Chr. Kaiser, 1986, 78-88.

————. "La théologie en tant que science et en tant que doxologie." *Irénikon* 33 (1960):291-310.

Old, H. Oliphant. *Themes and Variations for a Christian Doxology: Some Thoughts on the Theology of Worship.* Grand Rapids: W. B. Eerdmans, 1992.

Olivetti, M. M. "Sich in seinem Namen versammeln: Kirche als Gottesnennung." In *Gott nennen: Phänomenologische Zugänge.* Ed. B. Casper. Freiburg i.B.: Alber, 1981, 189-217.

Oppenheim, P. "Liturgie und Dogma." *Theologie und Glaube* 27 (1935):559-68.

————. *Principia theologiae liturgicae.* Turin: Marietti, 1947.

Pannenberg, W. "Analogie und Doxologie." In *Dogma und Denkstrukturen [Festschrift for E. Schlink].* Ed. W. Joest and W. Pannenberg. Göttingen: Vandenhoeck & Ruprecht, 1963, 96-115. (Reprinted in: W. Pannenberg, *Grundfragen Systematischer Theologie: Gesammelte Aufsätze.* Göttingen: Vandenhoeck & Ruprecht, 1967, 181-201). English translation: "Analogy and Doxology." In W. Pannenberg, *Basic Questions in Theology.* Vol. 1. London: SCM Press, 1970, 212-38.

Pascher, J. "Theologische Erkenntnis aus der Liturgie." In *Einsicht und Glaube [Festschrift for G. Söhngen].* Ed. J. Ratzinger and H. Fries. Freiburg i.B.: Herder, 1962, 243-58.

Pinto, M. *O valor teológico da liturgia.* Braga: Cruz, 1952.

Pius XII. "Mediator Dei." *Acta Apostolicae Sedis* 39 (1947):521-600.

Plathow, M. "Geist und Gebet." *Kerygma und Dogma* 29 (1983):47-65.

Power, D. N. "Cult to Culture: The Liturgical Foundation of Theology." *Worship* 54 (1980):482-95.

———. "Doxology: The Praise of God in Worship, Doctrine and Life." *Worship* 55 (1981):61-69.

———. "Two Expressions of Faith: Worship and Theology." In *Liturgical Experience of Faith.* Concilium series. Vol. 82. Ed. H. Schmidt and D. Power. New York: Herder and Herder, 1973, 95-106.

Prenter, R. "Liturgie et dogme." *Revue d'histoire et de philosophie religieuses* 38 (1958):115-28.

———. "Liturgy and Theology." In R. Prenter, *Theologie und Gottesdienst: Gesammelte Aufsätze.* Arhus: Aros; Göttingen: Vandenhoeck & Ruprecht, 1977, 139-51.

Rad, G. von. *Old Testament Theology.* Vol. 1, *The Theology of Israel's Historical Traditions.* New York: Harper & Row, 1962.

Richter, K. "Die Liturgie—zentrales Thema der Theologie." In *Liturgie—ein vergessenes Thema der Theologie?* Ed. K. Richter. Freiburg i.B.: Herder, 1987 (2d ed.), 9-27.

Ritschl, D. *Zur Logik der Theologie: Kurze Darstellung der Zusammenhänge theologischer Grundgedanken.* München: Chr. Kaiser, 1984. English edition: *The Logic of Theology: A Brief Account of the Relationship Between Basic Concepts in Theology.* Philadelphia: Fortress Press, 1987.

———. *Memory and Hope: An Inquiry Concerning the Presence of Christ.* New York: Macmillan; London: Collier-Macmillan, 1967.

Saliers, D. E. "Theology and Prayer: Some Conceptual Reminders." *Worship* 48 (1974):230-35.

———. *Worship as Theology: Foretaste of Glory Divine.* Nashville: Abingdon Press, 1994.

Sauter, G. "Das Gebet als Wurzel des Redens von Gott." *glaube und lernen* 1 (1986):21-38.

———. "Reden von Gott im Gebet." In *Gott nennen: Phänomenologische Zugänge.* Ed. B. Casper. Freiburg i.B.: Alber, 1981, 219-42.

Schaeffler, R. *Das Gebet und das Argument, zwei Weisen des Sprechens von Gott: Eine Einführung in die Theorie der religiösen Sprache.* Düsseldorf: Patmos, 1989.

———. *Kleine Sprachlehre des Gebets.* Einsiedeln: Johannes Verlag, 1988.

———. "Kultisches Handeln: Die Frage nach Proben seiner Bewährung und nach Kriterien seiner Legitimation." In *Ankunft Gottes und Handeln des Menschen: Thesen über Kult und Sakrament*. Ed. P. Hünermann and R. Schaeffler. Freiburg i.B.: Herder, 1977, 9-50.

———. "Kultus als Weltauslegung." In *Kult in der säkularisierten Welt*. Ed. B. Fischer et al. Regensburg: Pustet, 1975, 9-62.

———. *Religionsphilosophie*. Freiburg i.B.: Alber, 1983.

Schermann, J. *Die Sprache im Gottesdienst*. Innsbruck: Tyrolia, 1987.

Schillebeeckx, E. "The Liturgy and Theology." In E. Schillebeeckx, *Revelation and Theology*. Vol. 1. New York: Sheed and Ward, 1967, 218-22.

Schilson, A. "'Gedachte Liturgie' als Mystagogie. Überlegungen zum Verhältnis von Dogmatik und Liturgie." In *Dogma und Glaube. Bausteine für eine theologische Erkenntnislehre [Festschrift for W. Kasper]*. Ed. E. Schockenhoff and P. Walter. Mainz: Matthias Grünewald Verlag, 1993, 213-34.

———. *Theologie als Sakramententheologie: Die Mysterientheologie Odo Casels*. Mainz: Matthias Grünewald Verlag, 1982.

Schlink, E. "Die Aufgaben einer ökumenischen Dogmatik." In *Zur Auferbauung des Leibes Christi [Festschrift for P. Brunner]*. Ed. E. Schlink and A. Peters. Kassel: J. Stauda, 1965, 84-93.

———. "Gesetz und Evangelium als kontroverstheologisches Problem." In E. Schlink, *Der kommende Christus und die kirchlichen Traditionen: Beiträge zum Gespräch zwischen den getrennten Kirchen*. Göttingen: Vandenhoeck & Ruprecht, 1961, 126-59. English translation: "Law and Gospel as a Controversial Theological Problem." In E. Schlink, *The Coming Christ and the Coming Church*. Edinburgh: Oliver & Boyd, 1967, 144-85.

———. "Die Methode des dogmatischen ökumenischen Dialogs." *Kerygma und Dogma* 12 (1966):205-11.

———. *Ökumenische Dogmatik: Grundzüge*. Göttingen: Vandenhoeck & Ruprecht, 1983.

———. "Die Struktur der dogmatischen Aussage als ökumenisches Problem." *Kerygma und Dogma* 3 (1957):251-306. [Reprinted in: *Der kommende Christus und die kirchlichen Traditionen: Beiträge zum Gespräch zwischen den getrennten Kirchen*, 24-79]. English translation: "The Structure of Dogmatic Statements as an Ecumenical Problem." In *The Coming Christ and the Coming Church*, 16-84.

———. "Wandlungen im protestantischen Verständnis der Ostkirche." In *Der kommende Christus und die kirchlichen Traditionen: Beiträge zum Gespräch zwischen den getrennten Kirchen*, 221-31. English translation: "Changes in Protestant Thinking about the Eastern Church." In *The Coming Christ and the Coming Church*, 269-84.

Schmemann, A. *Introduction to Liturgical Theology*. Portland, Maine: American Orthodox Press, 1966.

————. "Théologie liturgique: Remarques méthodologiques." In *La Liturgie, son sens, son ésprit, sa méthode: Liturgie et théologie.* Ed. A. Pistoia and A. M. Triacca. Rome: CLV Edizioni liturgiche, 1982, 297-303. English translation: "Liturgical Theology: Remarks on Method." In *Liturgy and Tradition: Theological Reflections of Alexander Schmemann.* Ed. T. Fisch. Crestwood, N.Y.: St. Vladimir's Seminary Press, 1990, 137-44.

————. "Theology and Liturgical Tradition." In *Worship in Scripture and Tradition.* Ed. M. H. Shepherd. New York: Oxford University Press, 1963, 165-78. Reprinted in: *Liturgy and Tradition: Theological Reflections of Alexander Schmemann,* 11-20.

Schmidt, H. A. P. "Lex orandi lex credendi in recentioribus documentis pontificiis." *Periodica de re morali canonica liturgica* 40 (1951):5-28.

Schöfer, F. O. "Die Liturgie als gebetetes Dogma." *Eine Heilige Kirche* 17 (1935):111-15.

Schorlemmer, P. "Der liturgische Charakter der dogmatischen Theologie." *Eine Heilige Kirche* 17 (1935):115-21.

Schückler, G. "Legem credendi lex statuat supplicandi: Ursprung und Sinn des Liturgiebeweises." *Catholica* 10 (1955):26-41.

Schulz, H.-J. *Ökumenische Glaubenseinheit aus eucharistischer Überlieferung.* Paderborn: Verlag Bonifacius-Druckerei, 1976.

Seckler, M. "Theologie als Glaubenswissenschaft." In *Handbuch der Fundamentaltheologie.* Vol. 4, *Traktat theologische Erkenntnislehre.* Ed. W. Kern et al. Freiburg i.B.: Herder, 1988, 180-241.

Steinheimer, M. *Die Doxa tou Theou in der römischen Liturgie.* München: K. Zink, 1951.

Stenzel, A. "Liturgie als theologischer Ort." In *Mysterium Salutis.* Vol. 1, *Die Grundlagen heilsgeschichtlicher Dogmatik.* Ed. J. Feiner and M. Löhrer. Einsiedeln: Benziger, 1965, 606-20.

Stevenson, K. W. "Lex Orandi and Lex Credendi—Strange Bedfellows?: Some Reflections on Worship and Doctrine." *Scottish Journal of Theology* 39 (1986):225-41.

Stevick, D. B. "The Language of Prayer." *Worship* 52 (1978):542-60.

————. "Toward a Phenomenology of Praise." In *Worship Points the Way [Festschrift for M. H. Shepherd].* Ed. M. C. Burson. New York: Seabury Press, 1981), 151-66.

Stock, A. "Zur poetischen Theologie von Huub Oosterhuis." *Theologische Quartalschrift* 167 (1987):45-55.

Stuiber, A. "Doxologie." In *Reallexikon für Antike und Christentum* 4 (1959):210-26.

Suttner, E. Chr. "Glaubensverkündigung durch Lobpreis: Zur Interpretation der byzantinischen gottesdienstlichen Hymnen." In *Unser ganzes Leben Christus unserm Gott überantworten: Studien zur ostkirchlichen Spiri-*

tualität [Festschrift for F. von Lilienfeld]. Ed. P. Hauptmann. Göttingen: Vandenhoeck & Ruprecht, 1982, 76-101.

Theodorou, E. "Theologie und Liturgie." *La théologie dans l'Eglise et dans le monde.* Chambésy: Centre orthodoxe du Patriarcat oecuménique, 1984, 343-60.

Theologia in Hymnis, oder: Universal-Gesangbuch. Ed. J. J. Gottschaldt. Leipzig: J. C. Martini, 1737.

Theorie der Sprachhandlungen und heutige Ekklesiologie. Ed. P. Hünermann and R. Schaeffler. Freiburg i.B.: Herder, 1987.

Triacca, A. M. "Le sens théologique de la liturgie et/ou le sens liturgique de la théologie: Esquisse initiale pour une synthèse." In *La Liturgie, son sens, son ésprit, sa méthode: Liturgie et théologie.* Ed. A. Pistoia and A. M. Triacca. Rome: CLV Edizioni liturgiche, 1982, 321-37.

Tyciak, J. *Theologie in Hymnen: Theologische Perspektiven der byzantinischen Liturgie.* Trier: Paulinus-Verlag, 1973.

Tyrrell, G. *Lex Credendi, a Sequel to Lex Orandi.* London: Longmans, Green and Co., 1903; new impression, 1907.

———. "Lex Orandi, Lex Credendi." In G. Tyrrell, *Through Scylla and Charybdis, or: the Old Theology and the New.* London: Longmans, Green and Co., 1907, 85-105.

———. *Lex Orandi, or Prayer and Creed.* London: Longmans, Green and Co., 1906; new impression, 1907.

Umberg, J. B. "Liturgischer Stil und Dogmatik." *Scholastik* 1 (1926):481-503.

Vagaggini, C. *Theological Dimensions of the Liturgy: A General Treatise on the Theology of the Liturgy.* Collegeville, Minn.: Liturgical Press, 1976; from the Fourth Italian Edition, revised and augmented by the author.

Vaquero, T. "Valor Dogmatico da Liturgia ou Relaçoes Entre Liturgia e Fé." *Revista eclesiástica brasileira* 9 (1949):346-63.

Vinel, J. A. "L'argument liturgique opposé par Saint Augustin aux Pélagiens." *Questions Liturgiques* 68 (1987):209-41.

Vonier, A. "The Doctrinal Power of the Liturgy in the Catholic Church." *Clergy Review* 9 (1935):1-8.

Vorgrimler, H. "Liturgie als Thema der Dogmatik." In *Liturgie—ein vergessenes Thema der Theologie?* Ed. K. Richter. Freiburg i.B.: Herder, 1987 (2d ed.), 113-27.

Vries, W. de. "Lex supplicandi—lex credendi." *Ephemerides liturgicae* 47 (1933):48-58.

Wainwright, G. "Adoration." In *The Westminster Dictionary of Christian Theology.* Ed. A. Richardson and J. Bowden. Philadelphia: Westminster Press, 1983, 6.

211

―――. "Doctrine, Liturgy and." In *The New Dictionary of Sacramental Worship*. Ed. P. E. Fink. Collegeville, Minn.: Liturgical Press, 1990, 349-58.

―――. *Doxology. The Praise of God in Worship, Doctrine and Life: A Systematic Theology*. London: Oxford University Press; New York: Oxford University Press, 1980. Second edition, London 1982, New York 1984.

―――. "Der Gottesdienst als 'Locus Theologicus' oder: Der Gottesdienst als Quelle und Thema der Theologie." *Kerygma und Dogma* 28 (1982):248-58.

―――. "Gottesdienst. IX. Systematisch-theologisch." In *Theologische Realenzyklopädie* 14 (1985):85-93.

―――. "A Language in Which We Speak to God." *Worship* 57 (1983):309-21.

―――. "The Language of Worship." In *The Study of Liturgy*. Ed. P. Bradshaw et al. London: SPCK; New York: Oxford University Press, 1992 (2d ed.), 519-27.

―――. "Lex orandi, lex credendi." In *Dictionary of the Ecumenical Movement*. Ed. N. Lossky et al. Geneva: WCC, 1991, 600-604.

―――. "Liturgy and Doctrine." In *The Blackwell Encyclopedia of Modern Christian Thought*. Ed. A. E. McGrath. Oxford; Cambridge, Mass.: Blackwell, 1993, 339-44.

―――. "In Praise of God." *Worship* 53 (1979):496-511.

―――. "The Praise of God in the Theological Reflection of the Church." *Interpretation* 39 (1985):35-45.

―――. "Tradition as a Liturgical Act." In *The Quadrilog: Tradition and the Future of Ecumenism [Festschrift for G. H. Tavard]*. Ed. K. Hagen. Collegeville, Minn.: Liturgical Press, 1994, 129-46.

Ways of Worship. The Report of a Theological Commission of Faith and Order. Ed. P. Edwall et al. London: SCM Press, 1951.

Welte, B. "Religiöse Sprache." *Archiv für Liturgiewissenschaft* 15 (1973):7-20.

―――. *Religionsphilosophie*. Freiburg i.B.: Herder, 1978.

Werlen, I. *Ritual und Sprache: Zum Verhältnis von Sprechen und Handeln in Ritualen*. Tübingen: G. Narr, 1984.

"Worship and the Oneness of Christ's Church." In *The Fourth World Conference on Faith and Order. The Report from Montreal 1963*. Ed. P. C. Rodger and L. Vischer. London: SCM Press, 1964, 69-80.

Zeller, D. "Gott nennen an einem Beispiel aus dem Psalter." In *Gott nennen: Phänomenologische Zugänge*. Ed. B. Casper. Freiburg i.B.: Alber, 1981, 13-34.

II. Charles Wesley's Hymns

Adams, C. *The Poet Preacher: a Brief Memorial of Charles Wesley, the Eminent Preacher and Poet*. New York: Carlton & Porter, 1859.

Adey, L. *Hymns and the Christian "Myth."* Vancouver: University of British Columbia Press, 1986.

Algermissen, K. "Methodisten, Methodismus." In *Lexikon für Theologie und Kirche* 7 (1962 [2d ed.]):369-72.

Anderson, L. *The Doctrine of Christian Holiness as Found in the Writings of John Wesley and Reflected in His Hymns.* M.A. thesis, St. John's University, Collegeville, Minn., 1969.

Baker, F. *Charles Wesley as Revealed by His Letters.* London: Epworth Press, 1948.

———. "Charles Wesley's Letters." In *Charles Wesley: Poet and Theologian.* Ed. S T Kimbrough, Jr. Nashville: Kingswood Books, 1992, 72-84.

———. "Charles Wesley's Productivity as a Religious Poet." *Proceedings of the Wesley Historical Society* 47 (1989):1-12.

———. *Charles Wesley's Verse: An Introduction.* London: Epworth Press, 1964; 1988 (2d ed.).

———. "The Prose Writings of Charles Wesley." *London Quarterly and Holborn Review* 182 (1957):268-74.

Beckerlegge, O. A. "An Attempt at a Classification of Charles Wesley's Metres." *London Quarterly and Holborn Review* 169 (1944):219-27.

———. "Charles Wesley's Poetical Corpus." In *Charles Wesley: Poet and Theologian*, 30-44.

———. "Charles Wesley's Vocabulary." *London Quarterly and Holborn Review* 193 (1968):152-61.

———. "The Development of the 'Collection.'" In *A Collection of Hymns for the Use of the People Called Methodists.* Ed. F. Hildebrandt and O. A. Beckerlegge. Oxford: Oxford University Press, 1983, 22-30.

———. "John Wesley and the German Hymns." *London Quarterly and Holborn Review* 165 (1940):430-39.

———. "John Wesley as Hymn-book Editor." In *A Collection of Hymns for the Use of the People Called Methodists*, 55-61.

———. "A Man of One Book: Charles Wesley and the Scriptures." *Epworth Review* 15 (1988):44-50.

———. "The Sources of the 'Collection.'" In *A Collection of Hymns for the Use of the People Called Methodists*, 31-38.

Benson, L. F. *The English Hymn: Its Development and Use in Worship.* New York: Hodder & Stoughton, George H. Doran Co., 1915.

Berger, T. "Charles Wesley: A Literary Overview." In *Charles Wesley: Poet and Theologian*, 21-29.

Berger, T. "'Theologie die man singen kann.'" Christologische Titel im methodistischen Gesangbuch von 1780." *Una Sancta* 47 (1992):123-29.

Bett, H. "German Books on Wesley's Hymns." In *Proceedings of the Wesley Historical Society* 21 (1938):180-81.

———. *The Hymns of Methodism in their Literary Relations*. London: Epworth Press, 1913; 2d ed., 1920; revised edition, 1945.

———. "John Wesley's Translations of German Hymns." *London Quarterly and Holborn Review* 165 (1940):288-94.

Bettermann, W. *Theologie und Sprache bei Zinzendorf*. Gotha: L. Klotz, 1953.

Brailsford, M. B. *A Tale of Two Brothers: John and Charles Wesley*. New York: Oxford University Press, 1954.

Bryant, B. E. "Trinity and Hymnody: The Doctrine of the Trinity in the Hymns of Charles Wesley." *Wesleyan Theological Journal* 25/2 (1990):64-73.

Bucher, A. J. *Ein Sänger des Kreuzes*. Basel: Spittler, 1912.

Charles Wesley: Poet and Theologian. Ed. S T Kimbrough, Jr. Nashville: Kingswood Books, 1992.

Charles Wesley: A Reader. Ed. John R. Tyson. New York: Oxford University Press, 1989.

Charles Wesley's Earliest Evangelical Sermons: Six Shorthand Manuscript Sermons now for the first Time Transcribed from the Original. Ed. T. R. Albin and O. A. Beckerlegge. Ilford: Wesley Historical Society in association with R. Odcombe, 1987.

Clark, E. T. *Charles Wesley: The Singer of the Evangelical Revival*. Nashville: The Upper Room, 1957.

Clark, G. "Charles Wesley's Greatest Poem." *Methodist History* 26 (1988):163-71.

A Collection of Hymns for the Use of the People Called Methodists. Ed. F. Hildebrandt and O. A. Beckerlegge. Oxford: Oxford University Press, 1983.

A Collection of Psalms and Hymns, [Charles-Town 1737]. Reprint ed. F. Baker and G. W. Williams. Charleston, S.C.: Wesley Historical Society, Lewis Timothy, 1964.

Colquhoun, F. *Charles Wesley, 1707–1788: The Poet of the Evangelical Revival*. London: Church Book Room Press, n.d.

Creamer, D. *Methodist Hymnology; Comprehending Notices of the Poetical Works of John and Charles Wesley*. New York: Joseph Longking, 1848.

Dahn, K. "Die Hymnologie im deutschsprachigen Methodismus." In *Der Methodismus*. Ed. C. E. Sommer. Stuttgart: Evangelisches Verlagswerk, 1968, 166-84.

Dale, J. "Charles Wesley, the Odyssey, and Clement of Alexandria." *Methodist History* 30 (1992):100-103.

———. "Some Echoes of Charles Wesley's Hymns in His Journal." *London Quarterly and Holborn Review* 184 (1959):336-44.

————. *The Theological and Literary Qualities of the Poetry of Charles Wesley in Relation to the Standards of His Age*. Ph.D. dissertation, Cambridge University, 1960.

Dallimore, A. A. *A Heart Set Free: The Life of Charles Wesley*. Westchester, Ill.: Crossway Books, 1988.

Damm, U. F. *Die Deutschlandreise John Wesleys: Grund—Orte—Begegnungen—Auswirkungen*. Stuttgart: Christliches Verlagshaus, 1984.

Davie, D. *Purity of Diction in English Verse*. New York: Oxford University Press, 1953.

————. *The Eighteenth-Century Hymn in England*. Cambridge: Cambridge University Press, 1993, 57-70.

Davies, H. "Charles Wesley and the Calvinist Tradition." In *Charles Wesley: Poet and Theologian*, 186-203.

Demaray, D. E. *The Innovation of John Newton (1725–1807): Synergism of Word and Music in Eighteenth Century Evangelism*. Lewiston, Queenston: E. Mellen Press, 1988.

Doughty, W. L. "Charles Wesley, Preacher." *London Quarterly and Holborn Review* 182 (1957):263-67.

Eißele, K. G. *Karl Wesley, Sänger des Methodismus*. Bremen: Anker-Verlag, 1932.

Ekrut, J. C. *Universal Redemption, Assurance of Salvation, and Christian Perfection in the Hymns of Charles Wesley, With Poetic Analyses and Tune Examples*. M.Mus. thesis, Southwestern Baptist Theological Seminary, Fort Worth, Texas, 1978.

Elert, W. *Morphologie des Luthertums*. Vol. 1, *Theologie und Weltanschauung des Luthertums hauptsächlich im 16. und 17. Jahrhundert*. München: Beck, 1952 (2d ed.).

England, M. W. "The First Wesley Hymn Book." *Bulletin of the New York Public Library* 68 (1964):225-38.

Findlay, G. H. *Christ's Standard Bearer: A Study in the Hymns of Charles Wesley as They are Contained in the Last Edition (1876) of A Collection of Hymns for the Use of the People Called Methodists by the Rev. John Wesley, M.A.* London: Epworth Press, 1956.

A Flame of Love: A Personal Choice of Charles Wesley's Verse. Ed. T. Dudley-Smith. London: Triangle, 1987.

Fleming, R. L. *The Concept of Sacrifice in the Eucharistic Hymns of John and Charles Wesley*. D. Min. thesis, Southern Methodist University, Dallas, 1980.

Flew, R. N. *The Hymns of Charles Wesley: A Study of Their Structure*. London: Epworth Press, 1953.

Frost, F. "Biblical Imagery and Religious Experience in the Hymns of the Wesleys." *Proceedings of the Wesley Historical Society* 42 (1980):158-66.

Gallaway, C. *The Presence of Christ with the Worshipping Community: A Study in the Hymns of John and Charles Wesley.* Ph.D. dissertation, Emory University, Atlanta, 1988.

———. "Tradition Meets Revision: The Impact of the Wesley Hymn Corpus on the New United Methodist Hymnal." *Quarterly Review* 9 (1989):64-79.

Gill, F. C. *Charles Wesley, the First Methodist.* New York: Abingdon Press, 1964.

———. *The Romantic Movement and Methodism: A Study of English Romanticism and the Evangelical Revival.* London: Epworth Press, 1937; 1957 (2d ed.).

Hart, E. H. *The Influence of Paradise Lost on the Hymns of Charles Wesley.* M.A. thesis, University of British Columbia, 1985.

Heitzenrater, R. P. "Charles Wesley and the Methodist Tradition." In *Charles Wesley: Poet and Theologian,* 176-85.

———. "The Present State of Wesley Studies." *Methodist History* 22 (1984):221-33.

———. "The Quest for the First Methodist: Oxford Methodism Reconsidered." In R. P. Heitzenrater, *Mirror and Memory: Reflections on Early Methodism.* Nashville: Kingswood Books, 1989, 63-77.

Henry, M. *An Exposition of the Old and New Testament: Wherein Each Chapter is Summed up in its Contents; Each Sacred Text Inserted at large, in Distinct Paragraphs; Each Paragraph Reduced to its Proper Heads: the Sense Given, and Largely Illustrated; with Practical Remarks and Observances* [1708-1710]. New edition. 4 vols. New York: Fleming H. Revell Company, n.d.

Hildebrandt, F. *Christianity according to the Wesleys.* London: Epworth Press, 1956.

———. *From Luther to Wesley.* London: Lutterworth Press, 1951.

Hymns that Live: Their Meaning and Message. London: Hodder & Stoughton, 1980.

Jackson, T. *The Life of the Rev. Charles Wesley, M.A., Sometime Student of Christ-Church, Oxford: Comprising a Review of his Poetry; Sketches of the Rise and Progress of Methodism; with Notices of Contemporary Events and Characters.* 2 vols. London: John Mason, 1841; New York: G. Lane and P. P. Sanford, 1844.

Jarboe, B. M. *John and Charles Wesley: A Bibliography.* Metuchen, N.J.: Scarecrow Press, 1987.

John and Charles Wesley: Selected Prayers, Hymns, Journal Notes, Sermons, Letters, and Treatises. Ed. F. Whaling. Ramsey, N.J.: Paulist Press, 1981.

216

John Wesley. Ed. A. Outler. New York: Oxford University Press, 1964.

Jones, D. M. *Charles Wesley: A Study*. London: Skeffington (1919).

The Journal of the Rev. Charles Wesley. To which are Appended Selections from his Correspondence and Poetry. 2 vols. Ed. T. Jackson. London: John Mason, 1849.

The Journal of the Rev. Charles Wesley: The Early Journal, 1736–1739. Ed. J. Telford. London: Culley, 1910; reprint ed., Taylors, S.C.: The Methodist Reprint Society, 1977.

Kimbrough, S T, Jr. "Charles Wesley as a Biblical Interpreter." *Methodist History* 26 (1988):139-53.

———. "Charles Wesley and Biblical Interpretation." In *Charles Wesley: Poet and Theologian*, 106-36.

———. "The Charles Wesley Society." *Methodist History* 29 (1991):251-62.

———. *Lost in Wonder. Charles Wesley: The Meaning of His Hymns Today*. Nashville: Upper Room Books, 1987.

Kirk, J. *Charles Wesley, the Poet of Methodism: A Lecture*. London: John Mason, 1860.

Langford, T. A. "Charles Wesley as Theologian." In *Charles Wesley: Poet and Theologian*, 97-105.

Lloyd, A. K. "Charles Wesley's Debt to Matthew Henry." *London Quarterly and Holborn Review* 171 (1946):330-37.

Lofthouse, W. F. "Charles Wesley." In *A History of the Methodist Church in Great Britain*. Vol. 1. Ed. R. E. Davies and G. Rupp. London: Epworth Press, 1965, 113-44.

[Luther, M.] *D. Martin Luthers Werke: Kritische Gesamtausgabe. Weimarer Ausgabe*. Vol. 40, 1. Weimar: Hermann Böhlaus Nachfolger, 1911.

Manning, B. *The Hymns of Wesley and Watts: Five Informal Papers*. London: Epworth Press, 1942; 1948 (2d ed.).

Marshall, M. F. and Todd, J. *English Congregational Hymns in the Eighteenth Century*. Lexington: University Press of Kentucky, 1982.

Maser, F. E. "Charles Wesley and His Biographers." *Methodist History* 21 (1990):47-51.

Mayer, E. *Charles Wesleys Hymnen. Eine Untersuchung und literarische Würdigung*. Ph.D. dissertation, University of Tübingen, 1957.

Der Methodismus. Ed. C. E. Sommer. Stuttgart: Evangelisches Verlagswerk, 1968.

Morris, G. L. *Imagery in the Hymns of Charles Wesley*. Ph.D. dissertation, University of Arkansas, 1969.

Myers, E. P. *Singer of Six Thousand Songs: A Life of Charles Wesley*. London: T. Nelson; New York: T. Nelson, 1965.

Neues Geistreiches Gesang-Buch, auserlesene, so Alte als Neue, geistliche und liebliche Lieder, Nebst den Noten der unbekannten Melodeyen, in sich haltend, Zur Erweckung heiliger Andacht und Erbauung im Glauben und gottseligen Wesen. Ed. J. A. Freylinghausen. Halle: Verlegung des Waysenhauses, 1741, 1763.

Nichols, K. "Charles Wesley's Eucharistic Hymns: Their Relationship to the Book of Common Prayer." *The Hymn* 39 (1988):13-21.

Nicholson, R. S. "The Holiness Emphasis in the Wesleys' Hymns." *Wesleyan Theological Journal* 5 (1970):49-61.

Noll, M. A. "Romanticism and the Hymns of Charles Wesley." *Evangelical Quarterly* 46 (1974):195-223.

Nuelsen, J. L. *John Wesley und das deutsche Kirchenlied.* Bremen: Anker-Verlag, 1938. English translation: *John Wesley and the German Hymn: A Detailed Study of John Wesley's Translations of thirty-three German Hymns.* Keighley: Mantissa Press, 1972.

Nuttall, G. F. "Charles Wesley in 1739. By Joseph William of Kidderminster." *Proceedings of the Wesley Historical Society* 42 (1980):181-85.

Olney Hymns, in Three Books. London: W. Oliver, 1779.

The Poetical Works of John and Charles Wesley. Reprinted from the Originals, with the Last Corrections of the Authors; together with the Poems of Charles Wesley not before Published. 13 vols. Ed. G. Osborn. London: Wesleyan Methodist Conference Office, 1868–1872.

Quantrille, W. J. *The Triune God in the Hymns of Charles Wesley.* Ph.D. dissertation, Drew University, Madison, N.J., 1989.

A Rapture of Praise: Hymns of John and Charles Wesley. Ed. H. A. Hodges and A. M. Allchin. London: Hodder & Stoughton, 1966.

Rattenbury, J. E. *The Eucharistic Hymns of John and Charles Wesley.* London: Epworth Press, 1948. Revised edition ed. T. J. Crouch. Cleveland, Ohio: Order of Saint Luke Publications, 1990.

———. *The Evangelical Doctrines of Charles Wesley's Hymns.* London: Epworth Press, 1941, 1942 (2d ed).

Representative Verse of Charles Wesley. Ed. F. Baker. London: Epworth Press; New York: Abingdon Press, 1962.

Röbbelen, I. *Theologie und Frömmigkeit im deutschen evangelisch-lutherischen Gesangbuch des 17. und 18. Jahrhunderts.* Göttingen: Vandenhoeck & Ruprecht, 1957.

Rogal, S. J. *John and Charles Wesley.* Boston: Twayne Publishers, 1983.

Routley, E. "Charles Wesley and Matthew Henry." *The Congregational Quarterly* 33 (1955):345-51.

Schmidt, M. *John Wesley*. Vol. 1, *Die Zeit vom 17. Juni 1703 bis 24. Mai 1738*. Zürich: Gotthelf-Verlag, 1953; Vol. 2, Das Lebenswerk John Wesleys. Zürich: Gotthelf-Verlag, 1966. (reprinted in 3 vols., 1987–1988). English translation: *John Wesley: A Theological Biography*. 3 vols. Nashville: Abingdon Press, 1962–1973.

———. "Luthers Vorrede zum Römerbrief im Pietismus." In M. Schmidt, *Wiedergeburt und neuer Mensch: Gesammelte Studien zur Geschichte des Pietismus*. Witten: Luther-Verlag, 1969, 299-330.

———. "Methodismus." In *Konfessionskunde*. Ed. F. Heyer. Berlin: Walter de Gruyter, 1977, 595-605.

———. "Methodismus." In *Religion in Geschichte und Gegenwart* 4 (1960):913-19.

———. "Teilnahme an der göttlichen Natur. 2 Petr 1,4 in der theologischen Exegese des Pietismus und der lutherischen Orthodoxie." In M. Schmidt, *Wiedergeburt und neuer Mensch: Gesammelte Studien zur Geschichte des Pietismus*, 238-98.

Schneeberger, V. *Theologische Wurzeln des sozialen Akzents bei John Wesley*. Zürich: Gotthelf-Verlag, 1974.

Sermons by the Late Rev. Charles Wesley, A.M. London: Baldwin, Cradock, and Joy, 1816.

Short Hymns on Select Passages of the Holy Scriptures. 2 vols. Bristol: Farley, 1762.

Smith, T. "The Holy Spirit in the Hymns of the Wesleys." *Wesleyan Theological Journal* 16 (1981):20-48.

Stevenson, R. "John Wesley's first Hymnbook." *Review of Religion* 14 (1950):140-60.

Telford, J. *The Life of Rev. Charles Wesley, M.A.* London: Hodder & Stoughton, 1886.

Townsend, J. A. *Feelings Related to Assurance in Charles Wesley's Hymns*. Ph.D. dissertation, Fuller Theological Seminary, Pasadena, Calif., 1979.

Tripp, D. H. "Clement of Alexandria and the Wesley Brothers." *Proceedings of the Wesley Historical Society* 49 (1994):113-16.

Tyerman, L. *The Life and Times of the Rev. Samuel Wesley, Rector of Epworth and Father of the Revs. John and Charles Wesley, the Founders of the Methodists*. London: Simpkin, Marshall, 1866.

Tyson, J. R. "Charles Wesley and Edward Young." *Methodist History* 27 (1989):110-18.

———. "Charles Wesley and the German Hymns." *The Hymn* 35 (1984):153-57.

———. *Charles Wesley on Sanctification: A Biographical and Theological Study*. Grand Rapids: Francis Asbury Press, 1986.

————. *Charles Wesley's Theology of the Cross: An Examination of the Theology and Method of Charles Wesley as Seen in His Doctrine of the Atonement*. Ph.D. dissertation, Drew University, Madison, N.J., 1983.

————. "Charles Wesley's Theology of Redemption: A Study in Structure and Method." *Wesleyan Theological Journal* 20 (1985):7-28.

————. "Transfiguration of Scripture: Charles Wesley's Poetic Hermeneutic." *The Asbury Theological Journal* 47/2 (1992):17-41.

The Unpublished Poetry of Charles Wesley. 3 vols. Ed. S T Kimbrough, Jr. and O. A. Beckerlegge. Nashville: Kingswood Books, 1988–1992.

Völker, A. "Gesangbuch." In *Theologische Realenzyklopädie* 12 (1984):547-65.

Wakefield, G. S. "Charles Wesley's Spirituality and Its Meaning for Today." *The Charles Wesley Society Newsletter* 3/2 (1993):2-25.

Waterhouse, J. W. *The Bible in Charles Wesley's Hymns*. London: Epworth Press, 1954.

Welch, B. A. *Charles Wesley and the Celebrations of Evangelical Experience*. Ph.D. dissertation, University of Michigan, 1971.

Wesley Hymn Book. Ed. F. Hildebrandt. London: A. Weekes and Co., 1958; 1960 (2d ed.).

Wesley-Langshaw Correspondence: Charles Wesley, his Sons, and the Lancaster Organists. Ed. A. W. Wainwright. Atlanta: Scholars Press for Emory University, 1993.

[Wesley, J.] *The Works of John Wesley* (until 1984, The Oxford Edition of *The Works of John Wesley*. Oxford: Oxford University Press; from 1984 onward, The Bicentennial Edition of *The Works of John Wesley*. Nashville: Abingdon Press).

————. *A Collection of Hymns for the Use of the People Called Methodists*. Vol. 7. Ed. F. Hildebrandt and O. A. Beckerlegge. Oxford: Oxford University Press, 1983.

————. *Journal and Diaries I (1735–1738)*. Vol. 18. Ed. W. R. Ward and R. P. Heitzenrater. Nashville: Abingdon Press, 1988.

————. *Letters I, 1721–1739*. Vol. 25. Ed. F. Baker. Oxford: Oxford University Press, 1980.

————. *Letters II, 1740–1755*. Vol. 26. Ed. F. Baker. Oxford: Oxford University Press, 1982.

Wesley's Prayers and Praises. Ed. J. A. Kay. London: Epworth Press, 1958.

Whitehead, J. *The Life of the Rev. Charles Wesley, M.A., late Student of Christ-Church, Oxford, Collected From His Private Journal*. Dublin: John Jones, 1793; 1805 (2d ed.).

Wilder, F. *The Methodist Riots: The Testing of Charles Wesley*. Great Neck, N.Y.: Todd & Honeywell, 1981.

Wiseman, F. L. *Charles Wesley and His Hymns*. London: Epworth Press, n.d. (1938?).

————. *Charles Wesley, Evangelist and Poet*. New York: Abingdon Press, 1932.

Wood, A. H. "Charles Wesley's Hymns on Holiness." In *Dig or Die: Papers Given at the World Methodist Historical Society Wesley Heritage Conference, 1980*. Ed. J. S. Udy and E. G. Clancy. Sidney: World Methodist Historical Society, 1981, 67-76.

Zehrer, K. "The Relationship between Pietism in Halle and Early Methodism." *Methodist History* 17 (1979):211-24.